Also by Paul Shovlin

Bills of Exchange and Other Negotiable Instruments

When Push Comes to Shov

A Memoir

PAUL SHOVLIN

ISBN: 978-1-300-88859-8 (sc)
ISBN: 978-1-483-40160-7 (e)

Lulu Publishing Services rev. date: 6/14/2013

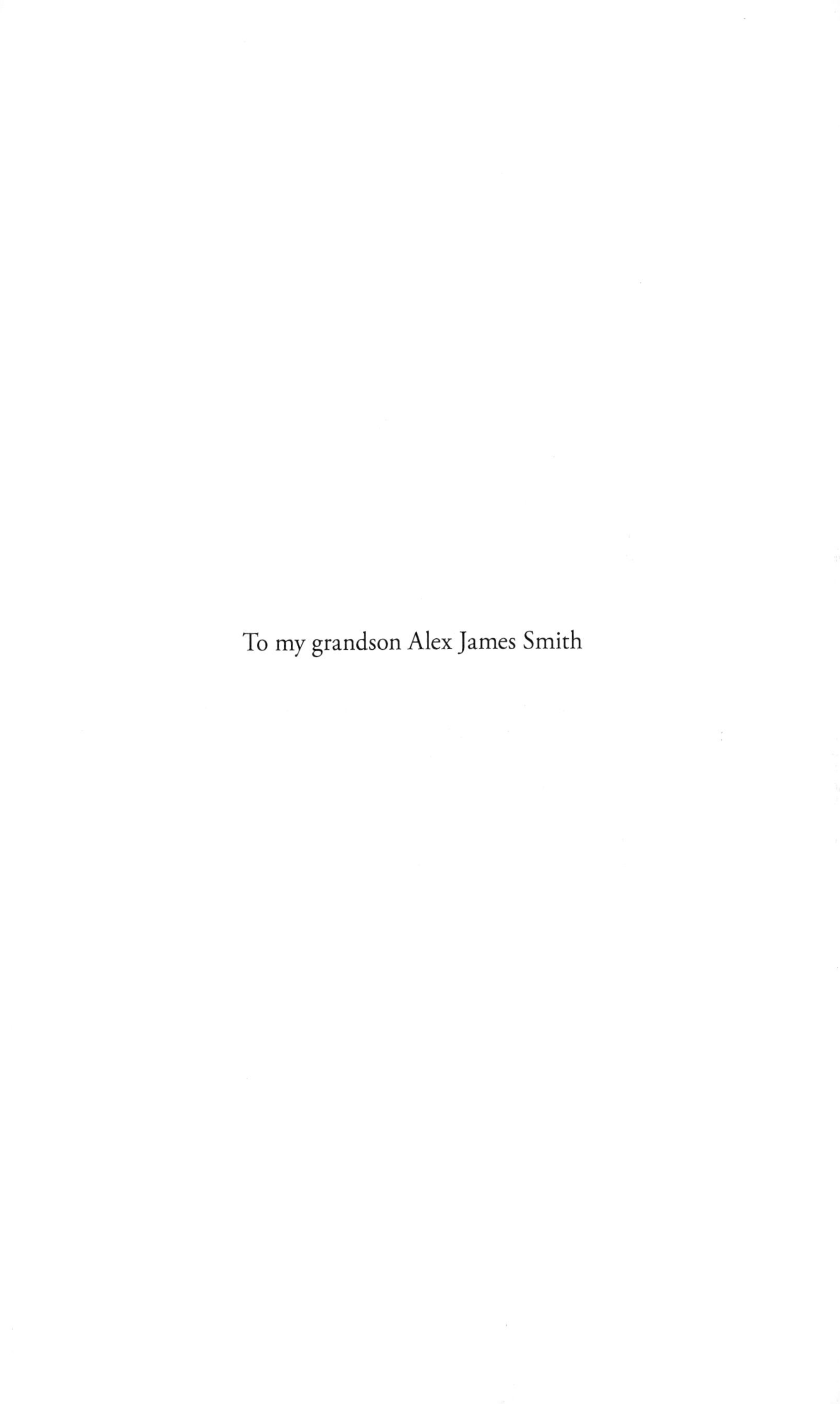

To my grandson Alex James Smith

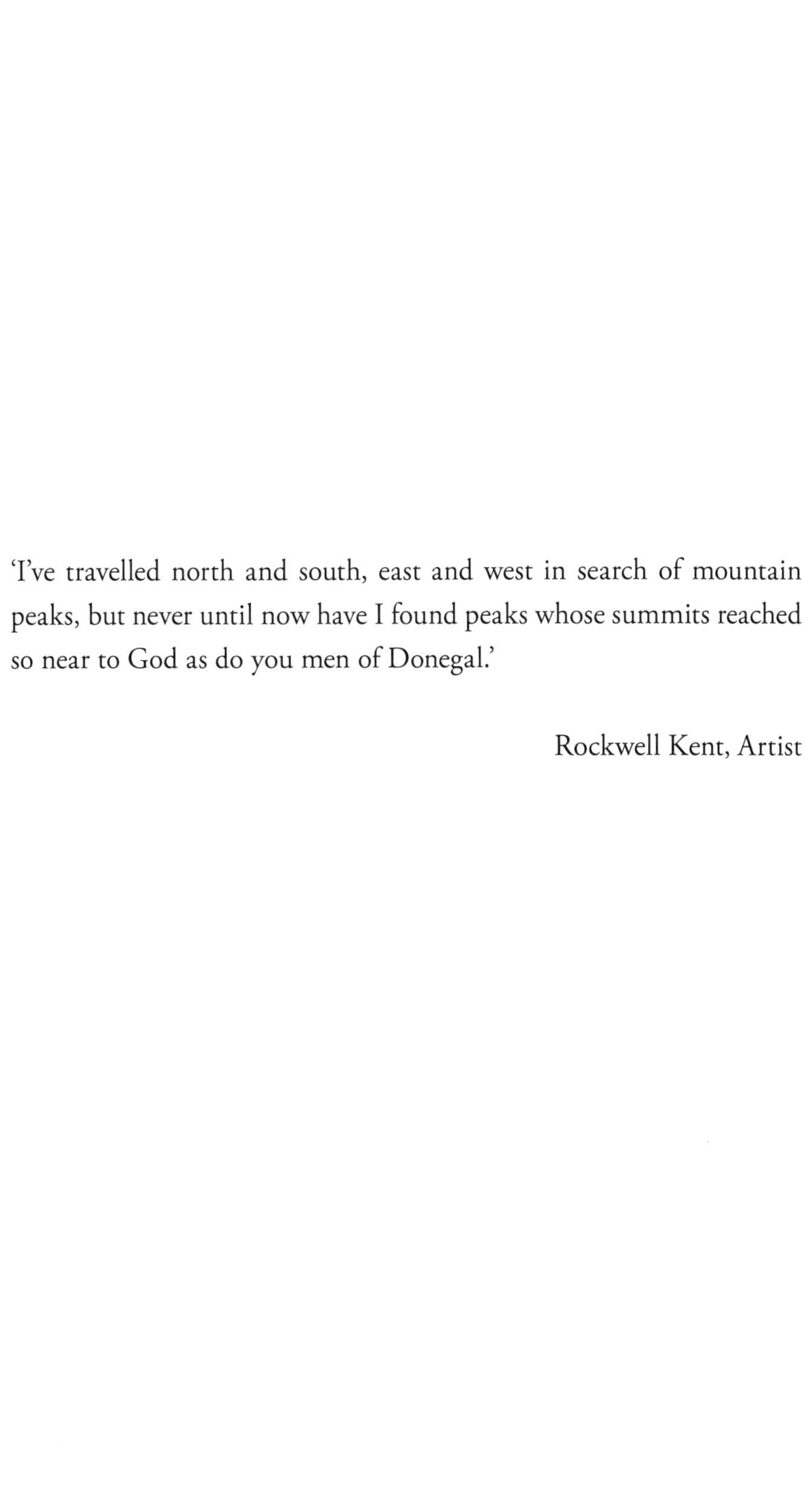

'I've travelled north and south, east and west in search of mountain peaks, but never until now have I found peaks whose summits reached so near to God as do you men of Donegal.'

Rockwell Kent, Artist

Contents

Preface

When I first put pen to paper to write this memoir, I did so without much conviction. I realised that there are many like me who could write their life story: the difference perhaps is that to do so, you need an element of egotism! However, I was strengthened in my resolve to pursue the project to a conclusion by the words of technology pioneer Steve Jobs: 'Remembering that you are going to die is the best way I know to avoid the trap of thinking you have something to lose'. So, my motto has been 'just do it' and hopefully raise some funds for charity in the process.

It is over ten years since I finished with full-time employment, leaving my position as chief executive of Barclays Bank Ireland. Since then, I have had the opportunity to use my skills in different ways, such as volunteering with charities and 'not for profit' organisations and have lived life to the full, travelling with my wife, Mary and enjoying my grandchildren. This ten-year period has been adequate, I feel, to allow me some perspective in viewing my life.

An important motivation for me in writing this memoir was to pay tribute to my wonderful parents. As I get older, my appreciation of my parents deepens: this is probably true for most people. Both my parents had so little in terms of material things or of wealth. Yet they sacrificed everything to help my brother Conal and myself make our way in the world. That they were both from modest backgrounds did not limit their vision for us and their determination that we would avoid the drudgery experienced by themselves. Also in my mind was the general goodwill and kindness of our neighbours, relations, friends and otherwise. They provided a warm and wholesome background in which to grow up.

Equally cherishing was the beautiful natural environment of the rugged coast of west Donegal, in which I was fortunate to live as a child, and the simplicity and adventure of life on a small farm. I realise that my roots in Donegal run deep, and have shaped so much of my life. To be born and raised in Donegal brings with it a powerful sense of place, clan and ancestry that has given a clarity to my sense of identity which has remained with me for a lifetime

On a broader perspective, I come from probably the last generation in Ireland to grow up without a car, television or telephone. People of my generation uniquely straddle the age of the donkey and cart and the age of the smartphone. That journey is in itself, I think, worthy of reflection.

My grandchildren may find it hard to be separated from whatever device they may be using to read what to them will look like a fairytale. However, should they ever wish to track back into their ancestry, I hope that this piece of writing will help them.

I hasten to add that I have not found writing this memoir to be an easy exercise. Indeed the book's gestation has been a fairly lengthy one since I first put pen to paper in 2007. However, in writing this memoir, I received help and advice from many people. I would like to acknowledge the role of one key person above all: that is my wife Mary, who has not only supported me in this project but in all my endeavours throughout my life and careers. She is truly an unsung hero for her support from the night we first met.

A final observation here is that times long past now hold much more enthusiasm and interest for me than, say, yesterday and I seem to be able to view them with greater clarity. That seems an odd thing, but it is true.

Paul Shovlin
Dublin 2013

CHAPTER ONE

PACKIE AND BRIGID

In October 1944, my mother, Brigid McGill, came to live in Sandfield, having just married my father, Packie Shovlin, a Sandfield native. The townland of Sandfield is in the parish of Ardara, and is situated three miles north of Ardara village in the south-west of County Donegal. As was often the case at that time, the newlyweds moved into Packie's family home with Granny Shovlin, called Brigid or Biddy, as she was widely known. My mother was also known as Biddy 'Condy' after her father, Condy. She had been born and raised in Largynaseeragh, a townland in the south-western extremity of the parish, a remote and mountainous part of the peninsula which extends into the Atlantic Ocean, stretching from Killybegs on the southern side to Ardara at the northern end. This peninsula is locally known as 'In Through'. 'In Through' is quite different from other parts of County Donegal: the landscape is mountainous and bleak, but the scenery is breathtakingly beautiful. There are spectacular cliffs, many lakes and fast flowing rivers and streams. The north-western part of the peninsula includes the townlands of Port and Glenlough, which are extremely remote and no longer inhabited. It was in Glenlough that the well-regarded American artist Rockwell Kent lived for a period, during 1926-7. There, he produced paintings of the landscape and people, some of which are in The Hermitage Museum in St Petersburg. In summer the 'In Through' area is a haven for serious hillwalkers. It enjoys a strong reputation for Gaelic culture, greatly enhanced in recent years by the setting up of the innovative Oideas Gael summer school by Liam O'Cuinneagáin.

The 'In-Through' climate is generally wetter than in other parts of the county. The mountainous sea cliffs take the brunt of the rain clouds borne by the south-westerly winds arriving ashore from the Atlantic.

At the time when Brigid permanently departed her childhood home, the In Through people would have made their living from a variety of pastoral activities, depending on their location on the peninsula. Inshore fishing would have been an important additional income source in the coastal villages of the Malins, Teelin and Kilcar, for example, but subsistence mixed farming would have been the predominant occupation of most households. Mixed farming provided a high degree of self sufficiency. Foods such as milk, butter, bread and potatoes were home produced, as was peat for the hearth, which provided for heat and cooking. Unlike east Donegal, the west of the county is not suitable for tillage of any scale. The rocky soil's most prolific output would have been stones used for house and rough road building.

Brigid's family had around twenty-five acres of near-arable land in Largynaseeragh, which were worked to the limit. In those days no financial supports were available from the state, so people had to rely solely on their own initiative, and any surplus they produced, they would sell, provided, of course, there was a market for the produce. Sheep farming was a key activity. The monthly Ardara fair, which was always held on the first working day of every month, was an important market outlet for both sheep and cattle. The majority of these animals were ultimately destined for the more fertile and bigger farms of east Donegal and elsewhere in Ireland where they would be further fattened before being sold for slaughter. Sheep farming was regarded as by far the most important cash activity. The hardy Scottish horned sheep could survive and thrive in the rough terrain. Their coats were a source of marketable wool in addition to their value as meat. The bulk of the wool would be sold to specialist wool merchants. Some families, such as my mother's would retain a small residual supply of the wool for their own use. The women folk would card or knead this wool before converting it to yarn on the family spinning wheel. They would then knit the yarn into heavy sweaters, socks and other garments for family use. These sweaters would be ideal wear during the harsh winter months in south-west Donegal. Alternatively, the yarn would be handwoven into tweed, out of which would be made clothes, blankets and other household fabrics. There was a strong tradition of handweaving in the area at the time; Ardara, with its many young weavers, was the centre of the then commercial handweaving industry in County Donegal.

In Through was largely a Gaelic-speaking area. Noted Irish folklorists such as Seamus Delargy, Ignatius Lambert and other collectors spent time there and made the McGill homestead their base in the area. They deemed Largynaseeragh and the surrounding area particularly rich in ancient Irish folklore. The Gaelic spoken in the area was well regarded for its grammatical quality and clarity of expression. English was Brigid's second language which she only started learning when she was nine or ten years of age. Like other locals, she would have picked up English as she progressed at school and mixed with people from non Gaelic-speaking areas, especially from the towns and villages. Because of the external influences of trade, policing and other state services, the towns would have been ahead of the rural areas in their anglicisation. The fact that they spoke their native language set the In Through people apart from neighbouring areas and seemed to create a cultural cohesion that was less evident in other parts of Donegal. Irish music, storytelling and dancing were an integral part of social activity. Despite their lack of knowledge of English the In Through people seemed to be unusually cosmopolitan in their outlook. They had an intellectual curiosity which was surprising in people living in what was a remote and supposedly backward area. This curiosity and generosity of spirit reflected itself in a tradition of warmly welcoming visitors to the area.

My mother was the youngest of a family of three girls and one boy. Her mother, also Brigid, died at her birth in 1908. Condy, Brigid's father, along with his sister and mother raised the four children. The sad loss of his wife was compounded by a family row which erupted over her burial place. Condy's mother-in-law, Madge Heekin, demanded that her daughter be interred in the Heekin family plot in Glencolmcille, rather than in Condy's family grave in Ardara. She believed that Condy would re-marry and his second wife would also be buried in the Ardara plot and this was an outcome Madge Heekin was not prepared to countenance. She needn't have worried. Condy succumbed to the 1918 Spanish flu pandemic and died when Brigid was not yet ten years old. This was a severe blow to a family which had already been struggling without a mother. However, Brigid's grandmother and aunt, Margaret and Máire respectively, stepped into the breach, running the household and smallholding and providing for the four children as best they could. Whatever little money was earned from farming was supplemented by two other sources, one of which was doing embroidery for a local merchant. Once, Brigid told me about an occasion when her older sister Mary received a payment of ten shillings from the merchant for a stack of embroidery she had just completed. After the endless hours of eye-straining work required to earn these few shillings, she gifted the whole amount to the local priest as a Mass offering. This act of extraordinary generosity seemed foolish for a family so poor, but was a measure of the family's deep faith; although without knowing the exact circumstances, it also seemed unchristian of the priest to accept it.

As an additional income source the main family bedroom was made available for a lodger or two. The lodger was typically the current schoolteacher or a pupil in the local school—it was customary for young lads from other local districts, who were preparing for scholarship examinations, to spend time in Largynaseeragh immersed in daily spoken Gaelic. Most of these pupils were aiming for teaching careers. Two such examples were unrelated gaelic scholars Clement and Patsy Sweeney, who coincidentally were both from Beagh where Brigid was destined to make her home. This exposure to the education process was a formative influence on Brigid, who had a rock-solid faith in education as the access to life's opportunities. She held true to this principle for all of her life. Indeed, I have been a big beneficiary of this philosophy.

My father, Packie Shovlin, was born in 1901, the third child of Hughie and Brigid Shovlin. A late starter, he was forty-three years old when he married Brigid. He was a cerebral kind of fellow and would have enjoyed an interesting and diverse lifestyle. Both his parents, Hughie and Brigid, were alive. He was close to his bachelor uncle Denny who also lived in the family home. Denny was the local postman, who uniquely delivered the mail on horseback. He also ran a small roadside grocery shop on the family holding. By all accounts, Denny was a high achiever and generous in helping Hughie and Brigid raise their ten children. Packie was the eldest living son. Francis, the eldest boy, had also succumbed to the Spanish flu while working on a road-building project in Gortahork, a village in north-west Donegal; he was just twenty-one years old.

Packie would have mixed widely and would have had a pleasant social life, if not a bohemian existence by the standards of the day. He had a motorcycle for a period, which must have been pretty unusual in those days. As well as working on the family farm holding, he carted fish from Rosbeg, a local fishing port, to the nearby towns of Ardara and Glenties. Packie loved anything to do with horses. He would have ridden the family carthorse and exhibited it at the Ardara annual show, a social highlight of the year. In the local community he was regarded as a good horseman with the nimbleness and low weight associated with a jockey. The Shovlin household was socially busy and would therefore have been a good place to be a young man. Six adoring sisters and boyfriends possibly coming and going would have created its own buzz.

Packie's mother Brigid was herself an In Through native who came from Straleel near Carrick village. Straleel is a picturesque townland situated along the Glen River. The relatively lowland Straleel people would have perceived themselves as a notch up the social scale from the mountain people of Largynaseeragh. Such awareness would have done nothing for the relationship between the two Brigids.

Sandfield is in the Downstrands district of Ardara parish and the Shovlins would have seen themselves as Downstrands people, benefiting from a vibrant and mixed community. Although all in the same parish, the people of the Downstrands and Ardara ends of the parish are different in many ways. Downstrands has beautiful sandy beaches and a golf course and some of the land is suitable for farming. In common with Ardara, Downstrands is a religiously mixed community and relations between Catholic and Protestant have always been excellent. At the time my parents met, Downstrands would have been a popular holiday location for visitors from Northern Ireland, many of whom were Protestants, and as a consequence Downstrands people were more anglicised and worldly than their counterparts in the Ardara village end of the parish. For example, in my time Gaelic was almost extinct in Downstrands, being spoken in few homes.

The formative influences on Packie and Brigid were therefore quite different, although they were both born and raised in the same parish. Packie was what might be termed today a kind of 'Renaissance man' with an interest in the more abstract things in life. Unlike Brigid, whose growing up was dominated by day-to-day survival Packie would not have been concentrated on where the next meal was coming from. He was a bright man who would have been able to advance himself had he received education, but like many older sons in large families, his education suffered against the need to help out on the farm as soon as he was able to do so. In those days it was common in rural Ireland for the older children to enter the workforce early to help subsidise the rearing and education of the younger ones.

Farming was Packie's life and he was knowledgeable on the subject, but he also enjoyed his involvement in the Local Defence Force(LDF), an auxiliary arm of the Irish Army, as well the Ancient Order of Hibernians (AOH), an Irish Catholic equivalent of the Orange Order. Local history was a particular interest, which he shared with his friend 'Wee Paddy' McGill, an eminent local historian and schoolteacher. Both Packie and Brigid were intelligent and strong-willed people whose outlook extended beyond the parochial reach, but in different ways because of the cultural diversity of their backgrounds.

Adult conversation in the home between themselves and visiting neighbours, friends and relations would have centered around current affairs. Ours wasn't a home where there would be much sentimental chit-chat that might include us children, so whilst we were well educated in the affairs of the world, we were somewhat weaker in the area of small talk. To keep their interest in current affairs up to date, my parents always bought the *Sunday Independent* newspaper in Dan McLoone's shop after 11 o'clock Mass in Kilclooney chapel. It would be read from beginning to end by both parents. A daily newspaper was a valued item in our home. If Brigid or Packie had business in Ardara during the week a daily *Irish Independent* would be on the shopping list. This newspaper was particularly well regarded in rural Ireland because of its extensive death notices. At a time when there were no telephones or local radio in the countryside both national and local newspapers were held in great esteem as sources of information. As well as the national press, the weekly *Donegal People's Press* and the *Donegal Democrat*, which was then published by the King family in Ballyshannon, were more staple requirements. Indeed, it wouldn't be unknown for Packie and Brigid to take time out to read the newspaper in the middle of the working day. Brigid, however, wasn't always comfortable about such a leisurely approach in the summer: to her chagrin Packie tended to make world events a greater priority than ensuring the hay was gathered before the weather broke.

Brigid moved into the Shovlin family home with Packie after their marriage but their stay was to be short lived. The contrast in their individual backgrounds didn't affect their partnership, but it created a fault line between the two Brigids that made a happy existence impossible in Packie's family home. Granny Brigid, the Shovlin matriarch, was undoubtedly a dominant figure and central to life in Sandfield. Brigid, the newly-wed, would have been expected to seamlessly fold into the existing routines which would have been quite different to those in her own home. Brigid came from a small family unit where she would have enjoyed significant autonomy, having grown up without her parents. On the other hand the Shovlins were a large family unit, and would have been self-sufficient as a community within themselves. The cultural clash between the two In Through women was an added aggravation. Brigid, who in any event was not a compliant type of person, couldn't handle this arrangement so the inevitable crisis was triggered. On more than one occasion during this time she departed the Sandfield home and returned to live with her brother Paddy in Largynaseeragh. It was clear that something needed to be done. Packie, as the eldest surviving son, had been destined to inherit the family holding. Hugh, the second youngest, who was about to get married, was to move to a small thatched cottage and holding in the neighbouring townland of Beagh. The Shovlins had recently bought this property, the estate of Patrick Kennedy. As Brigid couldn't settle in the Shovlin home, it was decided that Hugh and Katie would now live in the ancestral home while Packie and Brigid would move to the old cottage across the river in Beagh.

Packie never spoke about this episode, but it must have been a harrowing experience for him. He had spent many of the best years of his working life building up the Sandfield holding in the knowledge that this is where he would stay and raise a family. At forty-four years of age, he was effectively starting from scratch in a rundown cottage on a 26-acre holding, half of which was subject to flooding from ocean tides. Moving out of Downstrands, albeit just across the bridge, alone would have been a cultural jolt for Packie, not to mention the challenges posed by the poor economics of the move. For Brigid's part, little did she think when she came down the Glengesh Pass to live in the lowlands of Sandfield, that such domestic turbulence awaited her. But there is no doubt that for my mother, independence was more important than material welfare. She was a resourceful and hardworking person and so not fearful of the challenges ahead.

Packie and Brigid got on with their lives in Beagh as did Hugh and Katie in the Shovlin family home.

In addition to Hugh, Packie had another surviving younger brother named Peter. Peter was much revered by everyone who knew him. He had a great sense of fairness and he was very much the 'glue' that held the family together, in spite of any turbulence. He maintained good relationships with all family members and indeed in-laws, such as Brigid, despite the family tensions which had arisen. He commanded enormous respect in the family and wider community. He was well known throughout the parish by virtue of his job as a life-assurance representative. Peter would, for example, often effectively mediate in family disputes that would come to his attention: his view would be sought out by his customers and taken seriously. If Peter had been alive in Roman times, he would undoubtedly have been a respected senator.

Hugh was more of a business type. He had a direct style and was highly commercially focused; a good judge of cattle, an important and valuable characteristic in farming circles. Local history or idle talk of matters that had no bearing on immediate prosperity and survival had no place in Hugh's firmament.

I was born on 27 June 1947, in the lower room of our three-roomed thatched cottage in Beagh. The cottage consisted of a kitchen/living room, wedged between two bedrooms, one at either end. The 'lower room', as it was called, was the best bedroom in the cottage. It had a white tongue-and-groove timber ceiling and a timber floor. This floor was never in good condition and if you weren't careful, you could easily put your foot down through it. The kitchen/living room had a floor of local blue flagstones laid on the earthen surface. Neither the upper bedroom nor the kitchen had ceilings; the rafters, lathes and the truss, known as a couple, all of which supported the peat-sodded under-roof, were visible. The thatch was applied on top of the sods (or *scraitheanna* as they were known in Gaelic). The external front and back doors lead directly to the kitchen, which made it a cold room in winter. Packie would place old overcoats or some other fabric at the bottom of the external doors to keep out the wind. Brigid always maintained a good fire burning in the open hearth which kept the kitchen very comfortable.

Like other homes in Ireland, we relied on the wireless radio for the essentials, such as the Radió Éireann news, the big Gaelic football matches and Irish music programmes. A great favourite was the céilí music programme 'Take the Floor'. Because the old radios relied on a cumbersome set of two batteries, wet and dry, it was switched on only sparingly to preserve power. There was no television until much later and when it arrived, few households could afford the sets and aerials. So, during my childhood, 'raking' was still an important source of entertainment and information. Raking is a colloquialism for visiting neighbouring friends and relations during the long winter nights. The frequency of raking to a house would depend on distance: people within a mile or so would rake with each other regularly; people further apart would visit each other once or twice over a single winter. Some relations would ensure that they visited each other at least once a year so that good contact would be maintained. My younger and only sibling, Conal, and I greatly looked forward to the rakers coming to visit because we could eavesdrop on the wide-ranging discussion on both local and current affairs. We eagerly anticipated return visits to our neighbours and relatives, particularly if they had children of similar ages. At the time, raking was generally but not totally a male preserve so it was Packie who did most of the raking in our home. My mother, not being a local, would do much less raking as she would not have been as close to or related to many local neighbours. She would rake in a few houses where the woman of the house, like her, would have been an In Through native like Mary Craig or another non-local, such as Bridie Nicholson. However, she would actively partake in the general conversation when rakers came to our house.

We particularly liked Christmas-holiday and weekend raking, because we would be allowed to sleep in the next day, after our late night. We were also lucky in that Packie was a sociable man, who enjoyed visiting friends and neighbours and who was happy to bring us along. Many parents didn't want their children to overhear adult conversation, unlike our parents, who were relatively lenient in that regard. Also, being a small family meant that Packie could bring us along, impossible in larger families, who would have to take turns, which would lead to inevitable conflicts and resentments. Adults were careful not to mention controversial or sensitive issues in front of the children in case they carried the stories to school. One memorable story that I do recall is about Isaac O'Donnell's poitín, an illegal spirit. He is believed to have lived in nearby Summy, on the farm which is now owned by the Crummer family. A drunken local man who had been detained in the Ardara police barracks to sober up, had overheard another local man reporting to the police that Isaac had a keg of poitín under his front-door flagstone. The policeman asked the drunk if he had heard anything, to which the drunk man said that he had.'Well,' said the policeman, 'be away with you'.The message to the drunk was that he should get a warning to Isaac that the police were on the way, so Isaac could switch the poitín to another hiding place. When the police searched under Isaac's flagstone, there was no poitín to be found, needless to say.

Things may have looked bleak when Packie and Brigid left behind the comfort of Sandfield but the Beagh cottage turned out to be a happy place where visitors received a warm welcome. My mother loved the outdoor farming life and thus was a real partner with my father in the farm work. She was hardworking, strong, healthy and did things right. I never recall her being confined to bed with an illness. Brigid was very knowledgeable about all farm animals, especially sheep. We soon acquired a few ewes to start the first sheep flock in the general area. We were then able to rent additional winter grazing for the sheep, which allowed the small enterprise become more viable. Traditionally, sheep farming was confined to the mountain areas, so we were breaking new ground, and now that we had become sheep farmers, a whole new range of contacts, mainly mountain people, opened up to us. Brigid revelled in reaching back into the community from which she'd come and in using her skills and knowledge, and Packie brought his forward thinking and vision to sheep farming. He pioneered cross-breeding, using a horned Scottish mountain ewe with a Border Leicester polly (unhorned) ram. This pairing, of a hardy Donegal ewe with a solid English lowland sheep, produced a heavier sheep; the additional weight meant a better market price for the grown lambs. Consequently, Packie gained a reputation for having a high-quality, albeit small, sheep herd and for being a hard-working and resourceful sheep farmer. My parents had truly made the best of their circumstances and in turn created a solid and loving home for us, giving us the example of their hard-work and balanced outlook on life to take us forward in life. I know that I owe any of my later success in life to them.

CHAPTER TWO

The Early Years

Compared to today's world of iPhones and i-pods, my time of growing up was a simple one. I had great times and have the happiest of memories: playing on the leanach, a stretch of land at the mouth of the Bellanagoal river; droving our cows home across the river at evening time; observing the high ocean tides, which regularly overflowed the nearby bridge across the river, leaving cars with no option but to detour inland by Tullymore or to wait for the ebbing of the tide.

Most of our spare time was spent helping out on the farm. There was no shortage of work to be done, whether after school or at weekends, the work varying according to the seasons. Helping with milking the cows, checking on the welfare of cattle and sheep and keeping vigil on the animals in case they strayed on to our own or neighbours' crops were typical chores. In this task, we were helped by the family dog and adored pet, a long-haired collie named Sport. He was a highly intelligent dog who seemed to almost know what you were thinking. Brigid often reminded us of the occasion that Sport placed himself on the riverbank between me and a high and rising ocean tide, which was just a few feet below where we were sitting on the grass. I do recall that incident but would not agree that I was vulnerable; my take was that of course, I was just enjoying the sight of the rising tide. I knew exactly what I was doing!

For Conal and me, life at home on the farm was much more interesting than school. There was a sense of freedom and the time didn't drag. The school clock seemed to take forever to get to the three-o'clock finishing time and the more often you gazed at it, the slower time seemed to pass. I know it is nostalgia, but during my childhood, all the summer days seemed to be long and the weather sunny. How we looked forward to the summer, when the big jobs on the farm would need doing, for example, the annual wool-clipping and dipping of the sheep. I was eager to help out with these tasks because they were perceived as adult jobs. Saving the turf in either Meenarilliagh or Beagh bogs was another summer job, or more accurately, a series of jobs, from paring the bank to cutting, spreading and 'footing' the turf. (Footing refers to the careful standing of the partially dried peat sods so that most of the surface dries in the sun and wind.) Saving turf is ideal work for young lads; it is light work but can be backbreaking. As a child, I used to enjoy the social aspect to days in the bog, when we would meet other young boys and men who would be saving turf on adjacent peat banks. When the turf was saved, we would transport the sods from the bank to the bog road, a roughly finished gravel track which ran along the end of each bank. If the bank was level and dry, the turf could be taken off the bank by donkey and cart or by a donkey with two creels on its back—today's quad bike is the true successor to the donkey and creels. More often the ground underfoot was not sufficiently stable to use the donkey, so we humans would carry creelfuls of turf on our backs. (A creel is a square deep basket specially handmade for carrying on a person's back). This is tough work and so turf banks which could facilitate donkey transport were, for obvious reasons, in great demand. The turf, which would now be ready for burning, was piled high at the end of the bank on the side of the bog road ready for transporting home.

We would take it home by donkey and cart as it was needed. Other families, who lived some miles from the bog, would hire a tractor to bring all their turf home before the onset of winter. Turf was our prime source of fuel for the kitchen, used in the open-hearth fire which served for both heat and cooking. In our home, as money became a little more plentiful, we installed a Number 8 Stanley Range that also used turf and later, a bottled gas ring which could boil water much faster than the turf fire.

A donkey and cart was a vital possession on a smallholding such as ours. Bringing home the turf was one of their uses but they had a range of uses around the farm as well as carrying commodities to and from the shops. Our parents used a bicycle to go to Mass and the shops, but like our cousins and other local children we walked. In later years as we moved schools, Packie bought us second-hand bicycles in Donal Byrne's shop in Ardara. Donal was good at refurbishing old bicycles which he would have taken as trade-ins from other customers. His son Don, a schoolteacher and well-regarded local poet, still provides a similar service in Ardara.

School soon became a central feature in the lives of myself and Conal, and we began our schooling at Beagh National School. The number of pupils was small and the teacher, Mrs Agnes McGill, took all the classes, which were conducted in a large room which had a roaring turf fire in winter. Mrs McGill's husband, John, was a prominent Ardara shopkeeper. As well as driving his wife to and from school every day, he ran an extensive drapery shop, which also supplied fishing tackle. The serious combination of teaching and shopkeeping meant that the McGill family were held in high esteem by the local people. They had a talent for music and John was a distinguished member of the local church choir.

You would have thought that, like many of my contemporaries, my primary school education would have begun and ended with Beagh, but this was not to be. My mother's desire that we receive the best schooling possible meant that she didn't hesitate to move us on to schools that she thought would offer us more. She deeply regretted upsetting local teachers, especially families for whom she had a high regard, but she felt that she had to follow her convictions. At the time, we simply did as we were bid, but looking back, I realise how much my mother's passion for education has shaped my life. There is no doubt that I would not have dreamed of other possibilities in life, were it not for my mother.

My memories of Beagh school are mixed. I enjoyed the camaraderie of the other children and making new friends from Beagh and Tullycleave, but I used to greatly envy the older children, who were on the verge of finishing school and the freedom that would bring them. And the older boys were also given the privilege of sweeping the timber school floor rather than doing schoolwork. Beagh school was within easy walking distance of our home, and we always walked with our Sandfield cousins, Hugh Francis, Seamus, Pat and Neil. Another neighbour, Donal Byrne, travelled the same road to school, but he cycled. Being a few years older than us he was a kind of protector. The Byrne family included Donal's older brother John, their parents William and Mary, as well as William's brother Michael, a war veteran, who lived with the family. Michael was disabled, having been injured fighting for the British at Gallipoli in the First World War. Donal was a very bright boy and cherished child. He was largely self-educated through reading encyclopedias and he picked up much knowledge from his uncle Michael. Thus, Donal would know the principles on which a jet engine worked, but know little about Gaelic poetry. Furthermore, his school attendance was erratic so his great talent was lost to wider opportunities, which would have required a more formal education.

There is a particular story about a morning that we and our cousins were very late for school, which Donal delighted in relating to Brigid. I clearly remember that day. As we arrived at the summit of Beagh Brae we heard a loud metallic noise coming from the direction of the school, which we correctly assumed to be a mobile stone crusher. This was an intimidating looking and very noisy machine, which dominated the roadway as it passed along. As soon as we heard the noise, we sought refuge on an elevated sod ditch near Kennedy's ('Tailor's') Lane to safely await the crusher's passing. We must have waited at least thirty minutes by which time we could have comfortably arrived at our desks. I can't remember who had the idea of waiting for half an hour for the machine to pass, but I'm sure that my cousin Hugh Francis would have been the major influence.

However, for me, the biggest and most memorable event in Beagh school was the then compulsory switching of my dexterity from left-handed to right-handed. I was naturally left-handed or a 'ciotóg', in Gaelic. At the time, the received wisdom was that being left-handed was an unfortunate aberration, which had to be corrected. There was nothing for it but to fall in line and learn to write with my right hand. It felt very awkward to be going against my natural instincts in this way, but more than that, it affected my learning. I seemed to be unable to do anything right. My handwriting was terrible and was destined to be never other than poor. I just couldn't get the hang of sums and my workings were a sight to behold, they were so messy. It was a difficult time for me at school. My parents would not have been aware of the degree of my incompetence. Later, I got to grips with simple arithmetic so I was inclined to conclude that the problems arose from the trauma caused by the changeover from left to right. I continued doing all other functions left handed such as manual farm work, handball, table tennis and other games requiring hand action.

Around the time of the change, my right eye coincidentally shut of its own accord. This endured for a period until our local GP, the brilliant James Boyle, forced it open, damaging the eyelashes, but my eye worked normally afterwards. Packie and Brigid were convinced that the eye closure was a direct result of the switch from left-handed to right-handed writing. It is entirely possible, but this practice was soon generally and rightly discontinued; my age group was probably one of the last to be switched. Mrs McGill was a God-fearing and kind woman, so I am sure she just followed the practice prevailing at that time.

Our Beagh school education was not destined to last long. Our mother was pleased that our knowledge of the catechism was proceeding apace, but she was concerned that we were making rather less progress in the basics of arithmetic, reading and writing. Moreover, it was increasingly evident that Beagh alumni rarely progressed to secondary school. It is true that many local parents were interested in their children finishing school as soon as possible so that they could work on the home farm or join the paid workforce, but it is also true to say that more pupils would have progressed if they had been allowed to reach the required scholarship standard. Nonetheless, Kilclooney Dallán Forgaill primary school in Downstrands (named after the sixth-century saint and celtic poet) began to emerge in Brigid's mind as an option. Although a much longer daily walk at over two miles, the distance was within an acceptable range. Master John Boyle, the principal, had an excellent teaching reputation. In common with Brigid he was a fluent Gaelic speaker and In Through native whose family she knew well and hugely respected. Furthermore, as the school had two teachers, learning would be easier and better. Although not a major consideration, our Sandfield cousins had already transferred to Kilclooney, where they seemed to be progressing well, so we also made the move. Of course, their Downstrands credentials were superior to ours. Their mother, Katie, was born and raised in Clogher in the Downstrands heartland. The validity of their pedigree gave them a strong cultural empathy with the other school pupils, which was clearly evident the first morning of our arrival in Kilclooney school. However, our first experience was far harsher than we could have imagined. The air of expectation and excitement that we felt at the prospect of beginning at a new school dissipated rapidly. Kilclooney was a much bigger and less homely school with twice as many pupils as Beagh. Master Boyle took the third through to seventh classes (in those days, primary school took us to age 14) and Mrs Eileen Harkin took the junior classes. I joined third class on my arrival. Desks were shared between the two halves of the school, with half the pupils standing and the other half seated at desks, which were then swapped over, depending on the class. There didn't seem to be a set pattern, but broadly, pupils doing reading, history and geography stood while those doing arithmetic and writing work sat at desks. The blackboard was the fundamental teaching tool but the stone mantelpiece was used for making more permanent notes in chalk. I recall the names of the two Roman cities of Herculaneum and Pompeii remaining written in chalk on the mantelpiece for most of my time at Kilclooney school.

One advantage of having so many classes in the same room was that you would often be attracted by the subject matter being taught to other classes. While this was distracting, it could also be an interesting diversion. The school was heated by a turf fire in each of its two classrooms. The turf was stored in a small shed adjacent to the toilets and brought in to the classrooms in bacáns (Gaelic for armfuls) by the pupils as required. The toilets, a sight to behold, were of the dry variety with strong chemicals added from time to time to neutralise the pungent odour.

Two new pupils who had not begun their schooling in Kilclooney were an oddity in the eyes of the existing pupils. It was like two stray animals joining an established herd; we were resented. It was not long before Michael 'MacSwine' Boyle threw a few warlike shapes in my direction. Although I defended the dignity of Conal and myself valiantly, I was roundly defeated by a stronger, older and better-supported opponent and left to pick myself up from a large rainwater puddle in the schoolyard. However, the air was now clear and the pecking order reinforced. The altercation did enhance my image among fellow pupils: from then on, I was seen as a person who would manfully put up a fight, however inadequate. There were subsequent occasions when discretion rather than valour proved the best tactic for survival! A cooling in relationships with the McGills did follow our departure from Beagh School. They were not the only party to have felt betrayed in such a fashion. Master Boyle was destined for a similar fate when my parents' initial expectations of Kilclooney were not realised. John Boyle had a serious illness just before we transferred to Kilclooney and it was thought that the high quality of his teaching had therefore suffered. Brigid moved into action again before we reached the end of our primary schooling. From her closeness to the schooling scene in Largynaseeragh she knew that herself and Packie were within their rights to send their children to a school of their choice. Any political awkwardness they felt was in their view a small price to pay for the opportunity of better schooling which might ultimately lead to secondary education and a possible job.

Nonetheless, we enjoyed good times in Kilclooney, despite the inauspicious beginning. We made good friendships, some lifelong, with most of the children our own age. Ourselves and our Sandfield cousins got on well, apart from the odd blip. The exceptions would be when I mightn't have taken as strong a supporting line as would be expected in the fistfights cousin Seamus would be having with others, mainly one Packie McLoone. Our support for Seamus would ebb and flow in accordance with our relationship with Packie. Seamus was very strong and would usually win these battles, but I wasn't quite as successful. I recall one serious altercation between Packie and me in the chapel sacristy before an evening service. There was close hand-to-hand combat using candle extinguishers as weapons. Fr McGroarty, the extremely devout local curate, who arrived on the scene, was so angry that he expelled me from altar-server duties for a period. This caused some difficulties, as a great deal of our social life revolved around the chapel. My parents were, of course, disappointed but this was tempered by their mature perception of Fr McGroarty as a zealot and the old adage that 'boys will be boys'.

Church attendance in Downstrands would have been close to 100% in those days. Going to and coming from the chapel on foot provided us with opportunities for socialising in an environment much less rigorous than school, with little danger from traffic; there were few cars and very few children had bicycles. The big church events during the year provided great opportunities to be out and about masquerading under the solemnity of religious services and we greatly looked forward to them. Fr McGroarty was extraordinarily dedicated to the faith. This was the 1950s and the glory days of the influence of the Catholic Church in Ireland. One of Father McGroarty's projects at the time was the completion of a grotto commemorating the centenary of the appearance of Our Lady of Lourdes. A site for the construction of the grotto was procured on Pat McLaughlin's small holding. People saw it as a great honour for Pat to be chosen to donate land for such an exalted cause. He probably did see it as a great honour such was the devotion of people of that generation, even if the sale of the land might be a source of prospective cash. Fr McGroarty's efforts, supported by the labour of local men, resulted in a beautiful shrine with floodlights and a natural stream.

Candlelight processions between the new shrine and the chapel were a regular feature at that time. These were exciting events for us youngsters. Great ingenuity was employed in making up the candlelight torches from glass bottles so that they would remain lit in the winds. What passing tourists, many of whom would have been Northern Ireland Protestants, made of it all I often wondered. The glowing snake–like procession of worshippers through the fading sunlight must have been a puzzling sight. But then Northern folk were hardly strangers to upfront expressions of religious fervour. The Catholic faith in Downstrands is today a paler version of what it was in those days. The nostalgia for those memorable times does not stretch beyond my own generation.

Emigration was a normal part of everyday life during my time in Kilclooney school. Many pupils, senior and contemporary to me, emigrated to England, never to return to Downstrands except on holiday. The boys would work in the building industry while the girls would seek work in the factories of the large British cities. There were traditional family ties between Donegal and Scotland, making Glasgow a popular destination. Emigrants returning for holidays were commonplace. Their nice clothes and different accents seemed seductive to us, who were occasionally contemplating our own futures, no matter how far ahead.

At school in those days, corporal punishment, comprising slapping on the hands with a rod or ruler, was normal. It was not a burning issue. Recovery was quick and worsening behaviour was deterred. For the victim there was a bravado gained among the peer group. John the Master was not a violent man and when he did slap it was deserved. Perhaps young people now would think this unlikely, but in those days, we saw corporal punishment as part of our daily school lives, and, unlike some teachers, the Master mainly slapped for disciplinary reasons.

Attending Kilclooney school was a happy if somewhat boring experience for me. Since moving from Beagh my increasing maturity with each year and my recovery from the left to right-handed switch meant that I was getting a better handle on school work. I had a sense that I was one of the best pupils in my class and probably one of the best in all the senior classes. Sometimes I felt compelled to hold back in case I would be seen to be showing off. Subsequent experience in secondary school shattered that illusion when I encountered fellow pupils who were better scholars than me. With John the Master, I always felt that he was slower to give me credit for my performance than he was to some classmates. Particular pupils seemed to be greatly commended when they came up with a rare correct answer to a question. This disillusioned me but was hardly psychologically damaging. Maybe it was a Downstrands thing as well as the notion of wholehearted endorsement being withheld from children who did not join the school on Day One. On the other hand it may have been the Master's psychological way of encouraging the majority of pupils, while not having to be concerned about those more eager to learn

Though few children came from other-than-ordinary circumstances, those from poorer families generally seemed to get a harder time from both peers and teachers. Perhaps that was just all in my mind. Children whose mothers did not come from the immediate area often befriended each other because they had something in common, as was the case with us and the Barney boys, as they were called, i.e., Paddy and his brothers. Their mother, Brigid, was a Gweedore native and like my mother, a Gaelic speaker. Of course, their father, Barney Boyle, would have been a friend of Packie's. In his younger days, Barney had done farm contract work in Beagh and Sandfield and so was well known to the Shovlin clan. Moreover he possessed a unique farm implement, a donkey plough which he improvised from old metal baths and timber, which he would kindly lend to Packie in late Spring when the potato seed would be sown. Packie, Conal and myself would use our own donkey and this plough to turn the clay on the young potato tubers.

Children who could speak gaelic were eligible for a government grant called a '*deontas*';£5 in those days. The school inspector tested Conal and I and while I shaded the test, Conal did not get through. Unfortunately, Conal was exposed to a longer period of questioning by the inspector, having been given a lift home in his car thus revealing cracks in his gaelic speaking. Although Brigid was a native gaelic speaker, Packie's lack of vocabulary meant that our oral gaelic was thin.

As children, we had great freedom, being unsupervised on our walks to school, and the two miles provided ample opportunity for mischief-making. Even better were the opportunities to get up to no good on the way home, free from the pressure of having to be in school on time. Our Sandfield cousins were on a tighter leash than us. Katie, their mother, ran a tight ship and 'loitering' or 'dallying' as she described it, was perceived as an ever-present temptation. Katie seemed able to manage her ten children better than another parent could manage one or two. Should there have been excessive 'dallying' Katie would greet us all near their home equipped with a sally rod or other tool of corporal punishment. She rightly judged that Conal and I were the prime 'dalliers', but despite many skirmishes, we never incurred anything beyond severe scolding and threat. There was one memorable occasion when Katie and ourselves were on opposite sides of the road and the situation looked particularly ominous. Fortunately we were able to move on swiftly under the cover provided by a passing truck.

Hugh Francis, the first born of our Sandfield cousins, assumed a kind of leadership, because he was a little older than the rest of us and we were happy to let him take charge. In school, Hugh Francis would stand in class with a kind of swaggering gait, with both hands in his trouser pockets. John the Master once joked that 'Proinsias', as he called him, was ready to give a half-crown to the first person with the correct answer to a question the teacher had asked of the class. This brought the class down in laughter and Hugh Francis instantly extracted his hands from his pockets. I can clearly recall that on that day we were all wearing knickerbocker-type trousers, which had been sent from our aunt in the United States. It was a great thrill in those days to receive parcels of used clothing from American relations. We were in bare feet that day as we often were in summer. Going barefoot was not seen as being out of the ordinary; indeed, we looked forward to the warm summer days when we could abandon our shoes. It was fun apart from when you walked over rough gravel.

Following a successful carpentry apprenticeship with James Gallagher, our aunt Marian's husband, in Ardara, Hugh Francis went off to work in Dublin.

James Gallagher was a quiet and diligent man who was prone to sudden bursts of wit. Every male that he met, was addressed as 'caddy'; normally caddy was a form of address to boys but James used the term more widely to include all males, young or old. He was a shrewd businessman and would say things like, 'it is not necessarily how much money you make that is important but how much you don't spend'.

On one of Hugh Francis's early visits home from Dublin he regaled Brigid and Packie, who were his godparents, with stories of his experiences. He had a knack of telling the stories in such a way that placed him as the key player. There was one story which he told Packie about 'Paul' doing a big job at the Airport. The only Paul my father knew was me, so he was intrigued as to what I was up to. The 'Paul' was of course the large contracting firm of John Paul to whom Hugh Francis referred in his own inimitable way. It was as if he and John Paul were longtime mutual acquaintances.

Our childhood weekends were usually spent helping out on the farm. The kind of work to be done depended mainly upon the seasons but there was rarely a weekend when there was not some chore connected with farm animals. Dealing with the cattle required caution as they could react violently to the administration of farm medicines, for example. We played football on Sundays with our cousins at any opportunity. These football matches were characterised by lots of shouting and minimal skill, played over rocky, uneven ground with our jackets as goalposts. The sessions could get pretty serious and fouling was par for the course. There was one memorable occasion when cousin Pat threw a soft cow pat at me as retribution for some smart trick I had played on his team.

The cow pat destroyed my nice cream and only Sunday shirt. The shirt absorbed the stain and no amount of water could restore it. This meant war: it was far worse than the usual bleeding elbow or knee, which would quickly heal. I dreaded having to face my mother with the prospect of having to replace the shirt with money being so scarce. But I realised that for Pat to have taken the matter literally into his own hands, as it were, he must have been severely affronted.

The neighbours and the local parish community was our world when growing up. Because no family owned any agricultural machinery, neighbours always cooperated on the big farm jobs, such as turf-cutting and bringing in the hay at harvest time. Boundary fences between farms were poor, so preventing cows from trespassing on neighbours' grazing was a constant challenge and sometimes it was tempting to overreact if neighbours' animals trespassed on your lands. A good deal of mutual cooperation and tolerance was required. However, the state of relations between neighbours could be confusing. They regularly complained about each other but when the need arose, they were quick to pull together. Adversity drew them together despite any petty bickering that went on from time to time. In those days, it was common for a cow to fall into a drain or hole from where she could not escape unaided. We children were often sent as emissaries to alert male neighbours to the emergency. They would arrive almost immediately equipped with ropes to help and in no time the suffering cow would be helped out of her predicament by the sheer strength of the local men. In our case it was generally our uncle Hugh, the McNelis brothers, Paddy Shovlin and Josie Martin, our near neighbours, who helped us out when needed.

Brigid perceived that learning progress was disappointingly slow in Kilclooney School. At the age of twelve, I was about to enter 6th class, so we were nearly out of time to catch up. However, Brigid and Packie quickly decided to transfer me to the three-teacher Ardara School where their friend 'Wee' Paddy McGill was the principal. At the time, this kind of chopping and changing schools was not done. Feathers were inevitably ruffled in Kilclooney but both my parents were prepared to take any resultant flak. It was only years later that I realised the extent of their courage. If it hadn't been for their persistence, I would have been destined for a life on the smallholding, where I would have struggled to eke out a living.

Packie bought me a second-hand bicycle and I cycled the three miles to school and back each day. Remaining in bed was a tempting prospect rather than face cycling uphill against the prevailing south-west winds. Also, I had to pass Beagh School on my way to Ardara regularly, encountering acquaintances whom I had abandoned several years earlier to transfer to Kilclooney. I sensed a certain understandable satisfaction on some of their parts that Kilclooney had not worked out for me. At the same time a neighbour, Deirdre Sweeney, had transferred to Ardara from Beagh. Deirdre was a bright pupil, who was marginally younger than me. We usually cycled home together in the evening and I think Deirdre's presence helped shield any ire which was coming my way. Deirdre sadly passed away when she was still a young mother. My good friend and contemporary, Pat Slowey, also attended Ardara school around that time.

The town school was an altogether different experience from Beagh or Kilclooney. It was evident that the children posed a greater challenge for the teachers. For a start, the level of bad language was of a higher order. Challenges to my fighting skills lay just below the surface, revealing themselves in football games on the concrete playing area. Fortunately, I was able to hold my own in these skirmishes as they would undoubtedly have been a prelude to tougher engagements. The fact that as a family we knew Paddy McGill's boys, Kieran and Lochlann, helped my street cred enormously with the boys in general. Another revelation to me was how big Gaelic football was in the town. Names that come to mind are Ronald Given, Patsy Gildea, Enda

Craig and Sean Campbell. These boys would all have been pretty good footballers, which would have given them a certain stature among the children generally. I got my first opportunity to participate in school Gaelic football by being a substitute on one of the two school teams. I remember Phonsie Bennett being our coach and a pretty good mentor he was for us young lads. As it happened, our team won the parish league and I was on the medal list.

Another feature of Ardara school was the intensity of learning and study, which was new to me. Wee Paddy was a superb and dedicated teacher. He didn't hesitate to use the cane, but he got through a great amount of subject material. My pace of education accelerated under his tutelage, although it was not always to my liking. Had I had a longer run with him, I would have been well prepared to seek a Donegal County Council scholarship to St Eunan's College in Letterkenny. Unfortunately, time ran out by the time my preparation would have been complete. I was to go to St Eunan's as a boarder, but my fees would have to be paid. I was now leaving primary school at 14 years old, and thanks to Brigid and Packie, who had the courage to move me on when needed, I was at a reasonably good standard of learning, even if I had no idea of what lay ahead in the tough world of a boys' boarding school.

CHAPTER THREE

College Boy

On Tuesday 4 September 1961, I began my new life in boarding school. Packie harnessed the donkey and cart and the two newly packed brown cardboard cases were loaded in preparation for the three-mile journey to Wee Paddy's house in Ardara. There we would rendezvous with Paddy, who had kindly agreed to take me with his son, Kieran, in their car to St Eunan's College in Letterkenny. Paddy's wife Kay, a County Laois born lady, joined us for the trip. We were expected to check into St Eunan's not later than 8 p.m. Kieran was entering his second year and was to be very helpful in introducing me to the setup and showing me the ropes.

Despite the differing social status of schoolteacher and smallholder, Wee Paddy and my father were friends; Paddy, who himself had grown up on a smallholding, was down to earth, without any social hangups. It also helped that both had similar political allegiances as well as a deep interest in local history. Paddy wrote extensively on local history while Packie was an excellent source of material both directly and indirectly from his wide circle of friends and acquaintances. Together, they had resurrected the Cnoc a Stolar stone flag on Mullavea Hill. This flag had once stood on top of the hill during the Penal Law period in Ireland, a time when the practice of the Roman Catholic religion was illegal and had been driven underground. The story went that if a white cloth was placed on the flagstone, it was a signal to the local Catholics that Mass was about to be celebrated nearby. The stone flag had lain neglected on the ground longer than any living person could remember. So Packie, together with a friend, local First World War veteran Tommy McLoone and other local men, hoisted the heavy stone structure into the upright position where it still stands.

We got the donkey and cart under way, up the Hanging Stone Brae out of the little valley where we lived in the basin of the Bellanagoal river. With parting handshakes, I said my goodbyes to my mother and to my brother Conal, crying my eyes out in the process. I dreaded leaving the friendly environment of family, cousins, friends and neighbours for a new and strange place. What made the event even more poignant was that Wee Paddy had told my mother that boys departing for the first time to St Eunan's were really leaving home for good. There was little likelihood that they would ever permanently return home again.

The big grey donkey that Packie bought from the McLaughlins of Lochside, was at the height of his powers at that time. Under Packie's command he energetically delivered myself and my two brand new suitcases to Ardara. The cases contained the full inventory of clothes, including bedclothes, which had been requested by the school, and which my mother had painstakingly assembled on a visit to Bridie Gildea's drapery shop, known as The Tailors, in Ardara. Bridie's own nephew, Dominic, was also entering St Eunan's the same year and over the years she would have supplied many other boys who were making the same journey.

Wee Paddy was getting geared up for the journey as we arrived at his home. We had to secure the cases with ropes onto the roof-rack of his black Ford Anglia 100E. Packie and I said our goodbyes with a handshake; hugs and 'male bonding' were not for real men in those days. He consoled me with the prospect that I would not feel the time passing until I was home on holidays. His emotions were probably mixed; between seeing me have an opportunity of a secondary education and the loss of much needed help to him on the farm.

Off I went to Letterkenny with the McGills. We duly arrived at St Eunan's College before the 8 p.m. deadline. As we drove through the front gate, I was in awe of the vista in front of us. The trees, especially the big weeping willow, the shrubs and the manicured lawns were beautiful, but it was the building that for me was an awesome sight. It just looked like a castle; a large square building in roughly hewn limestone with a round tower at each corner and castellated walls. Impressive large wood-panelled double doors led us into an inner open-air courtyard. The area around the front door was humming with activity as hackney drivers and parents arrived to deliver their sons to the college. Some, like me, were arriving for the first time while most were returning to begin their next year of study. The accommodation was fairly basic, with first year boarders allocated open cubicles in a dormitory, each containing a single bed, a wardrobe and a metal washstand with a white enamel basin, a jug of cold water and a chamber pot. The communal bathroom and toilets were off limits between lights out and the early morning rising bell.

Although I was lonely, I settled down that night, hoping that things could only improve. My neighbours on either side, James Harley and Cathal Casey, adapted to their new surroundings in contrasting ways. James, a laid back Frosses native, settled down quietly, but Cathal was a typically lively teenager and a bit more of a handful for the college authorities. He would strut around the top of the cubicle partitions after lights out. A college priest, the gentle Father Matthew Arnold, slept in a room at one end of the dormitory with the aim of deterring such misbehaviour. However, Cathal seemed to have the happy and enviable knack of timing his night walks to avoid detection and censure. It also helped that Father Matthew, a kindly man, didn't take his responsibilities too seriously. Cathal used to tell us stories about his brother Terry, who had a burning desire to become a jockey, going off to horse-racing stables. This was the same Terry Casey who, thirty five years later, would achieve the enormous success of training the 1996 Grand National winner, Rough Quest.

The loud bell ringing in the silence of the early morning was a shock. Add to this the prospect of washing in cold water and the challenge of getting ready; quite formidable. As soon as we washed and dressed we trooped down to the college chapel for daily Mass. Each boy was allocated his chapel seat in reverse order of his year and position in the alphabet. I was therefore allocated a seat on the front bench along with the fellow S's and other letters at the end of the alphabet. Apart from the undesired high visibility, the front seat was the least comfortable in the chapel due to the large space between your backside and the back of the seat.

Breakfast in the refectory followed Mass, consisting of porridge, sliced buttered bread and tea. Some boys enjoyed the luxury of their own jam which their parents had supplied. The jams were taken from a special press where they were stored between meals. Lunch was a slice of buttered bread and tea. The menu varied little; shepherd's pie was the main dinner item and was served after the first study period, at 7.45 p.m. We couldn't wait for dinner time to arrive as our lunch was such a miserable portion and by the time evening came, we were ravenous. For students who had regular pocket money there was always the college tuck shop as a source of relief from the hunger in the afternoon between class and study. Like many others, whatever little I would have been given at the beginning of term would soon be spent, my resistance worn down by my appetite. I have never lost the taste for Penguin bars and Choc Ices, which were the most desirable items in local shopkeeper Jack Harkin's college tuck shop.

Homesickness was evident particularly at bedtime, when darkness and aloneness were a new and unwelcome experience for all of us, who, for the first time, were missing a mother's care. Needless to say, none of us would admit to missing home as stoicism was the order of the day.

Homesickness revealed itself either in rowdiness or just a quiet sadness. For those boys who had older brothers the regime was more bearable as they had an idea of what to expect. My homesickness was tempered by my curiosity about this new environment. A positive aspect was the large number of potential pals who were all in the same boat. A less savory aspect was the inevitable emergence of the occasional bully from the more senior ranks ready to prey on vulnerable first years. You just had to do your best to avoid their clutches. We looked forward to holiday breaks at Christmas, Easter and Summer with same-day breaks on 23 September (St Eunan's Day), Halloween and St Patrick's Day. St Eunan's Day was particularly longed for but had the disadvantage of reminding you of the love and warmth you had given up at home.

On our first morning assembly, all seventy of us first years gathered to be divided into two manageable class sizes. Our numbers were swelled by a surge of day boys, students from the local Letterkenny area. They could be distinguished from the boarders in that they looked more 'cool'. Elvis hairstyles and tight blue jeans were the enviable marks of 'cool' in those days. We were split roughly 50/50 into 'A' and 'B' classes. The 'A' class was made up of scholarship boys, both County Council and Gaeltacht, supplemented with boys who had done reasonably well in the college entrance examination. Wee Paddy had not got around to putting my name down for the entrance examination as it was by no means certain that I would go to St. Eunan's. Were it not for the kindness of my mother's single sister, aunt Annie in America in meeting my fees, I would not have gone to the school. Scholarships meant that parents were saved the cost of college fees for the five years' duration in St Eunan's. Gaeltacht scholarships were awarded to children from officially designated Irish language speaking areas who achieved a defined academic standard. The 'B' class comprised the remaining boys. In the first rough cut, I emerged as 'B' class. After fine tuning, I was transferred to the 'A' class. For the first few terms a small number of boys were promoted and relegated within the two classes as in the football leagues. Thereafter the two classes settled into their final memberships.

Subjects such as Mathematics, Irish, English, History and Geography were on the curriculum as you would expect. Latin and Greek were whole new experiences, as was having a different teacher for each subject. Dr Daniel Cunnea, the college president, was our first Latin teacher. He spoke with a distinctive nasal twang, which he used to maximum resonance in delivering our first lesson. This was the declension of the Latin noun *mensa*. He seem to repeat the exercise several times to the extent that I have never forgotten the moment. This was indeed a strange new world.

Dr Cunnea sometimes exerted his authority vigorously and I remember vividly getting on the wrong side of him in the refectory one day. Occasionally there would not be enough gravy to go around so it was essential to get your hands on the bulbous bakelite-handled aluminium jug of hot gravy at the earliest opportunity. A bit of gravy made the most unpalatable meal wholesome. Cathal Casey and I grabbed the jug at precisely the same instant with the result that the hot gravy splashed into the air and all over the table. Dr Cunnea called us both outside the stained-glass refectory door so that we could explain to him what had happened. In unison, we sheepishly replied, 'Father, it was the gravy.' He retorted, 'I don't give a straw about the gravy,' before administering the most violent slap with his hand across the face to each of us. According to the kind of discipline prevailing at that time, this was deserved and so we didn't resent it. I was glad that I rarely crossed his path following that incident, but to be fair, I had no sense that he held it against me.

The refectory seating arrangements were similarly alphabetically determined as the chapel. However, a few migrant first-year students in the lower reaches of the alphabet, which included me, were not allocated fixed places, so as to be available to fill any casual vacancies that arose from boys being absent through sickness. This practice avoided food waste and the prospect of boys fighting over the extra meals. Ours was an unenviable status and invariably led to pudding confiscation by the older boys. The more senior the table at which you found yourself, the greater the likelihood of suffering this indignity. A migrant who had a feared and respected bigger brother student would be much less vulnerable to this practice. A big lad nicknamed Patrick 'Whang' McAteer was a serial pudding seizer, often aided and abetted by one Hugh 'Golly' Friel. Hugh was to become one of Ireland's most successful business leaders and one of the founders of the Kerry Group, the Irish food multinational. Both boys were natives of the Fanad peninsula in north Donegal. Fanad is a different place where the people are very resourceful and independent minded. There are several Fanad clans, of which Friel and McAteer are two prominent names.

In those days, 'Whang' was a kind of warlord who had a fearsome reputation among the junior ranks. On one memorable occasion he pillaged a bottle of orange squash from Hugh Tierney. Some days later he encountered Hugh once more and seized a second bottle from him and began to drink it with urgency until a look of horror came on his face. Hugh had filled an empty bottle with urine and was now standing directly in Wang's path. Hugh was a hero among the younger boys but fortunate to escape a beating from an angry Whang.

One way of whiling away our free time in St Eunan's was to continuously walk around the perimeter of the grounds. At the time it seemed to me such a futile activity, but it was nevertheless a useful way of both passing time and gaining exercise, as well as mixing with the other boys. However, most boys walked within a group that was made up of natives of their own home parishes. These groups were called 'buses'. Among others there was the Fanad 'bus' and the Kilcar 'bus'. I took every opportunity to avoid this endless walking by playing handball and table tennis, which I considered more useful activities, but latterly, Con Ward, Daniel McGeehan and myself formed an Ardara/Glenties bus and we did have a lot of craic.

In selecting boys that came from our own townlands and villages, we were reflecting the diversity of our county. Donegal people are by no means a homogenous lot. The county covers a large area compared to some other Irish counties, with roughly 161,000 people, according to the census of 2011. The inhabitants of Inishowen, Gweedore, The Rosses, In Through, Fanad, Ballyshannon/Bundoran are examples of these diverse regions. Inishowen people are more akin to Derry folk than to fellow Donegal people and they would traditionally have seen Derry as their local hub. Many Derry people have relations in Inishowen and vice-versa. The coastal populations would generally have had a strong Gaelic-speaking tradition with language survival more robust in some areas than others; the vast majority would be Roman Catholic. The fertile east Donegal region contrasts with much poorer land in the western coastal areas. East Donegal, where the majority of Donegal's Protestant population is concentrated, would enjoy strong ties with counties Tyrone, Derry and indeed Northern Ireland generally. The path of history and especially the Plantation of Ulster with Scottish settlers assisted the westward movement of the native population. The Ballyshannon area, for example, is closer in ethos and accent to Sligo and Leitrim than other Donegal districts. To the outsider the accents throughout the county may sound similar but the local ear will be aware of many variations.

When we weren't hanging around with the other boys or studying, Gaelic football was the dominant feature of college life and every student was supposed to be interested in playing, despite any personal reluctance. The inaugural fitting-out with new football gear was an exciting event for first-year students. The college ordered a selection of boots, jerseys, togs, socks and shin-guards and each of us was fitted out according to our size. We greatly looked forward to this shopping experience. For me, it was very much a triumph of optimism over ability. Hugh 'Hawk' Duffy, the senior Latin teacher, oversaw the distribution of the football kit. I asked Hugh to exclude shin-guards from my pack as it was equipment that I was not accustomed to ever using or needing; Hugh was not to know that I was trying to save my parents some money on the exorbitant expense of the kit, but he simply thought this was hilarious. 'You are exactly the kind of boy we are seeking to play football in St Eunan's, so tough that you don't need shin-guards,' he said. In the event, he did persuade me that I should take a pair for my protection.

What little football I played, I enjoyed, although it has to be said that the limited coaching available, and mainly from Michael 'Wart' Cullen, the Greek teacher, concentrated on prospective good players who would be destined to represent the college. Country boys rarely excelled at Gaelic football; at home in Beagh we were charged by our parents to help out on the farm when football would be going on in the town. Because the local pitches were convenient, it was the town lads who were generally the better players, with active GAA clubs in every town and sizable village. In line with the then GAA ban on foreign games, soccer was not permitted to be played. The ban on soccer was a deprivation for boys from north of the county, where soccer was traditionally prevalent. I wasn't a natural Gaelic player: my sporting activities at college were handball and table tennis, which I greatly enjoyed but at which I never excelled.

The holy grail of college football in Ulster was the MacRory Cup, the senior Ulster colleges championship. St Eunan's had never won this cup; the closest they ever got was a final under the coaching of a college teacher, John Wilson. This was the same John Wilson who had won an All-Ireland football medal with Cavan. He later became a career politician, culminating in being a government minister and then Tánaiste. During my time, teacher Michael Cullen, a local man, coached the senior college team. While we seemed to have great players, we didn't have the motivation to prise the championship away from the Northern Ireland colleges, which had a tradition of success. It seemed to me that those colleges had a more powerful drive arising from very good organisation and to a lesser extent on their valued Gaelic heritage. The same focus which I witnessed in these teams was clearly evident in the successful Tyrone and Armagh Gaelic football teams of the noughties.

One of the most enjoyable aspects of the college championship were the away matches. Final-year students were allowed to travel with the team to matches in Derry, Dungannon, Cavan, Monaghan and other venues. For us boarders the sense of freedom was uplifting: winning a match was a sensational experience.

I hadn't been in St Eunan's long when I received one of my regular letters from Brigid bringing me up to date on family and local news. I remember it well because it was at the same time as a terrible storm which uprooted trees and damaged buildings, the tail end of Hurricane Debbie. The letter brought news that my paternal grandmother Brigid, who was in her late eighties, had passed away. The news would have been more distressing had she lived with us in Beagh but she had remained in her family home in Sandfield with Hugh, Katie and their young family. My recollection of her is of an old lady with grey hair tied in a bun. She was always dressed in black and sat at the left-hand side of the kitchen mantelpiece on which two lovely ornamental dogs presided; they still do. As a child, she seemed to me to be of gentle disposition but in reality, she had a strong persona and very much the matriarch, as my own mother had learned. In what were surely tough times, she had raised a family of ten children, which included Packie and Hugh. Coincidentally Hugh and Katie also had a family of ten children, whom they reared while looking after Granny, who suffered from dementia in her later years. As is often the case in Ireland, it is the women who are the heroes in this kind of situation. Katie, a nonagenarian widow and the last remaining member of that generation, sadly passed away only recently; husband Hugh predeceased her more than twenty years ago.

Some of my memories of St Eunan's involve corporal punishment, which was the norm in those years. It generally took the form of lashing by a leather strap on either the hands or behind. The number of lashes varied in accordance with the gravity of the offence, but six was about the norm. Sad to say corporal punishment was meted out for academic underperformance as well as for the usual types of bad behaviour. Father Peter McMahon, known by his nickname, 'Pa Bear', a brilliant honours mathematics teacher, was a notorious corporal punisher in class. There was, therefore, a real premium in being good at maths in Pa Bear's class. Some pupils could be so terrified of him that they would lose their composure at the blackboard even though they were well capable of solving the problem. A pal of mine, Con Ward, had such an experience. As maths was taught in Gaelic at the time, Pa Bear directed Con to draw a 'léaráid' (Gaelic for diagram) on the blackboard. Con drew a circle, thinking he was being directed to draw a football or liathród, and earned himself a severe lashing. Another classmate, John McGill, was a wilier fellow. He had a premonition that his turn at the blackboard was due. John took protection by wearing his pyjamas under his trousers on the fateful day. Sure enough, Pa Bear called him to work out the problem on the blackboard, and, when John failed to solve the problem, he received the mandatory lashing on his behind. The sound of John's lashing was different, more akin to a bass thud than the usual slapping sound. This was one up for the boys: we suspected that Pa was not best pleased, eventhough he never commented.

I had my own moments with Pa Bear. Calculus was not my strong point, particularly where I could not envisage a practical application to the theory: rightly or wrongly, I believe that the experience of being forcibly changed from left- to right-handed writing hindered my capability in that area. In Pa Bear's class I therefore felt vulnerable to the threat of a severe lashing. I could see that the worst position in which you could find yourself was if you didn't own up when he enquired at the beginning of class if we'd got all the homework problems solved. Many of us in class would be in a position where we hadn't, but few if any would admit to it. Problems arose if one of us was unlucky enough to be picked at random to work out one of these problems on the blackboard. We were all acutely aware of the grave consequences of being found out. Having applied some thought to the issue, I employed a defensive tactic. When Pa Bear routinely asked if any of us had failed to solve any of the problems overnight, I would raise my hand if I had a difficulty with the problem. This meant that in one swoop I was free from the threat of being sent to the blackboard empty handed. Often, a classmate who didn't own up was selected and suffered the consequences. This was my earliest experience of what is now called risk management!

In my third year in St Eunan's, two of my Shovlin cousins, Pat and John, arrived. Pat was a Sandfield cousin and John, son of uncle Peter, lived in the local seaside resort of Narin. As we were relatives, we were allowed to room together, which was like home from home (in the prior year I had roomed with Downings boy, Colm Ward). On the other hand, we seemed quicker to plot mischief because we knew each other so well, especially Pat and I, who had shared many previous escapades. John, who was more of a town boy, was sensible beyond his years. He avoided some of our behavioural excesses which, on reflection, was probably because John benefited from growing up in the more cosmopolitan environment of his parents' guesthouse.

A common prank among us boarders was 'polishing', i.e., applying boot polish to the faces of selected fellow boarders after lights out. Pat and myself decided that this was an experience we couldn't miss. We identified the occupants of the nearby tower room as our targets. As a precaution to the inevitable revenge expected from our victims, we prepared our defences by moving cupboards and wash stands into place, to be pushed against our bedroom door. With barricades at the ready, individual victims divided up between us, and armed with brushes and black polish, we launched our offensive. We polished their sleeping faces and the soles of their feet and having accomplished our mission, we were safely back in our room within seconds. Retaliation was equally rapid and fierce. Our barricades were charged. They held firm, but our water jugs spilled all over the timber floor.

Still, the worst seemed to have passed. Our enemies retreated and the room fell into silence again, until we heard a gentle knock on our door. It was Dr Andy Carrabin, the college bursar whose bedroom was on the floor directly below our room. The noise had woken him up. He gravely enquired as to what was going on; water had apparently begun seeping through his ceiling! I, being the oldest of the trio, sheepishly mumbled some inanity. Dr Carrabin was a real gentleman and a person I deeply regretted upsetting, but nonetheless, I was relieved that it was he and not one of the other priests, who would certainly have resorted to a more violent outburst. It also has to be said that, as the years in college passed, we all matured some and became less enthusiastic about making mischief.

Cousin John's arrival in St Eunan's meant that his father, my uncle Peter, often gave me a lift home. Although Peter would have had to deliver our cousins Isobel and Nora to the Loreto Convent in Letterkenny, as well as John to St Eunan's, he always tried to make room for me in his car. Peter being the local insurance man therefore had a car for as long as I could remember.

In my final year at St Eunan's, my father had acquired a family car, an old blue Morris Minor. It was a terrible wreck and eventually caught fire while parked at our front door in Beagh. He had been about to drive it to Ardara and give a lift to a neighbour, Molly Martin. Luckily neither he nor Molly had boarded the stricken vehicle, otherwise they could have perished. Molly, who was not one to suffer fools gladly, was not impressed. Subsequently, Packie acquired a small Ford van, the registration of which I still remember: ZT 5839, which was used to ferry me to and from St Eunan's in the final school terms. This was great fun as I would be allowed to drive the van to Letterkenny. Conal, who was under age, would drive the return journey with Packie's cap placed on his head to effect a disguise. Packie, who had not learned to drive until his sixties, was not an enthusiastic driver, beyond going to local villages. He was therefore more than happy to delegate the driving to Conal and myself. The local police caught up with him on the Rosbeg road, which is off the beaten track, when Conal was behind the wheel. Packie was summonsed and convicted at Glenties District Court and fined £5. The galling part for Packie was that the policeman who had issued the summons was then a lodger in uncle Peter and Nora's guesthouse in Narin.

By fifth year in St Eunan's, school became easier to accept as the end of our incarceration loomed. In particular, our fourth year was more relaxed, leading into the serious final year when we would sit our Leaving Certificate exams. One of the treats of fourth year was getting time off study in May to help prepare the grounds for the annual sports day. The college bursar, the genial Dr Carrabin, supervised this project which was mainly restricted to boys who didn't feature prominently in football. I recall the mad scramble there would be to operate the motor lawnmowers; access to such technology would have been a novelty for most of us.

In 1966, the Leaving Certificate examinations arrived. As boarders, we had so much study time to prepare that we all should have achieved top honours. While the results showed that we did reasonably well, my results fell far short of what I expected. Reflecting on it now, I might well have done better with less study time, when I would have had to study at a greater pace, because I have always worked better under pressure. Nonetheless, my results did not continue the trend of high marks I had obtained in the Intermediate (Junior) Certificate two years earlier. Perhaps I had peaked too early! What I do believe is that subconsciously, I had no great desire to reap the consequences of high marks: a call to teacher training or a university scholarship. The allure of returning to Beagh and my local community then seemed more compelling.

St Eunan's was a tough environment and I couldn't wait for the end of the five-year period; it seemed like forever. Some boys hated it while others seemed to find it much more tolerable. To me, it was just about bearable. Having been reared in the open countryside, I particularly disliked the lack of freedom to leave the grounds. However, it was only on the occasion of the twenty-five year reunion of our class, masterminded by well-known political pundit Sean Donnelly, that I realised how terrible our schooldays must have been for some boys. They refused outright to attend the reunion because the thought of St Eunan's brought back such bad memories. While I could see their point, I did have fun there and made lifelong and good friends and I think that one of the outstanding benefits of such a boarding school is that it teaches you to hold your own in life.

CHAPTER FOUR

BORDER PATROL

I recall that day in August 1966 when the Leaving Cert results arrived, because my cousin Pat visited the house that morning, curious to know how the first local Shovlin cousin to go to secondary school had performed. Pat was a few years younger than me and had that gift of timing capable of piercing the most vulnerable point of your psyche. He seemed to have uncanny and intuitive detection skills and it was no surprise that he later became a successful policeman.

Conal and I were sleeping late but Packie informed Pat that we were already out herding sheep in remote Derryness and not expected to return for a few hours. Thankfully, I was therefore able to open the results envelope in relative privacy and to discover that I had got an honours result, but only just. My Gaelic result, which fell just below honours level, was a particular disappointment, because my mother was a native speaker. Deep down, I knew I should have done better in the exams.

Nonetheless, not everyone had the opportunity to obtain the Leaving Certificate, so I had the comfort of being in that privileged minority. Going directly into the workforce rather than to third-level education was the priority. Brigid would have loved to see me win a place in primary teacher training college but I had no ambitions in that regard, nor I had I the grades. Indeed at that time, I would have been quite satisfied to stay at home and work with Packie on the farm. As well as the variety of work which included cropping, turfcutting and animal husbandry on the farm, I enjoyed the social aspect with friends and neighbours. Furthermore, I had had my belly-full of the books and study. There were social pressures to try to make good use of this relatively high level of education; the Leaving Certificate was then the pinnacle of academic achievement for most boys and girls, but after the examination results were announced, I continued to live at home in Beagh without any clear idea or concern as to what career direction I should take. At that time our family still lived in the old thatched cottage, but Packie was trying to get the money together to build our new house on the site where our haystack had always stood. This location was in a nice position, slightly elevated on even ground and convenient to the main road. The existing thatched cottage had been built among rocks on one of the worst pieces of land on the holding. (In Donegal, it was customary for families to build the home on a poor piece of land so that no arable land would be wasted).

The new house was built in 1967 by a local craftsman, Brian Boyle. Not only was Brian great company to have around but he was also a brilliant all-round craftsman who, aided only by his sole assistant James Elliot, did all the work on the house. Of course Packie and Conal were around to do a lot of the heavy labouring work attached to the project. There was continual banter between Brian, Packie and Conal, which Brigid thoroughly enjoyed. At last we had our much-longed-for nice new house with running water and full sanitation. Ironically, by the time it was built, I was not living there any longer to enjoy our new home, but in my regular visits home it was wonderful to see Brigid and Packie in their new home.

In 1966, both Conal and I took the opportunity to serve our country by joining the FCA, the Irish auxiliary defence force. The only significant time demand was the two week training camp in mid summer at Finner military camp, near Ballyshannon. This was an enjoyable period when we learned how to fire a rifle, army drills and disciplines and watch the unforgettable world cup final, on black and white television and see England triumph. My conviction that schoolteaching was not for me hardened following stints as a substitute teacher at two local schools. Firstly, I taught in Kiltoorish school for a number of weeks in place of Nuala Harkin, who was on maternity leave. This was a single-teacher school in the small coastal community of Rosbeg. The offer of this temporary post was the first dividend of my attainment of the Leaving Certificate and I valued the opportunity to earn a few pounds and to see what teaching school was really like. The Rosbeg assignment also allowed me to visit Mary Harkin, an old friend of Packie's, who lived in a thatched cottage on the Rosbeg side of the school. As children, we had walked the several miles across the warren by Tramore beach to visit friends in Rosbeg and Mary Harkin's house had been the first port of call. Mary was an accomplished farmer and would always have a good stock of hens and other farmyard animals. Her interests lay in farm matters and the affairs that generally interested men; she had little or no time for housewives' chat. Like many Rosbeg people, Mary spoke in a loud voice: Brigid use to say that this was because of the background noise of the sea nearby. Curiously at the time, Mary lived with a man called 'Red' Sweeney, who did the heavy jobs around the smallholding. Red was perceived as more of a servant rather than a partner in the farm and it was obvious that Mary was the farm owner and very much the boss. It was not clear if their relationship extended beyond farm help, but this was not a subject on which any local would comment. Mary was a kind-hearted woman and insisted that I have my lunch in her house for the duration of my attachment to the school.

Later that year, I had another opportunity to teach, this time in Meenavalley school, which is on the Killybegs side of Ardara parish.

I was a substitute for the 'juniors' teacher, Eileen Curran, who again was on maternity leave. The principal and senior teacher was Gracie McGhee, whose son, Frank, had been in my year in St Eunan's and who had just started at University College Galway. Gracie was an extremely talented and good-hearted person. She was an extraordinary music teacher who had her own school band, having taught the schoolchildren to play a series of instruments. She also gave me lessons in playing the tin whistle in which regrettably I never progressed, but I had great fun working alongside Gracie in Meenavally.

However, teaching children was a valuable experience that convinced me that I did not have the aptitude for it, although the sense that I was doing a real job did bring the first and welcome assertion of my adulthood, after a grim five years of studentdom. I found that time passed very slowly, despite the working hours being short. I realised that I was more interested in tangible direct activity, where I was accumulating information rather than passing on static knowledge to others.

What career path I might follow was a constant presence on Brigid's mind. She felt that it was high time I found something to interest me in the world of work. Her good friend Jim Curran from Malinbeg was the electricity meter inspector at the time. When he called, he would always have tea and a chat about matters In Through. Jim was a particularly good source of local information because he called to houses in several parishes. At the time, Jim's nephew, Pat McLoughlin, was doing very well in the Irish Customs service. The thought of the Customs as a possible career for me was mooted, not least because it was a steady job, probably local on the Irish border, with clear prospects.

In Autumn 1966 I duly responded to a newspaper advertisement for entrants to the Irish Customs Service and sat the entrance examination, which was held in the Literary Institute in Letterkenny. Con Ward, a St Eunan's classmate, also took the examination. We both did well in the examination, but Con chose to join the mainstream civil service shortly afterwards, where he enjoyed a good career. I subsequently went through a series of interviews and was offered a job with the grand title of Assistant Preventative Officer. My final interview was conducted by a Patrick John O'Reilly, then a senior inspector in the Customs Service and father of the legendary Irish rugby international and highly successful businessman Tony (Sir Anthony) O'Reilly whose path I later crossed in my banking career.

Having been offered a post, my first assignment was in Dublin and I'll never forget arriving by bus on the Navan Road, hosts of red brick chimneys stretching before me. I associated the sight with the opening scene in the television soap, *Coronation Street*. Because this city environment contrasted so sharply with the open spaces, landscape and sea in Donegal, I was a little homesick. However, in my first week or so in Dublin my cousin, Greg Harkin, came to my assistance in putting me up in his flat in Home Farm Road, Drumcondra. I recall thinking that it was sheer luxury. Greg, who was already established in the insurance industry, could not have been more helpful to me as a rookie in the city.

There were new recruits from other counties in Ireland in the Customs Service. Among those I became friendly with were Colm Gleeson from Cork and John Hever from Sligo. The three of us took up lodgings in a house on Clonliffe Road on Dublin's northside, but we quickly moved on because it soon became clear to us that there was more social activity south of the river. This is where two of the most popular dance halls, the Olympic and the Crystal, were situated. Hence, we rented a small flat in Lennox Street, near the South Circular Road. The accommodation, which was in part of a fairly run-down old Georgian house, was grim. The owners lived on the ground floor and we occupied a large first-floor bedroom and had the use of an adjacent bathroom. Most inconveniently our kitchen was in the basement so we had to troop down all the way from the first floor; this was a real pain, particularly in the mornings when we were always under time pressure to get to work. There was also now no landlady to give us a morning call and make our breakfast, a major disadvantage of our new-found freedom. So, we ensured that we did not sleep late by placing an alarm ('pandy') clock on an upturned enamel basin to create the maximum sound effect. The resultant noise would 'waken the dead' and the owners were not best pleased with this loud intrusion into their home.

In the beginning all three of us were assigned duties in the Dublin area, but it wasn't long until we were dispersed further afield. My Dublin assignments consisted mainly of checking passenger and freighter arrivals at Dublin docks. Belfast train arrivals at Connolly Station, which was nearby, were also on my roster and my duties involved checking for large shopping items in people's belongings as they disembarked off the trains. (Restrictions on the import of goods into the Republic of Ireland were strict in that period before trade was liberalised). My only tangible result was a banned pornographic magazine dropped in my lap by a fleeing young man.

The British and Irish Steam Packet Company ships sailed between the North Wall and Liverpool regularly and I was a member of the Customs team that covered their arrivals. They would arrive in the early morning and the passengers would pour down the gangways through the Customs area. Occasionally, cars would be offloaded by crane; this predated the roll-on/roll-off ferries which now ply the Irish Sea. The passengers were mainly Irish emigrants returning either for short stays or coming back to Ireland for good. One particular passenger was Mick O'Connell, the famous Kerry footballer. Dressed in a dark blazer with a crest, he looked every inch the sports hero that he was.

The morning arrival of the Liverpool ship was the highlight of our day. Seeing the throngs and variety of people was exciting and I was intrigued with the inside of the ship, with its huge steel doors and high thresholds. Then there was the daily treat from the ship's kitchen. After all the passengers had gone through Customs, the catering staff would make up bacon butties for us, which we would devour.

Dublin Port was then divided into different docking areas, according to the type of ship. The passenger ships which plied between Ireland and Britain berthed at the North Wall, beside what is now the International Financial Services Centre. The big cargo ships docked further east in Alexandra Basin, close to the factories, such as Goulding Fertilisers, which unloaded raw materials directly from the ships into their premises.

Customs would be notified with the approximate docking times of ships due to arrive in the Port. We would remain in the small Customs office nearby until we were alerted by the pilot's office that the ship had arrived on the quayside. We were the first to board the ship as soon as the gangplank was dropped. We were greeted on board by the ships' captain, who would be prepared for the customs process, showing us to the spirits and cigarettes store, which my senior colleague ensured was sealed as a bonded store until the ship departed Dublin. It was not uncommon for the ship's captain to present the senior customs officer with a bottle of spirits before the store was sealed. No favour was sought or given, but the captain was merely acknowledging the provision of the service often at an unearthly hour.

That was 1967 and my uncle Paddy, my mother's brother, had been ill for some time with a serious form of cancer. I received a letter from Brigid to say that he had passed away; leaving his wife Cassie and two young children, Phelim and Mairead. As this was at a time when few rural houses had ordinary telephones not to mention mobiles, by the time I heard, the funeral had already taken place. Even though Paddy's death was expected, Brigid was heartbroken, although her natural stoicism would have concealed her sorrow. Brigid and Paddy were close, having grown up in adversity. Their sibling bond was all the stronger because of a childhood marred by the absence of parents.

Paddy and Brigid had lived in the family home until they each got married. I was fond of Paddy, who was very laid back, with a wicked sense of humour. He was a highly intelligent man whose competencies seemed well in excess of the demands being made upon him. Paddy was, in effect, the local citizens' advice bureau, advising on all sorts of form-filling and also running a sort of impromptu shop for the locals. Largynaseeragh was a long way from local shops and the road surfaces were uneven and rough, particularly in bad weather, when even the travelling shopkeeper, Charlie Craig, might not manage to get to the townland. Paddy stepped into the breach by maintaining at his house a small store of key provisions such as paraffin oil for lighting, cigarettes, pipe tobacco, sheep dip and other necessities. Cassie was a good-humoured but highly efficient woman who handled the money side of things. She ensured that her famous tin money box always had sufficient funds to pay due creditors.

I had stayed for short periods with Paddy and Cassie on several occasions during my childhood. There was always plenty going on. I remember clearly being there in 1956 when the rural electrification programme had just reached Largynaseeragh. Other areas in Donegal had already been connected. It was usual for the Electricity Supply Board to bring the supply to a meter inside the front door, however, it was up to the householder to arrange for their home to be 'wired' for lighting and plug points. The few electricians in existence lived in the towns, and were in strong demand to support the electrification programme. Most people had no option but to join the queue for their services. Not so Paddy, who was able to do the wiring himself. Having observed a local electrician wire a house just once, he was then able to replicate the process perfectly.

I remember being a teenager at the time Paddy had just taken delivery of his first car, a cream Ford Anglia. Paddy, being Paddy, was able to hop into the car and drive it with the minimum of tuition and he allowed me to drive the car as soon as I could see out over the steering wheel. I had already reached a reasonable level of competence from driving Packie's old blue Morris Minor. I remember Paddy and I flying along the road with me at the wheel at a place called Scadaman, below Glengesh Pass. I drove into a dangerous bend much too fast and it was a miracle that I avoided ending up in the field. Paddy just laughed. It was not that he was reckless, but he had probably reckoned, 'so what, the car might be damaged, we'll survive'. It wouldn't be the end of the world. That summed up Paddy's attitude to life.

Just months into my assignment at Dublin Port, which I was enjoying, word came through of a change. I was to transfer to Muff, a frontier post on the Donegal/Derry border. Muff is situated on the western shore of Lough Foyle in the Inishowen Peninsula. I had mixed feelings about the change. Bidding farewell to my pals was difficult as we were having a great time. We had money in our pockets and there was so much more to see and do in the city compared to Donegal. On the other hand, I was returning to my native county, which couldn't be bad; my Donegal colleagues would envy my move back home.

Muff Customs post consisted of a small grey galvanised-steel building with a public counter area in the front and a small private room at the back. Fred Furey was the preventative officer and person in charge at Muff and he briefed me on my duties. I would largely be dealing with car drivers and bus passengers crossing the border. There would be occasional foot patrols and on rare occasions, I would be a crew member of the mobile patrol attached to Muff. Fred, a serious man, was highly regarded in the local community and it was clear that he had my best interests at heart as the youngest and newest of his charges. Lodgings had already been arranged with Mrs McGee, a kindly lady, who lived with her husband John in a two-storey farmhouse a few hundred yards down the lane. In fact, the house was across the border in County Derry. John worked in the Dupont plant across the

Foyle estuary on the outskirts of Derry city. He was a feisty individual who had been through the mill with his health having fully recovered from a severe cancer that had left his face disfigured. He was proud of his nationalist heritage. During the IRA troubles of the 1950s, he had suffered a beating at the hands of the B-Specials, the reserve police force in Northern Ireland. Both John and Maura McGee were kind to me and I have fond memories of my stay with them.

Another Customs man and Gweedore native, Joe McBride, also lodged with the McGees. Joe was a quiet and genuine bloke. He drove a well-kept slate-grey Volkswagen Beetle which was the envy of myself and other carless young Customs men. Joe and I shared a double bed in the McGees spare bedroom; hard though it may to believe now, it was quite normal for same-sex lodgers to double up in the same bed back in those days.

I soon settled into the daily routine at Muff. My fellow Customs officers were a great bunch and couldn't have been friendlier. It helped that Pat Haughey, a brother of my good friend Kevin, was a senior officer there. It was great making the connection with Pat whose family Brigid knew and of course they lived in a neighbouring townland to my aunt Teresa's family in Carrick. Being a Customs officer was a new and enjoyable experience, particularly when compared to being stuck in boarding school, which I had been less than one year previously. I felt so lucky, as if life was just beginning.

I enjoyed watching the comings and goings across the border; Brian Friel, the playwright, who lived locally, regularly passed through and once I had to assist the Honourable Garech de Brún with the paperwork relating to a vintage horse-drawn carriage which he and his late father had acquired in Donegal. In common with most people travelling to and from Dublin they had to drive through Northern Ireland as this was the direct route, and a document issued at the point of entry to Northern Ireland demonstrating that the goods were sourced in the Republic of

Ireland was needed. The document was subject to inspection when re-entering the Republic, at Monaghan in this case. Garech de Brún stood out because he was dressed in very traditional Irish woollen fabrics.

Being a Customs officer in Muff provided the kind of excitement that you derive from a new toy: I was having great fun with this new toy but after a period a little restlessness was creeping in; the low-boredom threshold which drives such restlessness has always been a feature of my life. I felt that I needed a greater depth to my existence, not just a secure job and good pay. Being aware of former St. Eunan's classmates who had gone to university, I secretly pined for the additional horizons and knowledge that was open to them.

In the meantime, much of my spare time was spent visiting Derry city, which had nice shops. It also had a fine swimming pool where I advanced my modest swimming ability. Muff wasn't much by way of a town in those days but it did have one great asset in my eyes. That was the widely known Borderland dance hall in which all the best Irish dance bands of that time played. Big names, such as Jim Farley, Earl Gill, Roly Daniels, The Freshmen and The Cadets, all featured in Borderland. Muff was an attractive leisure destination for the people of Derry, because of the sense of freedom in the Republic that, even in those pre-Troubles times, was not present in the divided community of Northern Ireland. Of course, in just the following year, 1968, all hell would break loose in that city, with the arrival of the Civil Rights movement and subsequent clashes with the police.

For us country boys, the Derry girls had that tantalising allure of town sophistication which we knew we didn't have, but craved. Many of them worked in the shirt factories around Derry. They were, however, much more amenable to being chatted up by fellow townies than by a lad from the depths of rural Donegal. From the time I had started taking an interest in girls, I always found the town man to be formidable opposition. They seemed to have a self-assuredness that was missing in us country boys. They were more trendy in both the clothes they wore and the way they spoke. They were knowledgeable about football and played regularly. All in all, it was an unbeatable combination.

Within a few months, I was transferred from Muff to Lifford, a much larger and busier border post as well as being the local Customs headquarters. Lifford is on the west side of the river Foyle, which borders counties Donegal and Tyrone. Strabane is the town on the east side of the Foyle, essentially Lifford's significantly larger twin in Northern Ireland. Lifford customs post was much larger and a more serious endeavour than Muff. There were more officers, so new arrivals and departures were commonplace; the environment was consequently more impersonal and less friendly. I was to be a crew member of a mobile patrol unit which monitored the border outside the town. The experience turned out to be far less exciting than I had been expecting. The midnight jousts I had anticipated with local smugglers never materialised: it seemed like fishing; waiting for hours but catching nothing. The truth was that the professional smugglers were rarely likely to fall into the trap of mobile patrol checks. These guys would have studied the shift patterns of the mobile crews and timed their crossings accordingly. Moreover, the border with Northern Ireland is so riddled with small unapproved road crossings that it was virtually impossible to patrol effectively. Also, most of the people using these roads were simply doing so for convenience, and not for the purpose of smuggling. One of these was Phil Ward from Ardara, whom our patrol once stopped on the Clady crossing. Phil was employed by the Kennedy family of Ardara to collect hand-knitted garments from knitters across the border in Northern Ireland. Ironically, Phil's sister Bernadette was to marry my brother Conal several years later.

Some of the Customs boys took lodgings in Strabane and a vacancy was found for me with Maura McMenamin, a well-known and respected Strabane landlady. Maura ran a happy boarding house and she also did a meals-only service on a limited basis. The meals-only client I remember best was local tailor and gentleman Harry McNulty. I also remember that I had my first bath with running water in Maura's, which was quite a novelty.

The shift-work pattern and the tedium of being driven around the same border areas day after day began to be boring. My mind started rolling over other career options. I began to wonder if this was it. Was I going to see out my future life doing this? Granted, the Customs was a good job, but mental stimulation was a luxury, and I was missing it. Staying awake in the Customs patrol car became a challenge.

Listening to tales of Customs officers' exploits helped pass the time. One such story was of a man who cycled daily from Strabane across the Lifford border crossing, a small wooden box on his bicycle carrier. He became such a familiar sight to the Customs officers that they passed no remarks on his passage. They deemed that the small box probably contained personal belongings, nothing to worry about. One day, though, a curious officer asked to see inside the box. The box was empty; it emerged that the man had been smuggling bicycles for some time and had never been detected.

Nonetheless, I concluded that if I were to continue in this job, I would go to seed. No matter what the opportunities for promotion in the future, wouldn't the work be the same, I reasoned. I even surprised myself by dreaming about furthering my education in some way. The possibility of a bank clerical job had been a possible fallback option, which I had never let finally fade. My attention switched on to this option and I decided to do the Ulster Bank entrance examination. The seeds of the idea of joining a bank came from a family discussion with my uncle Peter whose son, Francis, was already developing a worthwhile career with the Belfast-headquartered Ulster Bank. Brigid would not have viewed a banking career as as attractive as teaching or indeed the Irish police service, but it was well regarded all the same. Although the initial salaries were relatively poor, there was a definite status attached to being a bank clerk in rural Ireland. Indeed, the local bank manager was regarded as the cream of small-town society.

In those days, your application didn't get off the ground without a nomination from a respected member of society—it now seems so old fashioned. The ideal person would have a bank account with Ulster Bank and/or have some other business relationship with them. The bank would only rely on the nomination by a reputable person, recognised by the bank. My family did not have a bank account, so we had to find a person of good repute and known to the bank who would nominate me. At the suggestion of Harry Clements, a friend of the Shovlin family and then Ulster Bank manager in Donegal Town, I approached David McC Watson seeking a nomination. He was then a senior partner in the much-revered and long-established accounting firm of Craig Gardner, but he was also a non-executive director of a number of companies, including Ulster Bank. Mr McC Watson regularly fished for trout in the Bellanagoal river, which flows within yards of our home in Beagh. His wife, a lovely lady, would often while away the hours visiting and chatting with Brigid in our cottage. It must have been such an extreme comparison with their fine home on it own grounds in Kilternan, County Dublin.

If Mr McC Watson judged me and my family on our then housing circumstances, I would have sought a bank nomination in vain. However, he didn't, but gladly obliged, so I was off to a good start. I followed up with the written examination which was held in the Royal Belfast Academical Institution, a renowned Belfast school. My results were adequate to lead me to an interview at the bank's head office in Waring Street, Belfast. The interview panel, which consisted of three executives, was led by Tom Daly, Head of Personnel. I recall the interview to have been quite a grilling, albeit a courteous one. The abiding memory that I have of that interview was the blinding sunlight shining in through the window facing me. Thankfully, I had the wit to ask them to draw the blind, rather than persevere in the blinding light. Armed with the confidence boost of this little incident I recovered my composure and ended up enjoying the experience. I discovered later that Tom Daly was a much feared interviewer so perhaps on reflection the sunlight wasn't accidental after all!

CHAPTER FIVE

ULSTER BANK

After filing the acceptable nomination papers, succeeding in an entrance examination and an extensive interview process, Ulster Bank offered me the job of junior bank official in 1967. Having grown up viewing the local Ardara bank manager and staff with some awe, the prospect of now moving to the other side of the bank counter did attract me.

I accepted the Ulster Bank job offer and resigned from the Irish Customs service. As a green 20-year-old, I simply hoped that a job in a bank might offer a stimulating and worthwhile career. Little did I know, my career in the banking industry would endure for 35 years and would prove both enjoyable and demanding, and through which I would be privileged to witness the great changes taking place in the country.

My first month in the bank was spent with the other new recruits at the bank training school, which was near to Queen's University in Belfast. The excitement of meeting new colleagues was like the Customs all over again, but that was where the comparison began and ended. The work would be entirely different: more concentrated, with less freedom, exclusively indoors and with my nose to the grindstone. No more the gold-braided uniform or the official-looking peaked cap. Worse still, the salary was lower and came with no shift premia. I had to remind myself more than once why I had decided to move.

At Ulster Bank, I was to renew my acquaintance with John McGill, a St Eunan's College classmate, who joined the bank the same day. During the training period, John and I shared accommodation at Bridie Duffy's house. Bridie was a sister of Katie, my aunt by marriage to my uncle Hugh. Herself, husband Paddy and family lived in Newtownabbey, on the northern outskirts of Belfast. Bridie was a gem, a brilliant cook and all-round nice person. Her eldest son Seamus, a child Irish-dancing prodigy, was the same age as John and I, so we had great fun. Bridie had lived in Belfast for many years, and had first worked in service with the Corscadden family. Harry Corscadden was a senior Ulster Bank director around the time I joined and Bridie had no hesitation in ringing him to mention my name. I don't know if I would not have got the job without Bridie's intervention, but I am sure it did help my case.

Towards the end of our month's training and after the customary new entrants' course photograph was taken we were all advised as to which bank branch we would be attached. We were all excited and intrigued. Generally, we were placed in accordance with our native jurisdictions i.e. Republic of Ireland and Northern Ireland. I was appointed to O'Connell Street, Dublin, the second largest branch in the Republic. The next four years would be spent there, initially as branch junior and general dogsbody. It was difficult to imagine what to expect but I eagerly looked forward to experiencing the new environment on Ireland's main street.

O'Connell Street had a staff of twenty-five or thereabouts, which included both male and female employees. Working with women would be a new experience and a refreshing change from the all-male environments of school and the Customs service. CFR (Ricky) Anderson, one of the bank's most senior managers, was in charge and his deputy was David Netterfield; both northern Unionist gentlemen. The impressive Tony Larney, an adroit Louth man, became deputy before I left. The counter staff, and particularly the cashiers, were top of the pecking order. Cashiering was the coveted job in those days as cashiers were paid a handsome daily allowance. I never could understand the logic of this allowance, which eventually disappeared from the scene.

I would take over the junior's duties from my predecessor, Eamon Stapleton. Eamon, a Waterford boy, was accomplished both academically and in sport, but he had no heart for bank work. He was far more interested in culture, especially the theatre, for which he was to leave the bank. Eamon showed me the ropes and we got on well together. A part of the job was to walk to the large College Green branch to do the daily payment exchanges with other Ulster Bank branches. There I would meet juniors from the other Dublin branches, thus extending my social network. One of these was Harry McCarthy, who had joined the bank on the same day as me in Belfast. It was in a conversation with Harry that I first heard the term 'working class', which I could not comprehend, such was my naïveté. Harry tried to subtly explain the concept but my mindset was then far too socialist a bent to contemplate that, for example, could he and I not be called working class—after all, we worked, didn't we? Ultimately, I grasped the concept that there was a middle class who indeed worked, but weren't called working class. Where did that leave me then, I wondered. I concluded that I was of peasant background, but well on my way to becoming middle class!

My immediate perception of my new circumstances was that the status I had enjoyed in the Customs was much diminished and the lower pay was doing nothing for my morale. Eamon's literary orientation was subconsciously influencing my demeanour and fuelling my rebellious instincts. I began placing quotes from some of the great poets on the wall which my desk faced. By deciding not to conform to the branch's male dress code of 'suit only', instead wearing an unmatching jacket and trousers, I was seen to be testing Ricky's authority. He made it known through my immediate superior that were I to continue to wear them, I would find myself transferred to the Ballyjamesduff branch in County Cavan forthwith. I got the message. Despite this little incident Ricky gave me a positive staff appraisal at the end of my first year at the branch. In response to a question on the staff appraisal form as to how far this person would progress, he wrote, 'definitely managerial if not executive level'. This was a good endorsement indeed from someone who was normally scarce with praise.

I have fond memories of Eamon, who mentored me in those early days. He pursued acting and writing careers, notably at the Abbey Theatre, and was one of the most genuine and sincere people you could meet. Sadly, he struggled with alcoholism in his life, but overcame it and later returned to his native Waterford. To my pleasant surprise, Eamon renewed contact with me a few years ago. Mary and I visited him in Waterford in 2010 and recognised his failing health. Sadly, some months later I was telephoned by an acquaintance of his informing me that he had passed away.

A key player in the O'Connell Street Branch was Owen Mulligan, the head porter, who came from Longwood, County Kildare. He was a good adviser to the younger lads, but you had to be prepared to see things Owen's way. Your stature improved if you could drink a pint. He was in absolute command of his duties but more importantly, he was Ricky's drinking buddy. Ricky rarely socialised with his management colleagues, let alone bank staff generally. He was a shy man with a low tolerance level for those he believed to be incompetent; few apart from Owen seemed to consistently pass the test of acceptability. Drinking generally was a great pastime among several of the male staff; the ability to hold your drink seemed to be a test of manhood. It was a skill which I was to develop before long, hastened by the supportive environment. Most of the drinking was done in Mooney's pub around the corner on Eden Quay.

There was one particular staff member in O'Connell Street who was different, counter hand Charlie Ruttle, who was a perfect, but alas, not-much-followed role model. He was born and raised in Rathkeale, County Limerick and was of Palatine stock.

I learned a lot from Charlie's example. He was generous in sharing his knowledge of how the banking system worked and with general advice on career development. He was brilliant at his job, and a nice guy with it. His personal presentation skills were equally good; in short, he looked the part. He was the first person that I had come across who had more than one suit of clothes. Charlie had grown up above the family drapery shop, so his dress sense was well founded. At our shared lodgings in Calderwood Road, Drumcondra, Charlie showed me how to press trousers by placing them under the bed mattress overnight. Some colleagues found Charlie's perfectionism irritating, but for me it was a learning experience. Charlie and I spent about three years as lodgers with Rose McManus, a Co. Fermanagh native. We both caught the bus daily from Marino to our work in the city centre until I acquired a second-hand Lambretta scooter. This vehicle greatly enhanced my transport efficiency around the city, especially when I began my degree studies at University College Dublin (UCD). The scooter could be dangerous on wet surfaces and I did take a potentially serious tumble in Marino, crashing into a student who was wheeling his bicycle across the street in front of me. I was relieved that he was on the nearside of his bicycle and so escaped injury; otherwise, he could have been seriously hurt. As for me, I was fortunate to escape with a very painful shoulder, which has troubled me on and off ever since.

Charlie and I were not the only lodgers with Rose McManus: a couple of Aer Lingus guys stayed there as did Michael Tobin, a civil servant at the Department of the Environment. Michael was a bright, ambitious and cocky lad. He lorded it over the rest of us as the proud owner of a Honda 50 moped, which was mostly used in the courting of his future wife, Maura. He and I shared the front bedroom. I have an abiding memory of Michael putting his foot up on the end of my bed late one night and polishing his shoes with vigour. Despite my protests as I lay in bed Michael continued the action which had an annoying vibrating effect on the bed. Michael achieved great success in the civil service and ultimately became Chief Executive of the Irish National Roads Authority.

A few months after joining Ulster Bank, I signed up for a Bachelor of Commerce degree course at University College Dublin. This possibility had originally entered my head while I was working in the Customs service. At the outset, the lure of mental stimulation rather than any high-minded career objective motivated me in the direction of further study. There was also a social aspect: a few of my St Eunan's classmates were still undergraduates at UCD and I fancied connecting up with them again. Shay O'Byrne, John McMorrow, Sean Donnelly and James Browne are names that come to mind. As it turned out, I had little time left to associate with these guys after my day's work at the bank and my attendance at lectures.

I signed up for the evening course which took four years, a year longer than the day course. Course registration took place in the Great Hall, Earlsfort Terrace, then the home of the university, since transformed into the National Concert Hall. During term-time, the Great Hall was the study hall and the library was next door in what is now the John Field Room.

By coincidence I met an old classmate of St Eunan's, Eddie Rowland, at the registration. Eddie had just moved to Dublin from Mayo with Ulster Bank. He was also enrolling in the Bachelor of Commerce class by evening course. It was great to meet up with Eddie and to have so much in common, but we would not have taken on this challenge if we had stopped to think about the mountain we had set ourselves to climb. The prospect that a university degree could widen my career options now greatly appealed to me plus the excitement of travelling on a new road while still having the security of a job at the bank. The disadvantage of an incomplete participation in student life with its consequent ample leisure time was well and truly offset by having money in our pockets.

Student life was very different to secondary school. In the lecture halls, there was tiered seating in a kind of amphitheatre with the lecturer standing at the lowest level. The lecturers were also very different in their approach to the students and the feeling of being treated as an adult was a welcome change. Some of the lecturers were colourful and eccentric. There were a few engaging communicators whose delivery of information was logical and well organised. Of course, there was also the boring lecturer who struggled to hold the attention of the students for the whole hour. The majority of the commerce subjects appealed to me from the outset. They seemed to be practical and related to the real world, in contrast to my classical secondary schooling. I could readily relate the material to the commercial activity I was seeing at the bank. English was the only non-business subject covered, which we took in our first year. We were fortunate in having Professor Gus Martin lecture to us. Gus Martin was a highly regarded scholar. His lectures were stimulating and lifted my understanding of English literature to a higher level. This was my first introduction to James Joyce; a new window on Dublin life and literature was opened to me.

There was one unique character who was an institution in Earlsfort Terrace at that time. That person was Paddy Kehoe, one of several college porters who manned the small station on the right-hand side as you entered through the main door. Paddy spoke with such wit and verbosity that it was impossible to understand what he was saying. I think he must have taken his cue from James Joyce. He feigned an attitude that if you couldn't figure out what his words meant, it was you who was intellectually deficient. Paddy was very popular with the students and added colour to our lives. He was eventually awarded an honourary doctorate by the College; a decision that was widely acclaimed by anyone who knew him at Earlsfort Terrace.

The late sixties was a period of turmoil in UCD. The 1968 student riots in Paris seemed to set the tone for more radical student politics across Europe, including Ireland. UCD had it own activist group called the Students for Democratic Action (SDA), the vehicle for protest in UCD. They were demanding a more democratic university with a greater role for students in the running of the college. Students Ruairi Quinn, Kevin Myers and John Feeney were some of the names I recall being to the forefront at that time. All three would become prominent figures in Irish life.

The student protests brought a great buzz around Earlsfort Terrace. You wondered where they were leading and what the eventual impact on the university might be. While the protests lasted, the SDA caused considerable disturbance. They barricaded themselves into lecture halls and led protests around the vicinity of the campus. The full-time students involved themselves in the protest activity to varying degrees, but the episode seemed over the head of the average student. We evening students did not have the time or motivation to become involved. My impression was that it was mainly students who were active in the major college political and debating societies that were dedicated to the protest activity. However, the college authorities response was well judged and the students achieved recognition for their Union by the governing body of the University.

The commerce and arts faculties transferred from Earlsfort Terrace to the new Belfield campus in 1969. That meant that we would have the additional journey from the city centre out beyond Donnybrook towards Stillorgan for the final two years of our course. This is when my Lambretta scooter came into its own.

I was working away at the bank and studying at night, and my life seemed very full, too full sometimes, so when the large Irish banks closed their doors for several months from May 1970, due to an industrial relations dispute between the banks and the staff union, the Irish Bank Officials Association, over better pay and conditions, I was relieved to have some time off.

In today's context, it sounds unbelievable that an economy could function without its core banking system. But this is what happened in Ireland in 1970. Talks between management and the unions were slow to achieve results. John Titterington, a powerful organiser and charismatic orator, was the full-time leader of the IBOA. An Englishman and experienced trades unionist, Titterington brought an edge to the hitherto quiet backwater of Irish bank industrial relations. Better pay and conditions were achieved but only after a six-month-long industrial dispute, which seriously inconvenienced the Irish public. Nowadays, the weight of public opinion exercised through the media would be an irresistible force for earlier settlement, and of course, Irish economic conditions are totally different. The economy is greater in scale, payments are electronic based and more international; it would be inconceivable to now countenance a similar situation.

Nonetheless, anticipating a lengthy dispute, large numbers of us went to to London to find work as soon as the banks closed. For many, the aim was to maintain some income but for others without dependents, the excitement of escaping the daily routine was paramount. Charlie and I joined the exodus. We made our way to Dun Laoghaire to catch the Sealink mail boat to England. We arrived in Holyhead port late at night and took the overnight train to Euston Station in London. Charlie, being Charlie, was perfectly organised for the journey with his boy-scout-like backpack complete with dangling cooking utensils attached. This was a time long before backpacks became the common feature they are today and he made an unusual sight. Like so many

Irish people, we made our way to the Kilburn area, a predominantly Irish emigrant enclave in north-west London, reckoning that it would offer us a good base from which to seek work. After a few nights in temporary lodgings, we were glad to find a small flat on Honiton Road near Willesden.

Charlie soon found a job in the local Wall's ice cream factory; there he settled for the few months we remained in London. With my farming background I preferred to find something out of doors, so I tried to find labouring work on the buildings. Steady work proved elusive so I turned my attention to London Bus, who were seeking staff. I was fortunate to be taken on as a bus conductor, working out of the Willesden bus depot. This turned out to be a really interesting job, which took me across London on the 6, 8, 176 and other routes. The work was more demanding than I had expected, but mitigated by the thrill of seeing so many of London's great tourist sites along the way. London bus conductors were made up of a mix of nationalities, including cockneys, West Indian and Irish. Morale was high among the staff and it was generally a good place to work. Before I commenced my duties I joined other new recruits on a short training course. We learned how to work the ticket machines and the supervisors checked out our numeracy skills. Our trainer was pleasantly surprised at my numeracy but I didn't dare let him know that I was a bank clerk in another life and that my stay with London Bus would be a temporary one. It quickly dawned on me that I should conceal my cash-counting prowess so that I would be above suspicion. Those ticket machines had held a macho appeal for me ever since I had seen our local bus conductor, John Gillespie, issue tickets on the Ardara-Portnoo bus when I was a child. I just loved that clicking sound as he turned the little ticket-winder.

Charlie was just as well organised in our north London flat as he had been back in our Dublin lodgings. If anything, there was more opportunity for him here as there was so much more to do; we now had to buy provisions and cook for ourselves, now that there was no landlady to provide meals for us. He ensured that both of us got out of bed in the morning and to my chagrin, he made sure that I did my share of the chores. We both began to enjoy London, visiting all the big attractions such as Madame Tussaud's. Going swimming in the excellent public swimming pools was a great treat.

During my time in London I had the opportunity to try out a few other jobs. I managed to do this through a combination of my regular days off and a small amount of accumulated annual leave. By far the toughest work I did was labouring on the buildings, especially concrete-laying. A feature of this work was the 'lump' system, which was largely confined to Irish workers, most of whom seem to come from Mayo. By standing at a particular point on the Kilburn High Street in the early morning, you were showing yourself to be available for hire. Invariably you would find yourself in the company of others also seeking work, or 'the start' as it was known, a colloquialism for a job with the mainly Irish subcontractors. These subcontractors were mostly labourers, who had been smart enough to spot the opportunity provided by the plentiful supply of good Irish labourers. The subcontractor was paid according to the amount of work done, say cubic feet of concrete laid. They hired men to do the work they subcontracted from the big name UK contractors; the names of Laing and McAlpine featured regularly. You were not always guaranteed to be hired. A subcontractor might not turn up or there might be more men available for work than were needed. In this scenario the strongest, biggest and most weathered looking would win out; guys of medium height and build such as me could often find ourselves disappointed, especially if work was scarce.

My labouring days consisted of wheeling barrowsful of wet concrete and breaking up old concrete paving with a jackhammer. After one of these hard days, I was so exhausted that I failed to materialise for my bus conducting work the next day. When I did return to work, I was immediately summoned to the garage manager's office. I recall his opening words: 'Where was you on Monday?' I sheepishly replied that I had been unwell. He was rightly unconvinced and left me in no doubt that my career with London Bus had suffered a setback. Before that misdemeanour, my prospects had been good with the hint of a bus driver's training course in the pipeline.

To us bus conductors, the bus inspectors were a constant scourge. It was with trepidation that you spotted an inspector board your bus, in case you had not got around to picking up fares before passengers alighted. Once, I had a run-in in the garage yard with an elderly inspector. I was on the bus, directing the driver to turn around, and had to shout at the man to get out of the way at the last minute. He gave me a right and deserved earful for not warning him earlier.

During my time in London, I also did shopfitting in Chelsea and wine bottling in a warehouse on the south bank of the Thames river. The wine bottling involved pumping wine from huge vats into bottles, which we labelled and corked. To my astonishment, wine from the same vat was being poured into bottles with different labels! Although I was not a wine drinker at that time, the incident did shake my confidence in the industry. To my relief, shopfitting was entirely different from concreting. The work was detailed and lighter. The workers, who were trained craftsmen, were predominantly cockney. I also learned an interesting lesson from an old labourer on this site on how to do as little work as possible and remain undetected by the foreman. The secret is that you must keep moving at all costs. This guy had an old brush which he used as a kind of prop, lightly brushing parts of the floor as he moved around the building. While watching him I could see that he was the perfect embodiment of his own philosophy.

It was very clear to me that in general the Irish worker tended to do the heavy unskilled work while the native cockney usually had a trade and thus operated at the higher-skilled end of the business. It was therefore not surprising that many labouring Irish workers in Britain were destined for hard times as they got older and their physical strength diminished. I was glad that my stint as an Irish labourer would be a short one.

When we returned to Dublin for November 1970, the banks were trying to process the huge backlog of work that had built up during the strike. The large supermarket groups and pubs had played a key role in recirculating cash during the strike by being prepared to hold masses of cheques. When the banks did re-open, all of these cheques needed to be processed. The retailers were fearful that there could be a number of forged cheques in the enormous bundles, but as it turned out the element of fraud was not significant. However, the resultant overtime, while mandatory, was enthusiastically grasped by bank staff as a way to top-up finances and in many cases to repay debts which had accumulated. For me, there was the added complication of my university studies, which I had neglected for the previous few months. My good friend and classmate Eddie Rowland was in the same predicament. He worked in another Ulster Bank branch. We both knew that because of our circumstances at work, just passing our final examinations was going to be a real challenge; any honours were out of the question. After Christmas 1970 the overtime programme, that had continued since we all resumed work, declined significantly. Eddie and myself then resolved to co-operate closely in our study programme towards the June finals. Because we had missed so many first-term lectures, we essentially had to squeeze the full final year's work into the last two academic terms. It was tempting to throw in the towel, but we thought we should give it a real go, despite the poor odds. Most subjects could be studied by intensive reading and re-reading, except accountancy. If we were to get through we would have to put real graft into practicing accountancy problems. For all subjects we reviewed past papers extensively and categorised the questions that would inevitably come up in some form.

We studied question options so that we could take a calculated risk in eliminating some areas of study. We practised the toughest examples and cross-tested each other. Most of our study work was done at Eddie's dingy first-floor flat on Harcourt Street with a terrible noise in the background from an office building project which subsequently became ACC Bank's head office.

June arrived, we sat the examinations and passed, a very positive result in the circumstances. Graduation day arrived and we all were presented with our parchments at the awards ceremony in the Great Hall at Earlsfort Terrace. Brigid travelled all the way by bus from Ardara to attend the proceedings. Being the great enthusiast that she was for education, she greatly enjoyed the occasion. Although I never admitted as much to Brigid until many years later, it was her enthusiasm that had sub-consciously prompted me to enrol at University College Dublin in the first place.

My life at the time wasn't all work and study, though. I had some great times with my friend and former St Eunan's classmate, Kevin Haughey, with whom I shared a flat at one stage off the North Strand Road. Kevin worked in the computer department of Aer Lingus and was one of the most knowledgeable people on popular music; he was particularly good at discerning the good material that would endure from the rubbish. During my time as Kevin's flatmate, my knowledge of 60's music significantly improved. I particularly recall being very taken with an album from the American band Creedence Clearwater Revival. Kevin's sisters, Máire and Irene, lived nearby, in accommodation also owned by our landlady, Brigid Lafferty. In conjunction with the Haughey clan, the Lafferty family, who were also Donegal people, created a fun and homely atmosphere. The North Strand was a typical inner-city area where people had little by way of possessions, but were open and friendly. I particularly recall us having a local family grocer, the ever-patient Joe McCabe, whom we pestered for small portions. Joe Cuddy, the well-known Dublin comedian and singer, was our local butcher.

Having a car was one of my early goals. As well as the important status aspect, it made getting around the city, and more importantly, the journey to and from Donegal, a lot easier. The outlay was still beyond our respective financial reaches, so Kevin and I pooled our resources to acquire an old bottle-green Ford Zephyr. We bought it privately from an elderly man in the Dublin suburb of Dalkey, who was quite amused at the joint nature of the transaction. The car had wings at the rear and I just loved the bench seat and the column gear stick. I recall one of our first trips back to Donegal in the Zephyr. Our first port of call was Kevin's parents in Roxborough, near Carrick. The warmth of the welcome given to me by Kevin's parents is something which I will never forget. Mrs Haughey cooked us a big fry-up which we surely relished after the long trip from Dublin. I carried on to Beagh then to see my parents.

However much I loved the car, it took an accident to make me realise that I had to be a bit more careful with my driving. Returning from Donegal alone in the Zephyr, I had a narrow escape from a serious accident on the Navan Road on the way into Dublin. I had nodded off to sleep behind the wheel. The sound of the car crashing into a series of tar barrels along the road woke me up. Luckily my car veered to the left, away from oncoming traffic and a certain head-on collision. The song 'Montego Bay' sung by Bobby Bloom, was playing on the car radio as I realised what was happening. This was but one of many near misses I have had during a lifetime of driving. With the much tighter enforcement of speed regulations, I now have to fight a lifelong addiction to fast driving. For me faster driving is safer driving as it improves my concentration, whereas I am dangerously prone to mentally switching off if I am just ambling along.

In Summer 1971 Kevin and I went our separate ways. My commerce degree brought me to the notice of head office and Ulster Bank offered me a position in their Belfast head office as personal assistant to William

Eustace Boyd, Deputy Chief Executive. This was touted as a great opportunity for a young lad, despite the fact that the pay was only marginally better.

It was with mixed feelings that I decided to accept the offer of the job in Belfast. I was sorry to be leaving my flatmate Kevin and friend Eddie, with whom I had soldiered through good and bad times at UCD. Furthermore, now that the intense studying was finished, I felt ready to enter the social fray with a vengeance. There was lots of social activity in the bank and generally around Dublin, and there were lots of girls in the bank. I was ready to bask in the glory of my academic achievement and was greatly enjoying the improved self confidence that came with it. However, the lure of a new challenge and what excitement Belfast might have in store, proved compelling. The early shoots of ambition were sprouting, fuelled by the wider business perspective experienced in university. I didn't stop for a moment to consider the Troubles which were raging on the streets of Northern Ireland at that time. I was sure they would soon fade and anyway, they wouldn't affect me. What a naïve perception that turned out to be.

CHAPTER SIX

BELFAST AND THE TROUBLES

I had exchanged my bottle-green Ford Zephyr for a two-tone blue Triumph Herald at this stage, and I drove it to Belfast to take up my new job in August 1971, the height of the Northern Ireland Troubles. The journey was one I had done before. Despite the hazard of hitting trouble spots, I was confident that I knew my way to Newtownabbey, where I would stay with the Duffy family again, at least initially. My confidence was misplaced. In Belfast city centre, I made a left turn prematurely off Royal Avenue. My aim was to get on to the Antrim Road, then a major road artery leading north towards Glengormley. The surroundings began to look quite unfamiliar when I discovered I was driving up the famous Shankhill Road, a notorious Loyalist district. This was one place that I, a green Southerner driving a southern-registered car, did not want to be. I had two choices. I could either find a side street to make a turn back to the city centre, or I could continue driving as I was pretty sure the Shankhill Road ultimately led to the country. From there I could plot a fresh itinerary eastward to the Duffy home. I was aware that just recently two soldiers from a Scottish regiment had been killed by the IRA just beyond the Shankhill district. I worried that spotted by a Loyalist gang, I would make a ready reprisal target. I thought it better than to be seen to be so obviously lost, to keep going and and treat the problem of finding my destination as a lesser evil than the risk of being seen in the Shankhill.

As I drove through the Antrim countryside, I came upon crossroads after crossroads. My sense of my bearings suggested to me that I should be turning right at some point in the general direction of Newtownabbey. I was now in a maze of minor roads with little recognisable signage. Rather than stop and study my position in unfamiliar countryside, I kept driving in the knowledge that sooner or later I would come across signs to recognisable destinations. A direction sign to Glengormley, which is in the Newtownabbey area, came into view. I breathed a sigh of relief. I was now able to figure my way to the Duffy household where I received the customary warm welcome.

Mrs Duffy's accommodation was to be a stopgap until I got myself a flat, preferably in the Queen's University area. I was anxious to share a flat with a work colleague if possible. The Duffy hospitality, including Mrs Duffy's renowned home cooking and the good craic with the Duffy lads made my stay longer than originally intended. It took a stiff resolve on my part to leave this congenial environment. A few months passed before I joined up with my good friend John Kelly, who, like myself, was a UCD night graduate and who would now also be working at head office. John's arrival was a godsend as now I would have a pal to go socialising with. I recall an instance where we both spent a July evening in the Loyalist Sandy Row area surveying the huge Twelfth of July bonfires. There was a festive atmosphere and none of the menace that has subsequently come to be associated with these tribal occasions. John remained in Belfast for a relatively short period before he departed Ulster Bank for a new bank being set up in Dublin. It turned out to be a good move as his banking career took off in the years that followed.

On that first morning I made my way to Ulster Bank's head office on Waring Street and sought out the office of Eustace Boyd. It was in the front of the main building directly above the incredibly ornate and beautiful banking hall. I would work in an office down the corridor from the deputy chief executive, facing on to Skipper Street.

As you become older and wiser, you realise that the porters are key people in such an organisation and that it is useful to get to know them. They are at the fulcrum in terms of knowing what is going on and who the key players are. The porters in Waring Street were no different; they were savvy guys and always helpful to me. I feel sure they secretly relished witnessing the induction of a greenhorn Southern Catholic to this citadel of Ulster commerce and seeing how it would play out. Chairman Sir Robin Kinahan's driver, Tom Barr, was a real elder among the porters; he was opinionated and forthright in the expression of his views, which were well right of centre. Occasionally I travelled with him if the chairman's car was the only one available to deliver important documents on behalf of our department. The car was a beautiful white Daimler and I recall being impressed with its elegant wooden dashboard and array of dials. I later learned that this man had once been driver to Lord Brookeborough, the former Northern Ireland prime minister. Because of this unique background, his views commanded attention. Needless to say, he was incensed by the activities of the IRA and he saw the problem in Northern Ireland in security terms; to be fair to him, he was just articulating what he among many Unionist people sincerely believed. Indeed, without a closer examination of the issues, this could be seen to be ostensibly true. Given my southern Catholic identity, it was difficult for us to have a meaningful dialogue. His Unionist view had an appealing simplicity which did not reflect the reality as it appeared to me. I saw a distinct parallel with the ultra-Nationalist view held by some southern politicians of that time. There were no grey areas. In a way this simplistic view of the Troubles was Unionist parties' propaganda at its most effective. A cohesive majority community, politically and economically secure in its perfect democracy, albeit one contrived by partition, was in no mood to be challenged. There was no incentive to take a longer view as clearly any Nationalist threat had no basis in logic, Unionist logic, that is. Therefore any realisation of this threat was beyond comprehension. Mind you I also failed to understand why a campaign of violence was necessary as the Civil Rights movement seemed to be achieving good progress.

From what I could see, the Unionist psyche seemed to be in a defensive mode while the republican counter-position had a momentum, due to their then-marginalised position in the society in terms of property and jobs. Of the two positions, the Nationalist position seemed to me to have more purpose and to have the capacity to last the course over many years. Moreover, adversity breeds tenacity, and, as far as I could see, the Nationalist emphasis on education, and the higher proportion of teachers as role models in that community, meant that it had a certain cohesion which I felt was missing at that time in extreme Unionism. The longer-term vision that was required within Unionism of an alternative political future, was unappealing, so, 'put off the evil day' seemed to be the motto. Not being a simple and straightforward issue, it demanded a more far-seeing and pre-emptive evaluation for which there was no stomach among influential and articulate Unionists. Whenever I discussed these kinds of issues with Unionist colleagues, they could just about see my point, but they weren't going to be seen to accept such an uncomfortable scenario.

Even though I had grown up in a mixed community in the west of the province of Ulster and thought I had a reasonable understanding of the Ulster Protestant mindset, I still had a lot to learn. What I hadn't sufficiently appreciated was how distinctly British they felt and the chasm between the Irish Nationalist/Catholic mindset and theirs. Many of my Unionist colleagues could accept that their employer was an all-Ireland organisation, but they saw their personal lives in a British context.

As I got to know Belfast, I soon learned that there were predominantly Protestant and Catholic districts. The easiest way to distinguish between them was the greater presence of flagpole holders above hall doors, the mark of Protestant districts. In summer and particularly during the month of July, Union flags and other British emblems flew from these holders. Some Catholic districts would equally have a surfeit of Irish republican flags but this demonstration of loyalty seemed much less widespread. Another one of my early first impressions was how grey Sundays felt. Unlike in the Republic, no small grocery shops were open; if you were short of provisions, you just had to wait until Monday for the shops to open.

When I turned up for work on that first morning, I was escorted to the Executive floor, where Mr Boyd had his office. His sphere of influence in the bank was called 'Related Banking Services', which embodied all the non-traditional banking activities of the bank. These included the Lombard and Ulster finance companies, the computer bureau subsidiary, which processed payroll for other businesses, strategic investments and others.

Eddie Johnson, whose position I was to fill, showed me the ropes on my first day at work. Eddie was a nice man who seemed happy in his job. Undoubtedly, he would have been happy to continue for many years were it not for his family circumstances in Waterford, which demanded his presence there. Although Eddie was not Catholic, his Southern roots also left him open to the prevailing banter.

I was introduced to Mr Boyd, who was not given to small talk but he monopolised the little conversation which took place in the quiet office, of which his secretary, Patricia Duff, and Eddie were the occupants. I quickly realised that I was going to miss the noisy freneticism of a busy bank branch, the camaraderie of friendly colleagues and the interaction with customers. This work would be more intellectual and proactive than the day-to day-routine of cashiering and daily cheque processing, but less sociable.

Lunchtime on my first day came around. I joined Eddie at his usual table in the staff canteen. Colleagues who joined us were Barry Craythorne, Albert Wilson, Jack Torney, Sterling McGuinness and others. Banter was the order of the day and Barry was banterer-in-chief. My arrival provided him with a new curiosity and a new target for healthy banter. At that early stage, I wasn't sure whether to take him seriously or not. He was on to the North-South/Catholic-Protestant issue pretty soon. This level of conversation surprised me. I had naively been expecting more serious conversation around the current political problems and strategic banking issues. Having wised up, I soon realised that I would not only be taking over from Eddie in the job but also as the butt of Barry's attention. Another colleague and good friend from the South, the urbane Ultan O'Reilly, would also meet the criteria. However, Ultan's job involved extensive travel so he rarely featured in the canteen, thus escaping focus.

To be fair, the banter was pretty harmless, light hearted and often good fun. Most of the guys were salt-of-the-earth colleagues; they were helpful to me both in doing my job and socially. Indeed, lunchtime in the canteen became a time to relish as an escape from the gravitas and quietness of the job. Indeed I found myself having a lot in common with some of these colleagues who were also from farming backgrounds.

Being PA to Mr Boyd turned out to be a unique learning opportunity. A key part of my job was to devil papers submitted to him. Many of these papers were of a strategic nature, involving the bank's subsidiaries and non-mainstream retail banking activities. Mr Boyd was their direct reporting line into Ulster Bank. Examples of issues that would come up were, applications for additional capital to expand businesses, senior management issues and acquisitions and disposals of businesses. All large-loan applications to the Lombard and Ulster banking subsidiaries crossed my desk for approval by Mr Boyd. These subsidiaries employed skilled lending managers so it was rare that any of their loan applications would be declined. My function was to read through them in detail and revert to the subsidiaries for any clarification or additional information which I thought was required to enable Mr Boyd reach a decision. This work was most interesting and very far removed from trying to balance a cash till at a busy bank counter.

In our portfolio entitled Related Banking Services were housed the bank's large corporate investments, including the activities of several shell companies. Prime examples were the Fitzwilliam Securities and Brooks Watson shell companies led by Tony O'Reilly and Martin Rafferty respectively. These businessmen were seen as being to the forefront in creating large companies. Their approach was, with the support of institutions such as Ulster Bank, to make substantial investments in smallish inactive companies that were quoted on the Dublin Stock Exchange. They would become active players on the boards of these companies in acquiring a number of smaller companies. The objective would be, through their business skills, to create an enterprise of greater value than the sum of the parts. A part of my job was to draft reports on behalf of Mr Boyd for the Ulster Bank board of directors in respect of these companies. This was the era of the shell company and corporate activity in them was frenetic. From my viewpoint this made them interesting.

I enjoyed my interaction with the business finance subsidiaries and non-banking divisions. The people were quite different from the typical bank official. Many of the managers and executives were lawyers and accountants, but with a more commercial edge than you would see in the bank. Banks, in those days, were very much institutional in mindset and at the same time large commercial businesses, but it didn't feel that way. Technical proficiency emphasising process rather than commercial achievement, seemed to predominate. The senior people in the subsidiaries were more individualistic; many would have already made career moves from other companies. Some senior people in the Ulster Bank would have regarded the non-bank people as being 'different' if not somewhat 'flaky'. There was a kind of puritanical ethos in the Ulster Bank in those days. For example, you would rarely hear of executives having extra-marital affairs; this was not the situation in the subsidiaries, where the gossip tended to be far more interesting. In the subsidiaries the girls dressed fashionably and therefore the ambience was more exotic. The bank girls were compelled to dress in a standard blue uniform.

A major distinction between the two kinds of organisations was that the Bank was long established and it saw itself having a proud and successful history to protect.

My job description was pretty flexible and really depended on what arrived on my boss's plate. In a non-business context he once got me to help prepare the accounts of his local church, where he was a member of the select vestry. I remember the exercise being an early test of my accounting skills.

In November 1972, I was one of two bank nominees selected to attend a cadet management course at National Westminster Bank's training college in Heythrop Park, near Chipping Norton in Oxfordshire. Heythrop Park, now a hotel and country club, is a magnificent 18th-century mansion situated in beautiful countryside. The other course nominee was David Smyth, a Belfast colleague. The purpose of the course was to provide early management training to bank staff members who were deemed to have potential for senior management. The course content was stimulating and spending a few weeks with colleagues from another country was highly enjoyable. It also provided a welcome respite from the ongoing Troubles.

In my period in Belfast, the Provisional IRA terror campaign was at its zenith. The day-to-day existence of the ordinary person was being seriously affected. The British Army was all over the city. Some streets were closed to cars and security barriers, which controlled access, were set up at street ends. Shoppers were monitored and searched in case the packages they carried were bombs. Cars were banned from parking in some streets and in others they were only allowed to park provided there was an occupant in the vehicle. This was a precaution to prevent car bombs being placed near shops, a favoured IRA target.

My first experience of an IRA bomb happened soon after I started work in Belfast. A warning had been communicated to the police that a bomb had been placed in the offices of the Hire Purchase Company of Ireland building across the street from the Ulster Bank. Offices and shops in the vicinity were evacuated. We all convened at a safe distance until the bomb exploded. I still recall the eerie sight of the clouds of dust emanating from the shattered windows. The damaged building was unfit for occupation until it had been extensively repaired: very often a building suffering bomb damage would be irreparable and subsequently would have to be demolished. As a precaution against the danger of shattering glass, all windows were sheeted with clear adhesive plastic. It wasn't long before our building was attacked. A car bomb was detonated in Skipper Street outside our office in the early hours. It left a huge crater in the narrow street and shattered the windows around it. I arrived in the office for work to find myriad pieces of glass, from the window just behind my office chair, pierced into the surface of my desk. The shards of glass were embedded in the desk as if thrown by a knife-thrower. I felt so lucky not to have been at my desk when the explosion occurred.

These conditions were becoming the norm in Belfast. The IRA seemed to be able to assemble and deliver bombs with near impunity. The economic damage was extensive and not every business could re-open after being bombed.

Bloody Friday, 21 July 1972, was by far the most memorable and terrible day for Belfast citizens. Twenty-two bombs were detonated in the city centre that day, in just over an hour. Warnings were received that several places around the city were being bombed, but either the warnings were not given in time or the police were overwhelmed by the number of warnings received on that fateful day, as great carnage resulted. A bomb exploded in the Oxford Street premises of Ulster Bank before all personnel could be evacuated. Serious injuries were suffered by some of the staff members. The result of Bloody Friday was nine dead and one hundred and thirty injured. There was the dreaded feeling that the IRA were now bombing civilian targets without warning. To avoid the possibility of injury, our senior management closed down the Waring Street building for the day and all staff were advised to go home. Walking through the city to my flat in Eglantine Avenue near Queen's University, I sensed an unreal atmosphere in the city as people hurriedly and quietly made their way home. There was talk of civil war from time to time; was civil war now about to break out, and what would that mean for everyday living? I also had to wonder what it would mean for me, a Southern Catholic living in Belfast?

The sound of gunfire during daylight and night time became one of the city's trademarks during this time. A group of us taking a lunchtime walk in the city witnessed an incident by now quite common in troubled parts of the city. A large British Army excavator, armour-plated and painted green, was attempting to clear debris off the street near the Divis flats. The excavator was being peppered with gunfire and bullets were ricocheting all around the area. I could hardly believe that what I was seeing was real. It was subsequently reported that Joe McCann, a notorious IRA leader, was the gunman firing at the excavator.

To hear the sound of machine-gun fire ringing out when I would be getting out of my car at the flat was an eerie experience. The gunfire sounded close in the still of the night, but it was some distance away; generally in west Belfast.

During that time, I spent many weekends at home in Donegal; they were a welcome respite from troubled Belfast. Although my job was interesting, there was almost no social outlet after work. Most people of my age and circumstances, from both sides of the political divide, did their socialising within their own communities. This would have been typical of Belfast even before the Troubles erupted. Unlike Dublin or London, there was hardly any transient young working population living away from home. Within Ulster Bank, a relatively large organisation, there was almost none at that time. John Kelly, a colleague and good friend, shared the Eglantine Avenue flat with me for a period, but as John's job involved travelling throughout Ireland, he was not around Belfast much. I was grateful that my old pal Eddie Rowland was now also assigned to head office, even if, like John, his job also involved extensive travel to the branch network.

By the early 70s, most of the Belfast dance halls and discos had closed and the prominent city-centre pubs tended to close after office hours. Any nightlife in the city centre was negligible. Fortunately two of the better pubs near Queen's University remained open: the Eglantine and the Botanic Inn. These venues were lively places in the evenings but mainly confined to students and other young people in that general circle. While I was fortunate in having these outlets nearby, it was nevertheless almost impossible to break into new social groups. I hung out with a few bank colleagues from time to time, among them John Todd, Sterling McGuinness and Arnie Wright. These were genuinely nice guys who were single in those days and were always friendly to me, even though they would have had their own circles of friends. I recall the excitement of going to the famous North West 200 motorcycle racing festival in Portrush with John Todd, travelling in great style: he had managed to borrow his uncle's Rolls-Royce for the day. Motor sport was and still is a big leisure interest in Northern Ireland.

Social Belfast was very different from Dublin and not just because of the Troubles. Certainly, there was more socialising done in the home, but people tended to marry much younger in Belfast, too, and there wasn't the same pool of young, single people. There was however a genuineness about people and very often senior colleagues would invite me to their homes. I recall in particular enjoying warm hospitality from Brian Cathcart and Jack Torney in their respective homes.

The period following Bloody Sunday in Derry in January 1972 was a nervous time. I was spending the weekend with my brother Conal at his Dundalk flat when the news came through of the massacre. (He was employed by the Irish Department of Agriculture at a local cattle slaughtering plant.) Bloody Sunday seemed to be a milestone in the further increasing of community tensions. There was a distinct feeling at the time that this dreadful incident heralded more terrible events to come because retaliation was a major element in the Troubles. Indeed, the Bloody Friday bombings were considered by some to be a retaliation for the massacre in Derry.

Another very different but equally scary time was when the parliament at Stormont was dissolved in March 1972 and both the IRA and the paramilitary Ulster Defence Association (UDA) were cranking up their activities. These big events made me resolve to increase my personal vigilance. I would vary my route home from work and I kept to well-lit streets at night where others would be walking.

Unofficial UDA street checkpoints were becoming a feature of driving in the city. One Sunday evening near the roundabout where the M1 motorway terminates close to Sandy Row, I was hailed down by a number of hooded UDA youths wearing parka jackets. I was returning to Belfast after a weekend in Dublin, accompanied by a hitch-hiking student who I had picked up at Newry. As we approached the checkpoint, the student strongly suggested that I ignore them and not stop. Fearing an onslaught if I drove through, I ignored his advice and stopped the car. I was interviewed by a UDA member, brandishing a spiked cudgel. When he requested proof of identity, I produced my Republic of Ireland driving licence. As the holder of a Southern driving licence in a car with Southern plates, we were extremely vulnerable to either a severe hiding or worse. We were both extremely nervous but I managed to hold my composure throughout the ordeal. There was not a sign of a policeman during the period we were stopped. To our eternal relief, we were waved through.

Some businesses in Belfast at the time were rumoured to be covers for British Intelligence, including the famous Four Square Laundry, and in my case, I had a close brush with the Service one night. One night, I got out of my car at my front door, when I noticed in the semi-darkness that the door was wide open. This surprised me, but I thought that another tenant had just left the hall door open by mistake. I pushed the timed stairwell light switch and proceeded to walk up the stairs to my first-floor flat. I found that the flat door was also wide open and the internal doors were ajar. My first reaction was that I must have been burgled but none of my possessions were missing. I thought it strange that the doors were all open and eerily my flat was in darkness. There was no neighbour to throw any light on the situation as the occupants were absent that night. I thought no more of it. However, I was later shocked to hear a strong rumour that the British Intelligence Service had rented the flat immediately before me. I instantly recalled the night I found all my doors open. I couldn't help wondering if a terrorist hit squad had outdated information on the occupants, hence the raid on my flat. Maybe I had been extraordinarily lucky not to have been home earlier that night!

The security situation also affected me in other ways during this time, some not entirely expected! My old schoolfriend and neighbour, Donal Byrne, was a person I regularly visited on weekend trips back to Beagh. There was always a warm welcome in the Byrne home, especially for young people. As well as being self-taught and extremely clever Donal was an expert fisherman and shot as well as being able to do engineering jobs without the benefit of formal training. It is therefore easy to understand why Donal was an attractive character for similar aged lads to be around. At the time, Donal had yet to marry his wife, Marian, and still lived with his mother, Mary, herself a jolly and warm person. Donal worked the family's smallholding, but his heart was not in farming: weaving Donegal tweed was his main source of income.

Donal was a man interested in a lot of things and his natural curiosity led him to explore how poitín was produced; the clear spirit was illegal, but still produced in many country areas, particularly in remotest Donegal and other western counties. The extinction of poitín making was a big priority for the civil authorities, because of excise-duty loss. The Catholic Church in Ireland was very much against it for reasons of addiction. Poitín consumption was seen as the curse of the Irish peasant class. There was a romantic aspect which suggested that the activity of poitín making was more common and widespread than it ever was in reality. The illegal and covert nature of the process made it the ideal subject of song and story.

The mystique surrounding poitín intrigued Donal to the extent that he had to test his ingenuity on the process. From snippets of information gleaned from poitín-making veterans still alive, he discovered how it worked. Donal had the engineering skills to manufacture the still, the copper worm and the other pieces of equipment needed. He produced his first batch of poitín and passed it around to friends and the few poitín connoisseurs who existed vouched for its good quality. I obtained a bottle which I shared with friends and colleagues at the bank in Belfast. They were so taken with the subversiveness of drinking this illicit mountain dew that they wanted to have their own bottle for sharing with their friends. I think it was the story they liked, even more than the enjoyment of the libation itself. Donal was happy to increase production to meet the demand, but there were risks for me in delivering even a few bottles to friends in Belfast. As a somewhat daring twenty-five-year-old, I didn't dwell too long on the risks, even though it was common for either the British Army, the RUC or the Ulster Defence Regiment (UDR) to search cars at random checkpoints at the border. Cars coming from across the border were prime candidates for such searches and mine was no exception. My car, then a Volkswagen Beetle was searched by British soldiers while I had one of these bottles in the boot. The soldiers must have assumed it to be either plain or holy water and no questions were asked. In the prevailing environment poitín was not on the risk radar; later in the Troubles, when bombs were being made from miscellaneous chemicals, a bottle of clear spirits may have raised serious suspicion.

Donal was delighted with the ten shillings per bottle that I procured from my friends; but the sense of adventure was the thing for him as he was one of the most unmercenary people I knew. Today, great emphasis is placed on academic achievement, but it isn't necessarily accompanied by the kind of intellectual ability or life skills that Donal possessed. He was an authority on local wildlife with a genuine love of the outdoors. He was a superb huntsman with a love and respect for the countryside. Sadly, he passed away in 1999 and the saying that 'we will not see his like again' has a ring of truth to it in his case.

The scarcity of social activities and the Troubles did not totally inhibit me from enjoying my time in Belfast. As time passed, I got to know more and more people and my social circle widened, although I would admit that my life there never really took off in the way I might have hoped. I was, however, learning a great deal in my job and especially from working with Mr Boyd. He could express himself very well on paper. A qualified lawyer, his previous job had been head of the bank's law department. Being exposed to his work was a great learning experience for me, particularly in the areas of corporate credit in the specialised sectors of housebuilding, leasing and hire-purchase finance, all of which would stand me in good stead later in my career. Not only was I dealing with two legal jurisdictions, Northern Ireland and the Republic of Ireland, but also multiple economic and business sectors. and I was now drafting monthly board reports and papers to the Chief Executive, Rowan Hamilton, an accomplished executive with a sharp eye for detail. Once, I would have thought some of his reactions and comments to be pedantic but increasingly grew to realise the value of such attention to detail. This was an area in which I would always have to work hard throughout my career; it was not a natural tenet of my personality. My inclination, as per the thinking of the US leadership guru Warren G Bennis, has been primarily 'to do the right things and then always do things right'. At least that is my excuse!

CHAPTER SEVEN

BREAK FOR THE BORDER

By now although only into my second year in Belfast, I was beginning to contemplate what my next career move would be. The security situation wasn't improving in Northern Ireland and I was witnessing my youth passing in this restricted environment. My job was stimulating if a little lonely. I was gaining good high-level experience in an executive environment, but I was not experiencing customer contact which, I was beginning to realise, was a key area in banking. Ultimately, I felt that the sacrifice of remaining in Belfast for the sake of my job was greater than I was prepared to tolerate in the medium term.

My mind was firming around the concept of relationship corporate banking rather than retail branch banking, but a big plus factor in not seeking change was that I seemed assured of an excellent career within Ulster Bank given the progress I had already made. Also having been earmarked for the Bank's senior management development programme, I was aware what I was giving up in career terms. Would I cope as effectively with the challenge of a different banking culture and having to prove myself again with new people? I concluded that continuous self improvement and challenge was likely to prove more conducive to career development than simply being well placed in an organisation.

An opportunity emerged which I felt would help further these career aspirations. Recent developments in the Irish banking industry saw the other three large Irish banks establish corporate banking subsidiaries to offer specialised banking services to larger Irish and foreign-owned companies. These services included corporate finance advice and investment management services to pension funds and other large investors. Ulster Bank had decided to fill this gap in its business portfolio by setting up Ulster Investment Bank (UIB). These new banking operations were not investment banks in the Wall Street mode but rather more corporate lending units. Within Ulster Bank, Eustace Boyd conceived and drove the idea for this new venture, in conjunction with Bill Johnston, Chief Executive of County Bank, National Westminster Bank's merchant banking arm; the London-based bank was the parent company of Ulster Bank. They hired Michael Meagher, a high-flying corporate banker from Citibank to run the new venture. He was only in his early thirties and was already head of Citibank's Irish corporate banking unit. (I remember that in my job interview I thought he looked rather old fashioned for his tender years with pinstriped suit and trouser turn-ups. He projected a Wall-Street rather than a City-of-London image.) Ulster Bank had hired a leader who was regarded as one of the best in the business; a Tiger Woods of corporate banking, with that same dedicated application. They assembled an experienced board of directors around Michael with Lord Killanin as chairman.

The establishment of UIB represented to me an ideal opportunity to meet my aspirations and I decided to apply for a job with the new venture. By virtue of my current job, I was in the picture early, and importantly, such a position would get me out of Belfast and back to Dublin. I had two immediate hurdles on the way to my objective. Firstly, I needed my boss, Eustace Boyd's approval to apply for a job with this new subsidiary. Secondly, I needed to be successful in my candidacy; in the event of my candidacy not succeeding, rolling the clock back with Eustace Boyd would be embarrassing and almost impossible. However, I felt that if I could persuade him to let me go forward, it would be difficult for Michael to turn me down, coming as I was from the staff of his boss.

Eustace Boyd expressed his deep disappointment at my readiness to give up the excellent career prospects which he perceived me to have with Ulster Bank. This conversation was made more difficult due to the respect I had for my boss. A stoical Ulster Presbyterian, he was a decent and highly competent person to whom I owed the valuable experience of working in his division. While flattered by the nice sentiment, I intuitively felt that I was doing the right thing for my career but, more importantly, for my social well-being. Michael offered me a role as a credit analyst which I was glad to accept as a secondment from Ulster Bank at an unchanged salary.

David Bingham was appointed to succeed me as Eustace Boyd's PA. Colleagues in Ulster Bank head office gave me a great send-off with drinks and a nice meal at the Conway Hotel. Indeed, I was pretty high on booze that evening. When I arrived at my flat I realised that I had mislaid my key. There was a spare key in the flat, but that was of no help in getting me inside. After a moment's thought, I knocked next door where my neighbour, Liz Armstrong, and her friend lived. They very kindly allowed me exit their first-floor window and negotiate my way by walking and clinging along the exterior ledges to my own bedroom window. In normal circumstances, I might have thought twice about such a venture but with several drinks in me, my confidence was exaggerated. Next morning, I failed to surface in time for my last day's work in Belfast, only to wake to hear my doorbell ringing. It was long after 10 a.m. and Sam McCarroll, the Chief Executive's driver, was standing on my doorstep. He had been sent out to check on my well-being when I hadn't shown up for work. With the security situation and my condition the previous night, they had been concerned for my safety: this experience was a measure of the thoughtfulness of colleagues in the bank in Belfast.

Coming back to Ireland's capital city after a two-year stint in troubled Belfast was a welcome prospect. I arrived bag and baggage in my light blue Volkswagen Beetle 1303, a more powerful version of the ordinary Beetle. Cars were cheaper in Northern Ireland and provided you owned the car for a stipulated period, it was possible to bring it into the Republic without paying additional tax. I had bought the car from a small dealer in Glenwherry, County Antrim. He was the boyfriend of a colleague who also worked in Ulster Bank Belfast's head office building. I traded my beautiful aubergine Ford Cortina 1600E for the Beetle, a decision I often regretted; the Cortina 1600E was to become a popular classic in years to come. I was particularly fond of the car, because I had bought it from a Belfast publican, Joe Murphy who, with his wife Phil and their family, regularly holidayed in Downstrands, where they had built a holiday home. Joe, a delightful guy, was selling the car on behalf of his late uncle's estate. The car was perfect and Joe gave me a good deal. Some years later, his health gave up and he passed away at a relatively young age.

My abiding memory of my return to Dublin was my subconscious habit of avoiding walking close to unoccupied parked cars on the street. In Belfast the presence of such a vehicle was highly unusual and normally represented a bomb threat. It took a while for this reaction to disappear.

Until I found accommodation, Ursula Kelly, John's mother, very kindly put me up in her Cabinteely home. The long-widowed Mrs Kelly was a resourceful woman whose main focus was looking after her daughter, also called Ursula. As well as John and Ursula, her son Michael also lived in the family home. The Kelly family had strong connections in County Cavan where husband and father Mick had been a branch manager with Ulster Bank. Mick was a close friend of the legendary bank manager and author of *Like Any Other Man*, Pat Boyle, who, coincidentally, was our local bank manager in Ardara when I was a child. Not wishing to outstay my welcome with Mrs. Kelly, I soon found a vacancy in Donnybrook to share an apartment with two Michaels. It was there that I took a call on the old black coin-operated phone from my brother Conal to tell me that my father had been diagnosed with cancer. To be told that the cancer was terminal and so would take my father's life was one of the most distressing experiences ever for me and overshadowed my return to Dublin. My grieving was done there and then. I wondered how I would face my father when I would visit him in hospital. Would the conversation touch on the fact that he would not recover, or would we avoid the subject, I wondered. I think if it was me, I would prefer to have an open conversation on the issue, but in the event I respected my father's choice not to dwell on the subject.

Back in Dublin, the acquaintance of new and former colleagues was to be enjoyed, a distraction from my upsetting family news. I was reconnecting with old friends and generally getting back into the social whirl of Dublin. It was, however, a reality check to find that things are never the same when you return to previous pastures. Some friends had moved on. They were no longer living in Dublin or had since married or had steady girlfriends. Still, I had lots of friends and was making new ones. Because of the varied background of my new colleagues, the daily work experience was quite different to O'Connell Street or Belfast. Most UIB people were university graduates, whereas most of my former colleagues had finished their education after secondary school. Also, unlike my Ulster Bank colleagues, who, like myself, were young country folk, most UIB workers were either Dublin natives or more urbanised country folk. Gerry Murphy, another UCD graduate, was also on secondment from Ulster Bank for a period. A few of us, including Gerry, Michael Griffin and Brian Kenny, would often lunch together in nearby Buck Whaley's restaurant. Michael seemed to get the best out of Gerry, who was unbelievably funny; it was pure theatre and Abbey Theatre material specifically.

The working environment at UIB was more hyped-up, more American, if you like. People used the phrase 'I guess', which I had only ever associated with returning Irish emigrants from the United States. First names were used across the board but in truth, people's feelings for each other were not necessarily warmer, in spite of the first-name usage. I began to understand what office politics meant and ways to impress the boss. Senior and aspiring senior colleagues would rarely leave the office before their bosses, even if their work was done for the day. This was particularly true for senior colleagues reporting to Michael Meagher, even though he didn't particularly seem to expect it. Impressing the boss in such a way was regarded by those who did it as a worthy practice. I rarely succumbed to such subtlety.

Shortly after UIB commenced business, David Went was also hired from Citibank to be head of the key banking department. This had to be one of Michael's best decisions. David was able, forceful, and very funny. It was not surprising that he went on to become Chief Executive with Ulster Bank and subsequently with Irish Life and Permanent.

After my first couple of years at UIB, I judged that my own career aspirations and UIB's vision of how far I might progress in the organisation were not convergent. There were two stigmas with which I was burdened, apart from the style of my work performance: firstly I had what was perceived as, the 'clearing-bank mentality'. This was an unflattering label which the inner core people at UIB attached to colleagues who had begun their careers in the large retail banks, whom they perceived as being old fashioned and institutionalised. This view was not without merit, but those old fashioned bankers had a strong set of ethics and other merits which were conveniently overlooked in the judgement. If you had a clearing bank mentality, you were perceived as a journeyman or utility player who would be lauded for being able to provide operational support to the high flyers. The use of the word 'Operations' was a code meant to indicate that the senior corporate levels would not be attainable for this category. The second stigma was not having an honours university degree or masters. Better still if you had a degree from a well-regarded American University. My pass B. Comm. was a pale shadow of the desired standard and barely worth a mention despite it having been attained in adversity.

The approach to credit assessment was also different to what I had been used to in Ulster Bank. The UIB approach to a corporate-lending proposition was more formulaic in that you had to do a long descriptive report, at the end of which you would draw the conclusion. My personal approach would be to read the papers and decide in my own mind at the outset whether to recommend a lending proposition or not; top-down rather than bottom-up, if you like. If I could not convince myself of the merits of the deal, I would not do a report. The UIB house approach introduced by Michael seemed to me to owe its origins to the American way of doing things. Although there would never be unanimity on any style selected, his approach did create a consistency and a very positive perception of UIB within the Ulster Bank Group and indeed the wider National Westminster Group. These considerations would be positive in helping to push the bigger lending deals through the head-office credit system.

My new job at UIB was to provide credit-analysis support to the senior bankers. These senior corporate bankers had been mainly hired from competitors. Citibank, unsurprisingly was the source of some of these recruits. This ex-Citibank group was destined to always be the inner core at UIB. I soon found myself solely supporting Cian McHugh, a former Citibank Dublin officer. He was a very clever and quick-witted guy. I enjoyed working with Cian and learned a lot, both technically and from his approach to corporate-banking relationship-development.

He was one of the few people I had encountered who seemed destined for a high-flying career as a Wall Street investment banker should he so choose.

There was quite an adjustment for me from being in a position where I had access to high-level material to being a small fish in a relatively small pond. I had that feeling of going from being a somebody to a nobody within a few months.

All in all, Ulster Investment Bank was a good learning environment. The leadership was youthful and energetic and the relatively small scale of the organisation meant that it was easy to get a good feel for the strategic direction of the business and the banking industry in general. Michael set an open tone with all written correspondence, both strategic and technical, freely circulating it around our small group. Michael's report writing skills were among the best I have seen. His reports on financial performance and new strategic initiatives, to both the UIB board and his superiors in Ulster Bank, were intellectually rigorous, and brought home to me the power of the written word. A board member who received one of Michael's reports recommending a course of action would be hard put to decline his recommendation, so tightly would the case be made. Issues were drawn out and closely argued into what seemed an unavoidable conclusion.

What I also learned in UIB was the power of budgets as an effective short-term planning tool. It amazed me to see the extent to which budgetary based target figures could be used to drive forward an organisation. Obtaining unanimous buy-in from departmental managers on next year's annual financial targets at the outset, can be the communal driving force that powers achievement of the target levels agreed. Being bound and driven by the targets leads them to become a self-fulfilling prophecy, in essence.

After a few stimulating years at UIB, I felt that my learning curve was beginning to flatten and my cursed low boredom threshold had been reached again. UIB's business activity was, in my perception, specialist and one dimensional while I yearned for a wider brief. It consisted mostly of short-term corporate lending to the large Irish and multi-national companies. Yet we were writing these long reports accompanied by robust balance-sheet analysis in support of their credit applications, when a brief note might have sufficed because of the strong credit standing of the borrowers. Indeed, micro-analysis tends to lead me to minimise my focus on the bigger picture; so this was a learning point for me personally This numerical analysis approach seemed like it was the beginning of a switch in emphasis generally across the whole corporate banking industry, from a traditionally more rounded approach to an increasingly deeper, but more narrowly focused, historical balance-sheet analysis of lending propositions. It looked and felt good but if it had a flaw, it was that it perhaps went too far and could lead you to fail to 'see the wood from the trees'. Having said that, I should add that UIB's bad-debt record was exemplary in my time there.

Indeed, it might be argued that some of the seeds of the Celtic Tiger economy and its subsequent demise lie in that very approach. This is recognisable in both economic management by the authorities and the reckless approach of many of the commercial banks in Ireland. These organisations were led by acknowledged competent, well-meaning and highly qualified people who could do their jobs technically well but perhaps were blind to the bigger picture.

Another issue that influenced my restlessness was that the perception of my role had evolved into one of a useful person to support newly hired high fliers; I was a utility player, if you like. Impatiently perhaps, I perceived myself as the prop to enable these guys further their careers on the back of my experience and ability. What they had, that I hadn't, was a string of honours degrees and maybe a CV that included more than one previous employer. I felt that I was trapped below the levels to which I aspired. And importantly, I was not good at handling the in-house politics. It was doing my morale no good to see that colleagues who had joined after me at my level had done so on an accelerated career path that took them sailing past me. The combination of creeping boredom, fading morale and the possibility of wider opportunity hastened my desire to exit. With the benefit of hindsight I now think that I was intuitively trying to find my way to the wider vista of business management as distinct from the daily grind of process.

At the time, the consequent negative impact of my distraction on the standard of my work suggested that it was time to move on.

There has always been debate in the corporate world about the value of academic achievement in the workplace. During my banking career, I came across university graduates in several business disciplines. My opinion is that the value of high academic achievement in the banking industry is overestimated. My own degree allowed me the luxury of an elevated status compared to contemporaries whose academic peak was the Irish Leaving Certificate. For those with postgraduate degrees, the difference in status was more magnified. In my view, university education is useful for fleshing out hard skills but cannot teach natural ability or integrity. Our system of written examinations favours academic prowess against natural ability, which cannot be objectively measured. In my later experience as an employer, I have found that some highly qualified university graduates have heightened expectations of career advancement that exceeds their abilities and experience as well as exceeding the capacity of their employer to give them senior roles at an early stage. These expectations can be challenging for the organisation to manage. Conversely, I have known many people with varying levels of formal education but with buckets of natural ability. These range from successful entrepreneurs to smallholders.

At that time opportunities were scarce; the Irish economy was weak and emigration a fact of life. The notion of ready mobility between the large banks, that is now taken for granted, did not then exist.

I had already accepted a permanent role at UIB, so was no longer on secondment from Ulster Bank. The kindly Jim McCombe, then Personnel Director at Ulster Bank, had sought to persuade me to stay on secondment so that I could retain a wider career choice. He assured me of opportunities within Ulster Bank, but I had got a taste for corporate banking which I now intended to pursue. Furthermore, I was well aware that because of its Belfast roots, Ulster Bank's career opportunities for me would more likely lie in in that city. Having spent a difficult period there I could not countenance a return.

UIB prospered and rightly gained a reputation as a centre of excellence within the Ulster Bank group. Michael Meagher earned a deserved reputation within the group and within the industry as an eminent banking practitioner. He combined the qualities of both a good technocrat and strategist. He had a profile within the parent National Westminster Bank and he looked destined to become chief executive of Ulster Bank. This process seemed in train when Michael abruptly resigned and joined Bank of Ireland, a major competitor, as managing director. This development came as a shock to senior Ulster Bank people. At that time it was rare for any employee to transfer between the large banks, not to mention a senior executive. In this respect, Michael was ahead of his time.

CHAPTER EIGHT

THE DONEGAL-DUBLIN DIASPORA

The old Irish refrain goes, 'You can take the man out of the bog, but you can't take the bog out of the man'. So it was with me and the Donegal Association, which I joined on my return from Belfast to Dublin in 1973. Being a Donegal person has always been an important part of my life, and something that I take great pride in. Maintaining my links with my native county and finding a group of men and women with whom I share roots in that county, has been a source of camaraderie to me over the years. It was particularly the case in the early 70s, when I found myself living and working in Dublin and building my career and family life.

The Donegal Association is similar to many other county organisations, which are particularly common in New York and London. When they were founded, they would provide a valuable social network to emigrants who originated in the same local area. They prospered in a time when Irish emigration levels were high and emigrants rarely returned home. It's probably true to say that nowadays, with Irish emigrants being better educated and easier communications and travel facilities, the need for these organisations has changed, but many are still active. Whereas in earlier times they provided support to young people newly arrived from Donegal, the current need is more of a social networking one for people already settled in their new environments as well as maintaining a connection between the Donegal communities at home and away. Donegal people still seem to attach importance to their shared roots, despite the emergence of the global citizen in a borderless world connected by social networking sites.

The Donegal Association, or Cumann Tir Chonaill, to give it its proper Gaelic title, was founded in 1935 in response to a specific need. Its foundation was prompted by a fundraising initiative after a drowning tragedy near Aranmore Island off the Donegal coast. Indeed, history seemed to repeat itself in January 1975 when the fishing trawler *Evelyn Marie* sank in the same vicinity near Burtonport in the Rosses. All aboard were sadly lost. We in the Donegal Association, similarly launched a big fundraising effort in the Shelbourne Hotel for the benefit of the dependents. I recall a huge and generous response from Donegal people in Dublin at that time. Association President Frank O'Donnell, himself a Rosses native, was much to the fore in the initiative. His brother-in-law, Padraig Browne, then General Manager of the Shelbourne Hotel, was of considerable help to us, offering the excellent venue for the fundraiser.

Primary school teachers and other state employees traditionally formed the core of the Donegal Association, which prospered for many decades at a time when there was little opportunity to visit home. Into the 70s, young people continued to arrive in Dublin, but social patterns were changing. Transport services to and from Donegal were improving with the result that the new arrivals returned home more regularly. They were therefore, finding it less necessary to seek out fellow Donegal folk in the city and more willing to mix within their own immediate work and local Dublin communities. As a consequence, the environment became more challenging for Cumann Tir Chonaill. Its traditional role of being there for new arrivals in the city was evolving into a social network for Donegal people who had made their permanent home in Dublin. There was also the opportunity to promote and support Donegal community interests in a national context. To do this, the organisation would have to attract and retain the attention of an active committee. Through difficult times, Cumann Tir Chonaill was sustained by committed and successful Donegal people now passed on to their rewards, for example, Charles J. Boyle, James Boyle, Cornelius Gallagher and Sean Logue.

A lack of volunteers resulted in me being appointed to the Committee at the first Annual General meeting that I attended. As a relative whippersnapper of 27 years of age, I became a noisy proponent of change in the organisation, which I felt had become stagnant. In my own now-advancing years, I realise how galling it must have been for those committed people to have to listen to suggestions for change from newcomers. We wanted to widen the appeal to a broader swathe of the Donegal community in Dublin, especially to younger members. We felt that to achieve this, the organisation needed a much higher profile and needed to take initiatives that were relevant to this wider audience. Understandably, the more established members were sceptical of the worth of ideas coming from a person inexperienced in such affairs. The addition of two other young committee members, Pat Dunleavy and John O'Donnell, contributed to the momentum for change. And, in spite of our overenthusiasm, we new members, who were largely from the private sector, helped create a new dynamism in the organisation. Pat Dunleavy, a natural public relations person, soon acceded to be chairman to be followed by me in the late 70s. We now had a good balance of experience and youth, which began to work well together.

Although the organisation was becoming stronger, we lacked a serious support base. I was aware of a new social organisation which had been established by two Ardara women, Kathleen Sheerin and Kathleen McCready. They were concentrating purely on the Ardara and Glenties area, but were making a great impact. It occurred to me that we should attempt to learn from them in Cumann Tir Chonaill. I approached the two Kathleens with a view to getting them to come on board. They gladly agreed, joining together with their committed husbands Brendan Sheerin and Kieran McCready, both of whom had a strong background in community activity. This was a seminal development for the organisation and a real step up in potential for future development.

We set in train a few new initiatives, the most enduring of which was the Donegal Person of the Year award. This award is made annually to a Donegal-born person who has distinguished him or herself in a particular field of endeavour. The annual award ceremony continues to be the highlight of the Cumann Tir Chonaill calendar. The inaugural award was presented to Father James McDyer, the famous Glencolumcille priest and community leader. He was presented with it at a dinner of Donegal people held in the Tara Towers Hotel in early 1979. The legendary Irish broadcaster Gay Byrne generously gave of his time to read the citation. The attendance of Gay and his wife Kathleen added a touch of glamour to the occasion.

Also present that night was Irish and European parliamentarian, Neil Blaney, the only politician to support the function with his presence. He was no longer a government minister but still a powerful player in local Donegal politics and nationally. I was embarrassed that as Chairman I mistakenly failed to acknowledge his presence at the event in public, much to his chagrin. In small talk at the end of the evening his body language made me aware of this, despite my acknowledging him on a one-to-one basis. He was that kind of person: he saw things in black and white, which meant you were either with him or against him, and he let me know that he had taken offence. My mother had a high regard for Neil Blaney, because she felt that he was one of the few politicians who genuinely used his influence to help local people. For that reason alone, I regretted my boob and apologised to him for the omission. Unfortunately, he didn't accept. I learned a valuable lesson in diplomacy that night!

During my years as Chairman, the facilities of Dublin's Baggot Inn, then owned by Donegal man Jim McGettigan, were kindly made available to the Association. I recall one night at a function there when the great Luke Kelly of the Dubliners walked in and gave an impromptu singing performance. We should have been delighted, but instead of welcoming him with open arms, we expressed our irritation at his intervention! Our lack of graciousness on the night is not something I am proud of.

I remained active with Cumann Tir Chonaill for a short period after my chairmanship ended in the early 80s, but continued to be an enthusiastic supporter of the organisation. Making new friends and working with good people made my involvement a very fulfilling one. It was a great education in learning how committees and boards function and the experience of chairing meetings was of enormous help to me in my subsequent career.

Cumann Tir Chonaill prospered through the 80s and 90s with the attraction of many excellent people on to the committee, no-one more so than the highly respected Vincent Conaghan, who edited the excellent Donegal Yearbook for several years before he became president of the Association. One of the greatest stalwarts of all down through the years has been Annagry born Charlie McGinley.

In the year 2000, I returned as president of Cumann Tir Chonaill for a three-year period. The presidency is a largely ceremonial role with no executive involvement in the organisation's affairs. Funding annual awards such as the Donegal Person of the Year is always challenging but we had some acute difficulties in my presidency. That was when I learned to appreciate people like Timmy Kelly, Mick McGinley, Enda Cunningham and Gerry McHugh, who rallied with financial support so that the show could go on. Thankfully, subsequent years have seen the organisation go from strength to strength by any yardstick. Enjoyable highlights of my Presidency were conferring Donegal Person of the Year awards on worthy Donegal natives such as businessman Sir Gerry Robinson, Northern Ireland politician Bríd Rodgers and Olympic athletics coach Patsy McGonagle.

Gerry Robinson had enjoyed great success in Britain as a businessman, notably as chief executive of Granada Television, and later as a broadcaster. With his wife, Heather, and family he had returned to live in Donegal. With an appropriate degree of fanfare we revealed Sir Gerry to our members in the Harcourt Hotel, Dublin, in the presence of Bertie Ahern, then Taoiseach. It was a great evening of Donegal bonhomie. While this was humble fare for Sir Gerry, he nevertheless appreciated being fêted by the folk of his birthplace.

Another famous Donegal man who was happy to be associated with the diaspora was the well-known Killybegs fisherman, Kevin McHugh, regarded as one of the most progressive in a business, which was prospering around the millennium and nowhere more so than in Killybegs. In August 2000, Kevin arrived in Dublin Port with his new supertrawler, *Atlantic Dawn*. Joey Murrin, a national figure in the industry and a former Donegal Person of the Year, arranged an invitation for me. *Atlantic Dawn* was a most impressive vessel bristling with technology and endowed with five-star creature comforts. A memory I have from the day was seeing Donegal parliamentarian Pat 'the Cope' Gallagher, another visitor to the trawler, frenetically using several cell phones at once. I thought, what a relentless lifestyle a politician has!

As well as maintaining good contact with the Donegal diaspora in Dublin, I always kept in touch with things in Beagh and was glad to be able to offer help to local people if I possibly could. I knew from Brigid that our next-door neighbours, the McHugh family were in need of a new home. The old thatched cottage which they inhabited was not in a good condition and their road access was difficult. The building of a local authority house on their holding was long overdue, but there was one major obstacle. The deeds of their small farm had been mislaid, so no progress could be made on transfer of the site to Donegal County Council to enable the house to be built. Without the deeds and a diligent solicitor prepared to try and re-create the title documents, they would languish in the deteriorating old house. Rose McHugh was a very good neighbour and always ready to help my mother with chores when we were growing up, and I felt I wanted to help them now. I decided to investigate the issue to see what could be done. I contacted the Irish Land Registry Office in Dublin as a first step. I was fortunate in making contact with a most helpful title examiner, Iseult Kennedy, who explained what was involved. Although normally the work of solicitors, she advised me that a lay person could do it provided they followed the procedures. Unfortunately these were not documented, but the Land Registry rules were a starting point. I studied the rules and with Ms Kennedy's help, I managed to construct information that would ultimately enable the Land Registry to issue a duplicate title document. The problem was complicated by the fact that the existing title was in the name of Sean McHugh, grandfather of Rose and Johnny. That meant that I had to check out other potential claimants to the holding. The principal surviving claimant was Rose's sister Mary, who lived in Mountcharles. Mary turned out to be most co-operative and helpful. After a reasonable period the Land Registry issued the duplicate title documents enabling Rose and Johnny to transfer the required piece of land to Donegal County Council so that they could erect the house. Rose, her husband John Connolly, and brother Johnny were thrilled with their new home. For me there was a great sense of fulfilment in seeing the thing through to a successful end.

Just as I had been able to help my Beagh neighbours, I, too, was helped by fellow Donegal people. During my early banking career, I was very aware of the presence of a fellow Donegal man, Ted O'Boyle, the Director in charge of Ulster Bank's Republic of Ireland operations. Ted took a great interest in any young Donegal person in the bank by encouraging them to progress their careers. In my early Ulster Bank days, I was the beneficiary of such encouragement, warmth and goodwill.

For the Donegal diaspora, not just in Dublin but around the world, 1992 was a year that will live long in our memories. That was the year the Donegal Gaelic Football team beat a fancied Dublin team to lift the Sam Maguire Cup for the first time on a memorable September Sunday afternoon. To Donegal folk with even the remotest interest in the game, this was an unbelievably joyous event. I was fortunate to view events from up close in Croke Park, having been kindly given a match ticket by Billy McCann, then Chairman of ESB, and joined his group of guests in the old Hogan Stand. The only drawback was that as the lone Donegal supporter among a group of non-partisans, I was somewhat constrained in expressing my true tribalism.

The feelgood factor continued into Monday when I was privileged to be invited to meet the players on their special team train before it departed from Dublin's Connolly Station to take the players to Sligo, to be bussed on to Donegal for all the celebrations. My invitation was through a good friend, fellow Donegal man, Frank Crumlish, then Treasurer of CIE. It was a particular pleasure to meet Ardara heroes, Martin Gavigan and Anthony Molloy, as well as Anthony Harkin, fitness coach.

Donegal folk, including myself, have long basked in the reflected glory of 1992. It was particularly pleasing to see Ardara GAA stalwarts such as Tommy (Tom) Boyle and (Big) Paddy McGill live to witness a first-ever Donegal victory. I recall a subsequent conversation with Paddy, on why victory never came before 1992, despite the presence of other great Donegal teams in previous generations. Paddy's view, which I respected, was that the success was down to a modern organisational approach around a great team of individuals and their management. Much the same could be said of present day Cumann Tir Chonaill.

The unbelievable occurred again in 2012 with Donegal winning the Sam Maguire for a second time. Such was the indifferent performance of Donegal teams since 1992, despite the presence of a reservoir of talented footballers, that the fantastic 2012 outcome was a great and delightful surprise. This again was down to excellent organisation and management under Jim McGuinness, combined with a talented group of players. Rare events like these always create an emotionally powerful focus for Donegal communities outside the home county.

CHAPTER NINE

Family Milestones

Following my father's diagnosis with stomach cancer in the early 70s, our family knew from the doctors that he would not recover so it was only a matter of time. He spent his final months in the Shiel Hospital in Ballyshannon, County Donegal. In contrast to Packie's expected demeanour in such circumstances, he was remarkably peaceful now. He had suffered quite a bit during his life from bronchitis especially in winter time, and whenever he was ill, he was not a good patient. His contrary demeanour at those times contrasted with his more resigned conduct now. Conal and I visited him fairly often and more adult conversation took place on those visits than in the totality of years before.

On one of my visits I recall showing Packie one of my business cards shortly after I had been promoted to the role of assistant manager at Ulster Investment Bank. He asked if he could keep it. This was the first explicit demonstration I had experienced of any interest in my career. I was touched.

Packie passed away on 15 August 1975. He was 74 years old. I received the message from Conal as I arrived in Roscommon to pick him up on my way to Donegal. Death was not a rare experience for us but something inevitable and natural. In our childhood we had attended many wakes and funerals in neighbouring houses. It was nonetheless a jolt to see my father's failed body on the cold mortuary slab. I had experienced my grief when I had learned that he would not recover and felt glad that I had had the chance to come to terms with it. The wake and funeral process was now looming in my mind. In rural Ireland and Donegal in particular, they are very open and public affairs, but bereavements bring a focus on family members and, as the eldest son, I felt this more acutely.

My mother was stoical about Packie's death. She was mentally well adjusted to the reality of Packie's loss. Her independent-mindedness and the fact of losing her own parents when a young child made her strong. Also, Brigid had a strong faith and saw death as a natural progression, expecting that one day she would meet Packie again.

We waked Packie in our Beagh home and he was buried in the graveyard adjoining Kilclooney chapel. Funerals were big occasions in West Donegal and still are. In my mind's eye, I can still see a sea of pressing faces standing in the back room of our home as we struggled to close the coffin. Among them were our cousins Colm Browne and his wife Joan, who themselves have since passed away. The attendance was swelled by the arrival of a large number of our extended family from within the county and beyond. Many local people attend wakes and funerals out of routine but Packie's death did evoke genuine sympathy across a broad spectrum of the community. He was well known locally and because he came from a large family, the circle of relations alone was wide. Packie was a fairly laid back individual with lots of time for relations and friends who would visit our home where he and Brigid always offered a warm welcome. He never let his own farm chores get in the way of a friendly chat. These chats provided a great forum for exchanging local news and gossip as well as exchanging views on the great events of the day, political and otherwise. This was a time when information did not circulate anything like as widely as today.

For most of Packie's life cars were scarce, making a phone call was a major challenge and there was no television or local radio. For returned emigrants and others seeking genealogical information on their relations or general local history, Packie was both knowledgeable and generous with his time. Both he and Brigid loved to see people call at the house when the kettle would always hang over the open hearth, later on the Stanley range, and the modest hospitality of tea and home made bread and butter would be laid on.

I was 28 years old when my father died. Packie loved life and had he lived to a greater age, I could have shared many experiences with him. With my base in Dublin and greater maturity I could have brought him to events that he would love to have experienced. We shared a love of horses, and the Dublin Horse Show and a race meeting would have been right up his street. He never had the joy of attending either of these. Then again it seems that it is only when the person passes away that you stop to think about what you might have done together. Too often, we neglect to do or say something presently, only to find that we have left it too late and the person has passed on.

Shortly after Packie's death, Conal transferred his job from Roscommon to Donegal and returned to live in Beagh with Brigid. He may always have intended to return one day, but Packie's death hastened the event. In the years that followed Conal improved the holding greatly and modernised the farm.

Packie's illness and death had taken place at a time when my life was beginning to settle down both in terms of my career and my own romantic adventures; the latter could best be described as being fairly nomadic. The central feature of my love life was a lack of commitment or serious intent. The ruling theme of my approach had been to avoid steady relationships that might in the slightest way be perceived as leading to the constraint of marriage. Over the years I had had a few nice girlfriends but these were short-term relationships which either they or I let peter out after a period. Usually the beginning of one marked the end of the previous relationship. That was until I met Mary O'Leary. It was winter 1974, at a wine-and-cheese fundraiser in the Ely Centre near St Stephen's Green. The fundraiser was run by the Glencree Reconciliation Centre. My good friend John Kelly, who was at that time associated with the Centre, had invited me and Eddie Rowland there and Eddie and I joined a few of the girls, including Mary, at one of their apartments to continue the party after the main event. There was something about Mary, despite the fact that she was unresponsive to my advances that evening. Her apparently serious, no-nonsense demeanour constituted a challenge which appealed to me. I arranged to meet Mary again at another function where she was looking after her wheelchair-bound Aunt May. May, physically disabled from childhood, was a trained schoolteacher with a formidable intellect. Mary was in great form that evening and she looked radiant. From then on, I began seeing her regularly.

Although I was going out with Mary, the relationship had not advanced to the stage that I could bring her to Donegal. Packie's funeral was premature and therefore not an appropriate first visit. I did later regret that she hadn't met him as I feel sure they would have got on well.

Within a year of Packie's death, I was married to Mary. Brigid seemed ambivalent to my marriage initially. Her preferred wives for her sons would have been native Donegal girls, who might ideally conform to a few stereotypes: a schoolteaching country girl would be a nice combination. As ever, she was obsessed with the education process; her vision of achievement for me would have been that I become a schoolteacher; gardaí were next in her pecking order of success. Many years later, when Brigid came to visit us in London, where I was working for a time, Mary and I brought her to see my office in the eighteen-storey building where I then worked. Her only comment was, 'Wouldn't you have been better off teaching?' It was difficult for Brigid to relate in any meaningful way to my banking job. The local bank manager was what she regarded as the pinnacle of the profession. This I had not achieved, even though she had my word that my status was at least as good, if not better.

In common with many parents at the time, Brigid was never one to boast about any achievement of her children. She sought no more for us than to have a reasonable standard of living. Indeed, her deeply held religious beliefs and natural stoicism would have conditioned her to prefer us not to rise above ourselves. A job locally would be preferred to Dublin or elsewhere in Ireland. She took great satisfaction in tracking the progress of other local young people and preferred to talk about them than about her own sons. Although she was I know, proud of our progress she preferred not to discuss it. Of all the local families her highest regard was held for the Gallagher boys in Beagh. Their apparent wisdom and common sense beyond their years held great appeal for her.

Mary and I became engaged to be married shortly after Packie's death. It did not cross my mind to bring Mary to Beagh to obtain Brigid's approval. We weren't the kind of family that went on with might be called 'palaver'. The idea of making a meal of my engagement appealed neither to me nor to Brigid. Ours was a home where world affairs were discussed, but none of us were big on sentimental issues, particularly if they pertained to ourselves; discussion was usually in the third person.

I did bring Mary to visit Brigid after the event as it were. Mary brought her a small piece of ornamental Aynsley china as a goodwill token. Mary wasn't to know that things which didn't have a practical use held no attraction for Brigid, nor did she have any regard for things like fresh flowers, which Mary loves. On our arrival at Beagh, Brigid was in the process of preparing a drink for one of her calves. Her welcome was businesslike and her demeanour suggested that the calf would have to be fed before there would be time for idle chatter. As you can imagine, Mary was pretty nonplussed, to put it mildly, with this reception but she managed to hold her counsel. Thankfully she was not put off. Above all else Brigid was a good farmer and care for the animals was always a priority. Because she was a mountain woman, her knowledge of sheep exceeded Packie's and she was tougher physically. If Packie was confined to bed she would 'pull' hay at the mouth of the haystack and bring this fodder to the cows, no matter how bad the weather. I really admired and never ceased to be amazed at her ability to do this: hay is so tightly packed in the haystack that it makes for a very physical challenge. In the harshest weather she would carry buckets of water from our well, even if she had to smash the ice on the frozen surface. As a child she was used to surviving in a hostile environment so this was just more of the same.

Brigid was not at all a cold-hearted person, but the opposite, in fact. Because of circumstance, she was conditioned early in her life to make a priority of the welfare of others. Sentimental chatter could follow, but should not be allowed get in the way of day-to-day survival.

Mary and I returned to Dublin after Mary's induction and got on with planning our wedding. Both of us resolved to have a small and unfussy wedding; now that Packie was no longer with us, I was not in a mood for a big splash. We were married in Donnybrook Catholic church on 8 July 1976. Only our immediate families, my godparents Hugh and his wife Katie, as well as Eddie Rowland, my friend and then housemate, were present. We had the reception in Jury's Hotel, Ballsbridge where Mary's brother John, now sadly deceased, was a manager. It was a happy and enjoyable day; the two families got on fine. Mary's parents Jack and Molly, were an affable couple and, being Dubliners, they seemed to enjoy the rare novelty of meeting and mixing with Donegal folk, who were unfamiliar with city ways. Mary's elder brother, Michael, and his wife, Anne, attended and their daughter

Geraldine was flower girl. Mary's cousin, Joan Lambe, was bridesmaid and Conal was my best man.

In her inimitable way, Brigid put her stamp on affairs by walking in protest out of the group photograph. She never liked photographs and eventually lost patience with the amount of time the photographer was taking. The performance was a reflection of her independence and wilfulness despite the importance of the occasion. She was a person who took and got her way even when Packie was alive. The wedding night was spent in the Montrose Hotel nearby and the next day, we travelled to Lahinch, County Clare, where we spent a week in the Aberdeen Arms Hotel. We then drove north to Donegal with an overnight in the Royal Hotel, Boyle, County Roscommon. In Donegal we spent a night in Roneragh House in Fahan and then onto the final destination of my family home.

In the early years of our marriage, we would often stay with Brigid. She treated me differently to Mary in that my breakfast cereal would be prepared while Mary was left to provide for herself in this regard. It was the rural Irish tradition of 'looking after the men'; women should look after themselves in a domestic context and not expect another woman to wait on them. Thankfully, Mary recognised the situation for what it was and was more amused than slighted.

The honeymoon produced the usual stresses and strains that come from two people being thrown together for the first time over a continuous period. Unlike the newlyweds of today, we missed out on the co-habiting-before-marriage experience. We belonged to almost the last such generation in Ireland. We did, however, manage to avoid 'killing each other' in the process. We got over the adjustment period and settled in Trees Road, in the Dublin suburb of Mount Merrion. Mary continued her nursing career at St Vincent's Private Hospital until she became pregnant with Catherine in 1978.

In the month before Catherine's birth, Mary's parents. Jack O'Leary and his wife Molly, were relaxing in our house. It was just after a lovely Sunday lunch which Mary, being the excellent cook that she is, had prepared, when Jack suddenly collapsed. We called the ambulance, which immediately brought him to St Vincent's Hospital Accident and Emergency unit. Sadly, Jack was dead on arrival there. Mary was close to her father, enjoying his wicked sense of humour. Remarkably, she retained her composure and the presence of mind to deal with the situation. A month before giving birth to Catherine was a traumatic point in time to suddenly lose the father of whom she was so fond.

On Sunday 15 April 1979, Mary gave birth to a beautiful baby girl weighing 6 lbs 8oz. This was a life-changing event for both of us with the baby becoming the new centre of our attention and our world. Names were a quandary for us but we eventually settled for Catherine simply because we liked the name.

In 1983, we made our first family trip to the USA, to visit my aunt Annie in Morristown, New Jersey. I was very close to Annie and wanted to introduce my new family to her. Annie was Brigid's sister, who had emigrated to the United States in her twenties. She trained there as a state registered nurse and finished a highly successful career as a senior theatre nurse in All Souls Hospital, Morristown. My memories of her few visits back to Donegal in my childhood are glowing. Without the burden of parental responsibility, she was switched on to us children in the way that our parents could never be. She was extremely generous too. Christmases and birthdays were never forgotten and a $5 or $10 cheque was always present when you opened the letter. It is to Annie, of course, that I owe my secondary schooling which provided me with the platform for my career. Were it not for her intervention, I would have been destined to remain in Beagh and inherit the smallholding.

Annie and her American-born nephew Franny, my first cousin, awaited our arrival at Kennedy Airport. Franny chauffeured us in

Annie's old blue Dodge car. That car felt like you were in a huge biscuit tin, floating on air with its bench front seat and column gear-change. We crossed Brooklyn Bridge, intending to take the freeway to New Jersey, but there was so much excitement and chat that Franny missed the turn-off, to Annie's feigned displeasure. She was extremely fond of Franny and would defend him and forgive any deviation; he could do no wrong in her eyes.

We eventually arrived at Annie's spacious apartment in South Street, Morristown. It was a lovely environment. The tree-lined streets were laid out in an open, easy-to-follow grid format. Catherine who was just four, was the centre of attention. Annie and her friends loved her, so Catherine had a ball. Mary and Annie got on well; both being nurses helped but Annie thought highly of Mary. The few weeks we spent with Annie were both memorable and enjoyable, taking in visits to cousins Tom and Eileen Morley and their families, who lived further west in New Jersey. Aunt Bella, Packie's sister, lived on the New Jersey coast where we visited her and her husband Charlie. Sadly, Bella was suffering from advanced dementia so she didn't recognise us. Her son Frank and his family lived further south in a neighbouring state. It was not until a few years later, on a business trip to Atlanta, that I had the pleasure of meeting Frank for the first time.

Annie was to visit Ireland one more time; that was for my brother Conal's wedding to Bernadette Ward in 1984. They were married in Ardara chapel and have two children, Joseph and Siobhan, now young adults. Annie was in good form and greatly enjoyed the visit and the wedding. Herself and Brigid had their usual quota of arguments and lively discussion. Brigid would lament the changes taking place in the world, a position which clashed with Annie's more modern outlook. She passed away a few years later in 1988, having suffered a severe stroke. As was her wish, the machine which was keeping her alive was switched off and nature was allowed to take its course. Annie is buried in a Philadelphia cemetery where I had the privilege of visiting her grave in 2001.

For a time after our wedding we lived in a small semi-detached house in Mount Merrion, where we remained until Catherine was two years old. That particular housing development was built right after World War 2 when good quality materials were scarce. While the location was good, the house needed considerable expenditure to bring it to a reasonable standard. Instead, we moved down the road to nearby Goatstown, a convenient suburb. There were lots of girls of Catherine's age in that vicinity, many of whom went to the same local school. This was a time when I was greatly absorbed with building a career with Barclays. The result was that Mary did not receive the support she deserved in those early years of bringing up Catherine. For example, I went to England for a three-week residential management course in the Barclays management training centre at a time when Catherine was not yet two years old. Seen through the lens of today such an absence was not on. Indeed even at the time, it was far too long to leave Mary on her own with our young child. I belonged to a period when the husband's role was confined to providing and leaving the greater weight of parenting to the wife. This is a huge and negative contrast to the new man of today who sees his role as equally sharing the parental responsibilities.

Catherine was a busy, curious and intelligent child. Like myself, she has a low boredom threshold. School, therefore, would have dragged for her, however, she made it through and procured a job in the insurance industry at an early stage. Catherine is self reliant, can be very focused and is capable of hard work. When taken with excellent interpersonal skills, this ensured she was able to move jobs readily and successfully. Into her career Catherine went back to college and obtained a degree in Human Resources Management. This was a remarkable achievement.

She is a great mother, combining this important role with a busy job which she shares.

Brigid passed away in 2003 at the full age of 95 years. In late summer of that year, Brigid began to suffer a series of strokes culminating in her death in early November. She had lived an independent life since she was widowed in 1975. Although she rarely travelled far, she kept herself remarkably up to date with affairs local, national and international. She had a wonderful memory and loved nothing more than reminiscing with old friends. If these old friends were In Through natives, such as her cousin Peg Molloy, then all the better. Because she was so up to date from reading the newspaper and watching television, she equally valued the company of younger folk. Again coming from In Through was a bonus; she particularly enjoyed chatting to James Hegarty, a great source of local gossip. She was a great source of wisdom in the family. Indeed a greater source than was sometimes welcome, because both Conal and I would often be truly upstaged by her take on issues. Needless to say, we often found it hard to admit that she was right and we were wrong.

My daughter, Catherine, grew up to be a stunningly beautiful young woman. She was and is popular with peers. Never short of suitors, she married Ken Smith, whom she met when they both worked in Canada Life Assurance. Ken is a good personality with a huge interest in most sports and particularly golf, which he plays well. His addiction is Liverpool Football Club, which he follows religiously. Catherine and Ken married in St Patrick's Church, Donegal, in September 2008. The reception was held in the excellent Harvey's Point Hotel on Lough Eske.

Just a year later, Alex, their baby boy was born. He is a special child and adored by both the Smith family and ourselves. In January 2012, our joy was repeated when Catherine gave birth to a bouncing baby girl whom they christened Zara. Mary and I feel very lucky to have Alex and Zara in our lives. Their trusting smiles are a delight and indeed a tonic in themselves. We take Alex every Friday, bringing him to his school in Glenageary during school term. Mary's favourite places to bring Alex are to see the ducks in the pond in Herbert Park, where she herself played as a child, and when it is open, the urban farm at Airfield in Dundrum. Alex is fascinated by animals and most particularly by our Jack Russell dog, Duke.

CHAPTER TEN

A World of Banking

In 1978 an employment opportunity arose for me with the arrival of Barclays Bank International (BBI) in Dublin. A discreet advertisement was placed by Price Waterhouse, acting as consultants, for a business development officer, and, having looked at the job requirements, I concluded that I was a suitable candidate. The economy was doing poorly so it was a tough time to set up a new corporate banking business in Ireland. However, I viewed this challenge as well mitigated by the high-quality name of Barclays. It was one of the largest banks in Britain and enjoyed a world-class reputation. BBI was the international arm of Barclays and a very substantial organisation in its own right.

Having got through the initial filtering process and on to the shortlist, I was interviewed by Bob Maw, head of the new Barclays office in Ireland. Together with his secretary Sue McCrory, he had set up a temporary office in Mercantile Credit's Dublin premises. Mercantile Credit was ultimately owned by Barclays. Bob came across as well spoken, charming and he looked every inch the city banker. He seemed the ideal choice to spearhead Barclays launch in Ireland. The interview went well and I felt I could get on with Bob. It did strike me that he seemed less apprehensive about business prospects than I would have expected, in view of the difficult conditions then prevailing in the Irish banking market. What I didn't realise, but learned later, was that Bob's role would be more presidential than I would have anticipated. His job would be more about developing profile for the new Barclays Ireland than about day-to-day driving and management of the business. The organisational structure was designed around Bob to facilitate this approach.

I then flew to London and for what would turn out to be the first of many times, entered the august head office building at 54 Lombard Street, right in the heart of 'The Square Mile'. There I was interviewed firstly by Alan Mitchell, Assistant General Manager, a larger-than-life Scot. He asked me few questions and with considerable bombast, did most of the talking himself. I had no sense of being tested, but I was not complaining! The next person to interview me was Patrick Perry, a high-level recruit from the Foreign Office and a rising star in Barclays. Because he had Irish connections, it was considered that he would be an appropriate interviewer in the circumstances. Patrick did indeed have strong family affiliations with north Donegal. I got on well with him and he and his wife Mary remain good friends until this day. Patrick progressed rapidly up the senior ranks in Barclays to ultimately hold the key position of group treasurer.

After the round of interviews I returned to Dublin to be offered the job by Bob Maw. I saw this opportunity as opening an exciting new phase in my life and I looked forward to what might lie ahead. I realised that there was a risk it might not work out but this did not worry me. Working in an international banking environment was bound to be a useful professional and learning experience. Moreover, having a name of the quality of Barclays Bank on my CV would be a positive should I have to move on again

Barclays opened for business in Dublin in September 1978. The fitting out of the new offices had taken place over the summer months.

Two floors of the newly developed offices at 47 and 48 St, Stephen's Green, were fitted out to a high standard, with extensive wood panelling on the ground floor. The banking-hall floor was adorned with a specially made Donegal carpet into which had been woven the Barclays eagle crest. These excellent preparations belied a less-than-due emphasis on business strategy. George Colley, then Minister for Finance, performed the official opening. The great and the good of the Dublin banking and corporate elite attended. A posse of Barclays senior executives had flown in from London and were led by Group Chairman, Sir Anthony Tuke. Bob Maw did a superb job on the arrangements for the opening ceremony and all went well. The main theme of the time was the Irish pound's break with sterling to join the European Monetary System. Sir Anthony commented to colleagues afterwards that Ireland's decision to break with sterling seemed to have an overriding political aspect in addition to the central economic case.

Among the head office group present that day was Peter S. Ardron, whom I observed holding forth to a sidebar within my earshot. In one fell swoop he dismissed the future of the new Irish branch with some vigour, declaring, 'we are never going to make our fortune in Dublin'. In the context of the large scale of the Barclays Group, this was true and genuinely felt. It was, however, deeply inappropriate and morale depressing for the new team.

A local Irish supervisory board was formed to foster and supervise the growth of the fledgling Barclays banking business in Dublin. The board was made up of two Barclays heavyweights, Derek Vander Weyer and Peter Leslie, as well as Bob Maw and local accountant Donal Flinn. Leslie, to whom Bob reported directly, was a very bright and articulate man who ultimately went on to vice chairmanship of the Barclays Group. Regarded as a moderniser, Derek Vander Weyer was often spoken of as the best chief executive that the Barclays Group never had: in those days, the job was always retained within the Barclays founding families. There was no room for the outsider, no matter how talented.

Ulster Bank Group, the employer I had just left to join Barclays, was represented at the launch by one of their directors. In a brief conversation, he commented to me witheringly, and in some pique, about my decision to leave the Ulster Bank Group. I was taken aback at this harsh attitude in view of my relatively junior status and youth, but of course this was a time when employee movement between the large banks in Ireland was rare and was perceived as a form of betrayal. In the years that followed, changing employers became a more regular feature of the industry and so wouldn't have drawn such hostility. The combination of Ardron and my former colleague seemed to conspire, but failed to dent, my enthusiasm for Barclays prospects in Ireland.

Most of the bank staff had been recruited by Bob's deputy, branch manager George O'Neill, and operations manager Robin Pomeroy. Both were Irish born and were experienced Barclays career bankers. George had been a branch manager in east London, a role in which he seemed to enjoy considerable autonomy and respect from his customers. He had an enviable reputation for working well with the Jewish and Indian business communities. It was therefore not surprising that he was unenthusiastic about a management structure in which he now had to report to a more senior person in Bob Maw, in the same office.

Apart from Robin, chief dealer Denis Holland, Bob's secretary Sue and me, the remaining staff were recruited by George. Denis and George struck up a good relationship, as did their families. Bob was undoubtedly the boss, but in the tradition of Barclays, George was the day-to-day enforcer. As time passed, I was to learn that Barclays Group management structures had a close parallel with the British army. There was a kind of officer tier, the most senior of whom were connected, albeit distantly, to the founding families of the bank; many of these people had served time in the more glamorous British military regiments. The day-to-day management of the bank was in the hands of a capable cadre of enforcers, some of whom had joined Barclays as young as sixteen years of age. Their careers had been built on ability and strength of character, rather than on their level of education or interpersonal skills. This approach well suited the context of the banking market of the time and produced many excellent bankers. In Barclays at the time, there was a premium on credit assessment through character judgement: eyeballing the customer. Legendary reputations were built on this approach. Marketing was a relatively new concept at this time. As an outsider, this approach felt old-fashioned to me, even at the time, but there was no doubt that it had worked for Barclays and other banks, who had built up enormous businesses over time.

Against this background it was not surprising that there was no clear business strategy or business plan for BBI. The only relevant documentation was a business development plan which Julia Russell, a Poole-based young management trainee, had worked up from desk research. This lack of serious attention to the fundamentals of business planning surprised me, to say the least. It seemed to be based on the fact that the Barclays brand name was so powerful that such niceties as a thought out strategy were superfluous. I believed that it foolishly underestimated our competitors in the Irish market. The general business approach evident here should have been an omen of the challenges that lay ahead.

Before commencing work in Dublin, I spent a week visiting head office departments in England. The purpose was twofold; to investigate customer introductions for the Dublin office and to familiarise myself with the Barclays Group. This trip was a revelation. I realised that there were two Barclays organisations, not one, and that they didn't relate well to each other. BBI was the organisation that had offices all over the world, with a particularly large presence on the continent of Africa. Barclays Bank Limited was the British clearing bank with branches in nearly every town in England and Wales. This was a powerful operation and one of the largest players in the British domestic banking market. The people in each of the two organisations were different. It was possible to draw broad comparisons between the two sets of bankers. The BBI people were outward looking and cosmopolitan. Some were graduates of Britain's best universities. They had good articulation and interpersonal skills. Communicating with different nationalities was second nature to them. The BBI people referred to their UK domestic colleagues, somewhat disdainfully, as 'limited' as in Barclays Bank Limited. On the other hand the UK bankers referred to their BBI colleagues as 'bush bankers'. There was an element of truth in both labels. While some of the domestic bankers didn't have the cosmopolitanism of their BBI colleagues, they were nonetheless good technical bankers. They enjoyed the self-confidence that comes from belonging to a company that is a dominant market player. The domestic banking operation was highly structured with well-resourced head office support functions. It was regionalised across England and Wales. Indeed, it was more a conglomerate of regional fiefdoms rather than a single organisation. The regional directors each had a fully functional local head office. These local leaders varied in status depending on such factors as membership or not of the founding families of Barclays Bank, and the economic scale of the individual regional business unit in its own right. Regions had the authority to approve very large loans without reference to head office. These large lending discretions allowed these regions to be powerful players in their own right.

To the uninitiated, the BBI head-office organisation was less clear. BBI's London head-office structure broadly mirrored the domestic bank's, albeit on a smaller scale. The BBI culture allowed for greater flexibility and discretion by senior managers. Due to their exposure to different cultures, the BBI people with whom I had contact were broadminded. I found them to be good colleagues.

With the benefit of hindsight, the nature of the Barclays organisational structure had the potential for challenges when it came to Barclays Ireland. Ostensibly, the business potential for Barclays in Ireland was significant, because of the dominance of Barclays in the British corporate banking market combined with the fact that Britain was Ireland's largest trading partner. However, the reality was somewhat different. The business cultures of both arms of Barclays were as different as if they had been completely separate and independent companies. Therefore, it was not possible for Barclays Dublin, as part of BBI, to fully leverage the powerful domestic banking presence across Britain. These branches had long been used to a protocol of referring the Irish connections of their customers to Allied Irish Banks. A strong correspondent banking relationship existed traditionally between both these banks. To attempt to revise this old and now inappropriate protocol was in itself a challenge, not to mention implementing it to the benefit of Barclays Ireland. This was a pity because the Barclays fledgling Irish corporate banking unit had more in common with the UK domestic bank than with BBI.

BBI's strength was in its extensive African network of banking operations, which had little synergy with Western markets such as Ireland. BBI was a serious banking outfit with long and deep roots in many former British colonies in Africa. These were independent localised banks often enjoying a dominant market position. Much to my disappointment, Barclays did not have long-established presences in the corporate banking markets of continental Europe or the United States of America. This was particularly difficult in the Irish market, because the United States was the source of significant corporate banking opportunities, given the steady flow of foreign direct investment into Ireland. Unlike the US banks represented in Ireland, Barclays market position in the U. S. was insufficiently entrenched to influence customer introductions to the new Barclays Ireland.

Here we now were, set up in Dublin, one of the world's well-recognised banking brand names. Fellow banking competitors might understandably have anticipated a serious challenge from Barclays; they needn't have worried too much.

The formal Barclays Dublin organisation chart had me reporting directly to Bob Maw. The logic was that Bob and I, either jointly or on an individual basis, would bring the Barclays message to potential customers. George would manage the office on a day-to-day basis and, with his lending background, specifically process new business lending opportunities. In theory, this was a sensible strategy but in the event, practice didn't match theory.

Bob was a superb public relations person with buckets of style, wit and charm, but his interest in the cut and thrust of dealmaking was limited. He seemed to have little corporate credit experience and a very low appetite for risk. Although this was somewhat of a surprise to me, it shouldn't have been as a closer look at Bob's resumé would have shown. His major recent experience was in representing Barclays in Madrid while making preparations for a launch of Barclays in Spain; Bob would have excelled in this self-starting type of role. His successful career, which was built largely in the Caribbean islands and African territories, would have been in the customer-deposit rather than lending-oriented banking. In any fledgling Irish banking operation, a strong lending capability was essential.

The Irish corporate banking market was growing slowly if at all, and the major local banking players were savvy and highly competitive. Barclays brand was little known in Ireland apart from the name recognition accruing from Barclaycard, the credit card. Potential customers would be slow to switch their allegiances from the well-entrenched local players of AIB and Bank of Ireland to an untested newcomer. Barclays was joining a number of equally big name foreign banks, none of whom had achieved scale in the Irish market. Moreover the Irish economy was performing poorly and consequently there was little corporate-credit expansion in which a new market player might participate. Corporate lending opportunities were largely confined to a premium tax-based loan product called Section 84 loans, for which demand was strong because of its low pricing. It was the major local banks that had this product available in large supply, thus creating serious competitive advantage for them.

While the external challenges were real, we nevertheless had a powerful, reputable and experienced name in Barclays behind us. However, the internal challenges were frustrating, if only because they were self imposed. The triangular relationship between Bob, George and I didn't help the business. Any evidence in George's eyes of me having a good working relationship with Bob militated against my relationship with him. George enjoyed a pivotal position in both running the office day to day, and being the credit risk officer for the business. In view of his grip on the day-to-day business routine and autocratic management style, he enjoyed great influence and control over staff. I struggled to gain support from George when I needed the help of colleagues in doing my job. We didn't have a shared vision. Achieving support for a business initiative with our treasury dealing room was a typical example. I saw the opportunity to leverage our strong treasury capabilities to gain competitive advantage with prospective corporate clients. BBI's London dealing room, HOFEX, was one of the world's biggest players in the foreign-exchange markets and operated on a global basis. Therefore, corporate foreign exchange was one of the few product areas of competitive advantage to Barclays in the Irish market. It could provide a door-opener for other product sales. The key person who was in a position to assist effect this strategy was our chief dealer, Denis Holland, who reported to George O'Neill. Although Denis was an experienced money dealer and a bright guy, he was not used to the corporate sector, having come from the Central Bank of Ireland, the

Irish financial regulator. My hopes of working with him in helping to build the customer base were quickly dashed. Without a directive from his boss to emphasise the corporate route, Denis was never likely to divert effort from the short-term profitability of interbank trading to the longer-term grind of building a commercial customer base. That interbank trading was producing quick profits militated against any desire for George to influence business strategy in the direction suggested by me.

What initially seemed like an exciting career path was turning out to be extremely challenging. Despite the presence of a world-class brand in Barclays, I felt we could do much more to set ourselves up to progress in what was already a difficult economic environment. It felt like driving a car with the handbrake engaged. Nonetheless, any temptation I had to give up the struggle was tempered by both the lack of similar employment opportunities and the eternal optimism that circumstances would ultimately change for the better. I was suffering in the short term but there was a longer game which I should see out.

I had little choice but to take a more philosophical approach. For the sake of my health alone, I was forced to lower my lofty vision of what Barclays should achieve; a bout of stress-induced shingles amounted to a sufficiently strong signal. Moreover, I conceded to myself that I had to lower my objectives in accordance with the constraints, both internal and external. In any event, overall business progress was not my primary responsibility; there were two senior people more directly in the firing line than me. In the way I did my job I tried to communicate strongly and equally with my two masters in order to minimise the fallout from my peculiar juxtaposition in the organisation. In this I was greatly helped by Bob's secretary Sue McCrory, a most competent and diplomatic person. She helped me to navigate a more productive relationship with Bob and George. My contribution was recognised as useful to both Bob and George and I tried my best to support them. To be fair to Bob, he was always very ready to acknowledge my efforts.

Despite some trials and tribulations, I was increasingly beginning to enjoy aspects of my career with Barclays challenging internal relationships notwithstanding. My involvement with colleagues in the London and European centres of Barclays was a new and interesting dimension to my work. Apart from a longstanding presence in France, Barclays was relatively new to these countries. Common problems created motivation and a unity of purpose for all of us. France was different. Barclays had had a banking presence in that country for several decades; a key raison d'être for its establishment was to serve British expatriate residents. Barclays France was therefore well established as a domestic bank, albeit foreign owned and quite French. From my visits there it was clearly evident that contact with other parts of the Barclays Group, including London head office, was not greatly welcomed. They had no real interest in co-operation with 'Johnny come lately' parts of Barclays, such as Ireland. One good example of the prevailing attitude was when Paris's turn came around to host the regular Barclays European business development conference. This conference rotated around European capitals and it was now Paris's turn. The host venue's chief executive would formally open the conference and in this case, the French chief executive did so, with an address completely in French, even though it was known that he spoke English. As a new boy, I was taken aback at what seemed to me a disrespectful attitude, particularly towards senior colleagues from London. The performance was no surprise to more seasoned colleagues, who had seen it before. While Barclays owned the French banking operation they seemed to have had little say and furthermore a lack of respect from local management. In the years that followed, it was no surprise that things were to change radically in this regard, with greatly increased intervention.

Through the Barclays European business development forum I met many interesting people. Barclays Spain was then represented by a Spanish Count, Carlos Martínez de Campos. As a member of the Spanish élite, he was held in high regard by the London hierarchy, as well as for his business abilities. He possessed an unsurprising sense of self belief that truly reflected his value to Barclays in Spain. Under his leadership, Barclays Spain embarked on an investment programme which resulted in an extensive retail banking operation. Carlos's remote connection with Ireland was that he had learned English in Dublin as a student.

International personal interaction was not confined to London and European colleagues. There was a continuous programme of residential management courses and conferences which enabled me to meet many interesting colleagues from Africa, the Americas and other places. At that time Barclays had a large banking presence in South Africa, Barclays National Bank, which was at that time bigger than any Irish bank. The South Africans, be they of English or Afrikaaner extract were among the most impressive people I met. A few of the British expatriate African country heads were equally impressive and seemed destined for senior leadership roles on their eventual return to London. Native African country heads were rare in those days but from the impressive African managers I had encountered on management courses, I could see it was inevitable that they would progress to lead their business units. The expatriates had the unique experience of independently managing large local businesses in a foreign market, a long way from head-office support. In the event, few of these managers succeeded in becoming top senior executives in the group. The reality was, that to succeed to the higher echelons, you were better off staying close to the source of power and influence; as they say, 'Out of sight is out of mind'! Those managers who set their sights on high office ensured that they would remain in or close to London and would endeavour to place themselves in senior general manager's assistant positions. Some of these high fliers also seemed adept at avoiding the really tough assignments that might potentially register a failure on their resumé. There was also a political factor that entered the equation. The top echelon at group level had their origins in Barclays Bank Limited, the big UK arm and consequently the serious opportunities seemed more restricted for BBI people. This state of affairs led to deep frustration and to the departures of many highly able people from the International side.

Barclays Dublin made steady if unspectacular progress, in line with the Irish economy's mediocre performance. Foreign direct investment was one of the few bright spots. Ireland's industrial development authority (IDA Ireland) continued to win foreign manufacturing investment into Ireland, mainly from the United States. The presence of Barclays in the U.S. might suggest that we were well placed to obtain a slice of the local Irish banking requirements from this investment flow, however, due to our corporate structure we could not offer the attractive Section 84 finance. I did raise the Section-84 issue, and at head-office level we discussed the possibility of converting our Dublin branch to a locally incorporated subsidiary. Through a subsidiary we could offer tax-based financing products. Senior colleagues understood my proposal, but they did not see its strategic value and may have considered it more trouble than it was worth. Two other considerations came in to play. Firstly, the proposal was of medium-term advantage and so would not generate significant value in the relatively short-term career horizon of senior colleagues. The words of P. S Ardron, the senior general manager whom I had overheard at the official Dublin opening, came back to haunt us. Secondly, such was the then-robust profitability of the big UK domestic bank that in the overall scheme of things, overseas operations would be no more than of marginal significance for the foreseeable future. I needed to absorb that reality.

The Barclays Group did own a well-established finance company in Ireland which long preceded the 1978 arrival of Barclays Bank, the aforementioned Mercantile Credit Company, which had acted as our temporary base. The UK based Mercantile Credit Group, together with its Irish subsidiary, were autonomous and independently separate businesses within the overall Barclays Group. It would have been sensible for both Barclays Dublin and Mercantile Ireland as relatively small players in the Irish banking market to co-operate closely with each other. Mercantile MD David Hogg and his deputy Josh Cunningham, were always pleasant and helpful at a personal level, but there was no compelling motivation for them to work closely with us. I recall presenting a paper at a Mercantile sales conference in the Killiney Castle Hotel on how both organisations might achieve synergy by working more closely. My message went down like a lead balloon. These guys were doing fine, enjoying a strong position in motor finance and really saw little advantage for them in a closer working relationship. In truth, the advantage would be more to Barclays Dublin and of course, to overall group benefit. In the absence of a group directive on co-operation in Ireland, no progress would be possible; no such directive was forthcoming. It would also be wrong to underestimate the challenge of marrying the two diverse cultures. Under Bob Maw's leadership Barclays Dublin would in Mercantile's eyes be perceived as having a superiority complex while Mercantile seemed to unjustifiably suffer from an inferiority complex, in the presence of their ultimate parent company.

It seemed that all possible routes to expansion of Barclays in Ireland were blocked. And then, in the early 80s, a small Irish bank, the Commercial Banking Company, came available for sale. It was owned by PMPA Insurance Company, a local insurance company controlled by the Moore family. PMPA provided motor insurance to the Irish public at affordable prices at a time when motor insurance was both expensive and difficult to obtain. The then financial regulator, the Central Bank of Ireland, had a policy preference that banks not be owned by non-banking companies. Hence, they were keen to see the Commercial Banking Company owned by another large bank. Donal Flinn, non-executive Chairman of Barclays in Ireland, envisaged the acquisition of this bank as a rare opportunity to enlarge Barclays footprint in Ireland. A former senior partner in accountants Coopers and Lybrand, Donal relished the challenge and higher profile consequent on this acquisition. Barclays Group reluctantly backed it, if only because it cost pocket money; a mere couple of million pounds to buy a bank. Unfortunately, the ultimate price of this expansion would turn out to be a great deal more.

To his credit, Bob Maw was lukewarm about this business proposition, which operated in a segment of the banking market unfamiliar to him. However, Bob's views didn't rate highly on the group's agenda at a time when his succession was becoming an issue in view of his impending retirement. Although the new business would work closely with the existing Barclays operation, it would remain separate and its management reporting line would be directly to London rather than the logical route, to Bob Maw. This state of affairs did not make for good working relationships between the two local arms of Barclays, a sharp contrast to what was necessary in order to achieve a better market positioning for the group in Ireland.

The acquisition of the Commercial Banking Company brought change for me. A year earlier, I had transferred from my original business development role to become Head of Operations. My reasons to seek the change were twofold. Due to the weak economy, new-business activity was low, so I was inclined to seek a fresh internal challenge. As the operations department had a wide brief, which included all back-office support activities, the change offered me the opportunity to deepen my general management skills. On the other hand, my colleague Robin Pomeroy, my predecessor as Head of Operations, was keen to widen his experience into the business development side of the business. One of my achievements in my new job was the successful introduction of the SWIFT international payments to Barclays Dublin. SWIFT is a secure global payments system owned by a group of major international banks.

The then major issue for Barclays was to fuse the recently acquired Commercial Banking Company into the Barclays Group. The intention was to allow this new banking vehicle to thrive in the freedom from Barclays bureaucracy while at the same time to let it harvest the good practices and general benefits of being part of a worldwide banking group. To assist them in achieving this objective, I was appointed deputy general manager of the company. My main functions would be to act as a communications channel between the new acquisition and the Barclays group as well as being a lightning rod on behalf of the group for issues arising in the Commercial Banking Company.

My early excitement at the prospect of this new role evaporated fairly quickly. This was going to be an experience all right but a difficult challenge. Skills in corporate re-organisation rather than banking or general management skills were to be at a premium.

There were a number of issues. Even before the ink was dry on the final purchase agreement to buy the bank, the signs were ominous. At the due-diligence stage, the Barclays inspectorate struggled valiantly to get to grips with an assessment of the quality of the loan book. The lending records were in the form of bulky files rather than the more normal comprehensive schedules showing all key information, especially security valuations as they related to loan balances. Much of the bank's lending was in the property, housebuilding and licensed trade.

I soon realised that this was an alien environment to me in that things were not as they appeared at first sight. The management style of the organisation was different to what I had been used to at Barclays. The context that prompted me to promote change was a Barclays context, which at that point was of course, alien to the incumbent managers. I realised that I would be on my own should I try to effect change and was forced to agree with the words of Matt Barrett, the Irish-Canadian who would become group chief executive, when he said, 'Guess what? If you stop knocking your head against the wall, you feel better'. There were echoes of this message here. A lesson learned from this experience was that when a company makes a new acquisition it should always appoint a minimum of two people to the unit to help bed in the acquired entity to the Group. A single person operating in isolation is ineffective if significant change is required.

It was not too long before the loan book at the Commercial Banking Company began to reveal faults that to date had not been evident. The practice of repeatedly extending loans beyond their original and revised maturity dates raised questions at the central advances department in London. This forced the Barclays Group to take a closer look at the bank they had acquired in Ireland. Although the bank had been bought for a paltry few million pounds, steady erosion of the loan book could make it a very expensive and loss-making venture. Some management changes were made to Barclayise the acquired unit at a faster rate and to facilitate succession in Ireland. The inherent weakness of the loan book continued to reveal itself through substantial bad-debt writeoffs. Barclays had bought something a great deal less valuable and more troublesome than it first appeared.

After less than two years after being appointed deputy general manager of the Commercial Banking Company, I was appointed to replace John Kidd as branch manager in Barclays Dublin, reporting to Bob Maw. Bob reached retirement shortly thereafter and he and his wife Elizabeth went to live in Sevenoaks, Kent. Sadly, Bob passed away a relatively short period after retirement. He was succeeded by Trevor Jones who would combine this appointment with his responsibilities at the Commercial Banking Company. By that time, Trevor had realigned the senior management in the Commercial Banking Company, now renamed Barclays Bank Ireland Limited. He had installed some experienced personnel from Barclays UK and had converted the head office into a large branch. Despite considerable investment of time and personnel the renamed and separately managed Commercial Banking Company did not prosper. Its attempts to grow were stymied by the very difficult economic backdrop of the 80's. Typical retail bank lending policies involving a mix of secured and unsecured business lending were adopted. Unfortunately, this business strategy failed mainly due to the difficult economic environment, but it also transpired that implementation of the change in business strategy was premature, because the skills required were not yet fully in place. The result was that while many of the building blocks were now in place, other factors conspired to deny success.

Eventually, the branch network was closed and the remnants of the business was merged into Barclays Bank Dublin. This assignment was left to David Burke, an experienced and adroit international banker who had managed Barclays offices both in London and overseas. He had already succeeded Trevor Jones, who had returned to a senior responsibility in London. David was new to Ireland, so, unlike Trevor, he had no baggage and proceeded apace to implement a rationalisation plan. This project, which marked the end of Barclays foray into the Irish retail banking market, involved branch closures and staff severances, which David handled as sensitively as possible. In my job managing the day-to-day corporate banking business of Barclays Bank Dublin, I worked closely with both Trevor and David, gaining valuable experience in the process. It was envisaged that David's Dublin assignment would be for a period of a few years, after which he would move to greater responsibilities; his key mission would be to complete the rationalisation programme. The possibility of me succeeding David was put to me on the proviso that I was prepared to spend a period working at head office in London. Having discussed the proposition with my family, I agreed to a two-year assignment in the corporate division in the City of London.

CHAPTER ELEVEN

KICK ON FOR LONDON

The three of us, Mary, Catherine and myself, departed Dublin in mid-1988 to live in Harpenden, a pretty commuter town in Hertfordshire. Ideally, we would have preferred to live in North London but we discovered that there was better renting value further out and train services were excellent into my new workplace in the City. Taking the availability of schools and the convenience of nearby Luton-Dublin flights into account, we chose Harpenden. We rented a nice old house on Browning Road within ten minutes of the train station.

It was heart-breaking to witness Catherine's sadness at leaving her school friends in Goatstown. The change was more of a wrench for her than we realised at the time. Although my new job at Barclays head office was a career-driven move, both Mary and I also saw it as a great opportunity to experience living in England. A permanent move there was never in our plans. We rented out our Dublin home to an American couple, Bill and Kathy Frake, and their children. Bill was an animator who worked on the Disney movie, *Who Framed Roger Rabbit*.

The period spent at head office was far more advantageous to my career than I had envisaged at the outset. Despite the large scale of the Barclays' organisation, I was able to develop personal networks that subsequently served Barclays Dublin well following my ultimate return to Ireland.

But I like to think that the move was good for us as a family, too. Harpenden was a nice place to live, with its rural setting. The houses on the streets were quite old and each one different to the other; they looked the better for being different. Internally they could be disappointing, being small and old fashioned. The tendency was for people to live in the most expensive location affordable to the extent of skimping on internal comforts, if needs be. Social class and home location were closely entwined. Neighbours were mainly middle-class professionals many of whom, like myself, commuted to work in London. People were reserved but friendly. There wouldn't be any rush to welcome new arrivals into neighbours' homes, so in our case, we made the the first move by inviting our neighbours into our home for a midday drink. We were in some trepidation that they might not come. We needn't have worried. Not only did they come in droves, but we had difficulty getting a few of them to leave before I ran out of whiskey!

A big difference that we immediately noticed compared to Dublin was that children did not play on the street after school hours. For Catherine, as an only child, this was an unwelcome change from Goatstown. Nor would children be in and out of peoples houses; their evenings would be planned around extra-curricular activities.

Another thing that surprised me at the time was the silence observed on the train journeys to London, which was remarkable. People who would see each other every working day would never converse except when there were incidents such as train cancellations or rail strikes. Many of us would be reading a newspaper or work papers; being without something to read one felt a distinct nakedness. It wasn't unusual to sense fellow commuters reading your newspaper over your shoulder without a hint of embarrassment. I would often have secondary readers for my *London Evening Standard,* which I regularly enjoyed after a day's work.

Having been used to reading newspapers which were full of Ireland, it was strange to me to find little mention of Ireland in the London papers. This experience was a useful and necessary revelation for me that the world didn't begin and end in Dublin. In a similar vein, I was enlightened to find that the typical English person didn't seem to distinguish much between people from north and south of the Irish border. I thought it a little sad, though, that an Ulster unionist person seemed to receive no greater feeling of wantedness due to his/her British allegiance. We were all simply Irish to the British.

Harpenden had a small Roman Catholic community, made up of local English parishioners and a few Irish. The elderly Canon O'Leary was the parish priest. He was much more ceremonial than what we were accustomed in Dublin. The burning of incense with its lovely aroma was a common practice and his Mass had a Tridentine feel to it. For the first time I understood what it felt like being a minority religion. There was a quaintness about our little community which for me mirrored the Protestant communities in the Republic of Ireland. Church fundraising had a tentative feel to it; despite the relative wealth of the community, there seemed to be a preponderance of copper over silver. Henceforth, I would treat garden fêtes in a more ecumenical light as previously I would have regarded them as being Protestant-only events. As an Ardara neighbour Josephine Maguire used to say, 'You can't beat the Protestants for making jam.'

The Catholic Church in Luton which we occasionally attended, was very different. The congregation was largely made up of people of Irish birth or descent but was less middle class. The atmosphere was more akin to what we had in Donegal. The parish priest contrasted sharply with our man in Harpenden. He was a well-nourished looking Irishman with a knowing eye, in sharp contrast to the unworldly and skeletal Canon O'Leary. The Harpenden worshipping experience was, not surprisingly, the more exotic to us.

We also found English pubs to be notably different to our own. The pubs ranged from yob emporia to small front rooms where the proprietors and customers seemed like all friends together. Our first foray into the Harpenden pub scene was an experience. We settled on visiting a small elegant looking bar on the High Street owned and managed by a most serious looking moustached gentleman. Customers had their own personal beer tankard which hung from a specially designed frame over the counter. Our arrival was greeted with enthusiasm neither by the owner nor his handful of customers. We were made to feel that we had travelled from Mars. The owner was clearly not motivated to increase his spread of customers. He was there to serve his existing customers whom he appeared to regard as friends. Drinks were served to us but the owner made the atmosphere distinctly uncomfortable by not lifting his eyes off us for the duration of our visit. To his relief and ours we were glad to drink up with no desire to return. The really nice pubs were out in the countryside. These were small, cosy venues full of character. Unlike our suburban Dublin pubs, they were neighbourhood gathering places which seem to put general bonhomie to the fore, rather than voluminous drinking.

For the duration of my two-year period in London, I would be attached to Peter Scott's property finance team at Barclays. This was the same Peter Scott to whom I had had an introduction when I joined Barclays back in 1978. Peter, a gentleman, was very bright and well connected; his family were the Scotts of the Glasgow shipyard Scott Lithgow. Peter could be creatively very intense and forward looking in devising finance schemes but his span of attention could be short. It was therefore important that others picked up and ran with the ball if Peter got bored. These were the years immediately before the property slump in London. Demand for offices and shops was still strong and Barclays, in common with other large banks, were doing lots of deals. Many of them were stand-alone projects, done with either limited or no recourse to the sponsoring company; in effect repayment of the loan depended on the success of the underlying project. I was a member of the Barclays team that assembled the financing of the huge Lakeside Shopping Centre in Thurrock, near the Dartford Tunnel and the large office development, One America Square, in London. Lakeside was well established before the downturn but the latter development missed the boom and struggled to establish itself. I was fortunate to be long gone back to Dublin before the slump and consequent loan write-offs emerged in the early 90s, but my attachment to Peter's team taught me quite a lot about property financing. The financial numbers were excitingly large and growth in values could be significant, but I never gained great enthusiasm for the industry. What didn't appeal to me was the highly cyclical nature and illiquidity of the business. Unlike other business sectors, there was a premium on timing rather than on skill and experience.

Our offices were located on the 18th floor of 168 Fenchurch Street, a building that Chris Bonnington, the famous mountaineer abseiled for charity while I was there. To allow for the redevelopment of the building, we later moved offices to Murray House at Royal Mint Court in east London. It was during that time that 54 Lombard Street, the Bank's flagship head office building across the street, was also redeveloped. A peculiar feature of this new building was that the size of the toilet cubicles was incredibly small. It was joked that the-then chief executive, Andrew Buxton, ordered them to be so designed as a productivity measure; none of us would be encouraged to prolong our stay there!

Half-way through my two-year stint in London, I was fortunate to be sent on a media training course as part of Barclays senior-management development programme. The excellent two-day course was arranged by Group Senior Public Relations Executive, Claire Mascall. The course took place at the premises of Capital Radio in London, so there was a strong emphasis on broadcasting including both radio and television.

Our little subgroup comprised colleagues Pat Noble of Barclays Africa and Caroline Dellinger from Barclays America, who hailed from Charlotte, North Carolina and myself. Participating in studio sessions with household broadcasting names such as David Perman, Paul Burden and Laurie Mayer, was a lot of fun.

Another surprise to me was that London was really two cities, and that the 'city' I worked in, the City of London, had its own dress code and behaviours. Both men and women wore dark clothes and in the men's case always a suit and very often a pinstripe suit with a striped shirt. The wider the pinstripe and the louder the shirt stripes, the further up the entrepreneurial scale; for example, investment bankers would be at the top of this pile. I was surprised at the regularity of seeing braces as a means of holding up trousers; the highly noticeable red variety were the most popular and indeed seemed to be worn as a mark of distinction. You immediately recognised a red-braces wearer as not lacking in self-belief. Another important lesson I learnt was that at that time, any serious banking person working in the city wore black shoes and the brogue style seem to be favoured; brown shoes were certainly out. Ocasionally, you would see men who seemed somewhat dishevelled looking, almost like they slept in their clothes. A ropey, frayed tie was the obvious trademark of this coterie. Their appearance was deceptive as, in fact, they tended to be bankers who were extremely wealthy in their own right and would probably be titled gentlemen. Their dress code seemed to suggest that because they were financially independent and their status was already acknowledged by their family title, they had no need to impress anyone. It would be a mistake to take any of these guys for granted because of their somewhat eccentric image; those that I encountered were professional, talented and thorough gentlemen.

London was a time of both personal and professional fulfilment. Before we left for London, I had been working on a banking book for publication and shortly after we arrived in England the book, *Bills of*

Exchange and Other Negotiable Instruments was published by Simon and Schuster. A bill of exchange is really an IOU, traditionally used in international trading of goods and the financing thereof; what is important about it is that its good standing is underpinned strongly in law. This project was the culmination of two years' work. The suggestion for a booklet on the subject had emerged from my membership of the education sub-committee of the Institute of Bankers in Ireland. It was to fit into a series of similar publications already issued by the Institute. The proposal was approved and I was mandated to write up the material. I duly did so. Sub-committee discussion on my draft seemed to drift on to the point when I gave up hope of ever seeing it in print. In a conversation with a Barclays London colleague, Dick Francis, himself a published author, although not the jockey and novelist of the same name, the subject of the booklet came up. Dick suggested that I should consider publishing it independently. He introduced me to Neil Wenborn, then Commissioning Editor with Woodhead Faulkner, a Simon & Schuster company. Neil was helpful beyond belief. Not alone did he accept my manuscript for publication, but he gave me the help and encouragement I needed to realise the project. The book of 141 pages had a classy hardback finish. I enjoyed the thrill of seeing it in print. I later learned that the subject had been covered almost 50 years previously by other authors but the books were long out of print. Thankfully, I was not aware of their texts, otherwise I might not have proceeded. Indeed the absence of the temptation to plagiarise their work was welcome! The content of my book was different however, in that it was a handbook based on the practical application of these instruments and did not pretend to be a definitive legal commentary. Although a powerful financial instrument, the bill of exchange had long ceased to be fashionable for contemporary usage. The book, therefore, achieved little profile, apart from the initial reviews in specialist publications. I did enjoy a few thousand pounds in royalties out of it, which I used to purchase a nice rolltop desk from the local antique shop in Harpenden. Seeing my humble effort on the shelves of business book shops in the City of London was a nice experience for me.

At the same time as I was writing my book I had dialogue with John Byrne of the Commerce faculty in University College Dublin. John encouraged me to submit the manuscript for consideration in their postgraduate degree programme. I worked closely with John on the project. The result was that I was awarded a Master of Commerce degree in late 1988, following submission of my work. The award was inconsequential from a career perspective, but was nevertheless personally satisfying. The graduation ceremony provided a reason for Brigid to rendezvous with us in Dublin on a brief return trip from England. It was the kind of occasion she greatly enjoyed.

Now an octogenarian but healthy and active, Brigid's natural curiosity motivated a visit to Harpenden. She flew from Knock Airport to Luton with Ryanair. Although Brigid was an avid television viewer and newspaper reader, she remained in a time warp as far as the value of money was concerned. She was frugal in things for herself but generous towards those in need; she abhorred the waste of money on what she termed luxuries. Her life experience, in which money was extremely scarce and precious, conditioned her high regard for the care of money throughout her life. The total amount of money she brought on that trip was a paltry £5! Of course, she rightly relied on her son to meet any expenses on her visit to England. We all had an enjoyable few days visiting sights in the local area as well as in London.

We enjoyed our two years in Britain and we made the most of everything. What we never did before or afterwards was take enjoyable skiing holidays in Austria and Slovenia. Places on continental Europe seemed to be much more readily accessible from London than Dublin. There were many flights at a reasonable cost. I was also privileged to entertain bank customers at both Ascot and Cheltenham racecourses.

These were great days out but I found the sheer throngs of racegoers at these popular venues made enjoyment of the pure racing aspect difficult. I am a horse lover and have derived endless pleasure from the sport. Around that time I made a small investment in the Pipe Racing Club which was set up by the horse trainer Martin Pipe, who was then winning races all around. The Pipe Racing Club was a syndicate made up of a large number of horse-racing enthusiasts who each paid a relatively small amount into a fund managed by Martin. He would buy a few horses out of the monies and train them. As in most racehorse-owning scenarios, the quality of the horses acquired ranged widely. I regret having missed the open days at Pipe's Somerset yard for club members to see his establishment. Part of the fun from the investment would have been a day out seeing how a successful trainer operated. Needless to say, there was, as I expected, no return on my investment, but it provided an interest when horses owned by the club were racing. For a modest outlay. I had learned a useful early lesson in the financial futility of the racehorse ownership for which I often pined.

As a family, we found Harpenden a beautiful place to live. The weekends were particularly pleasant especially in summer when the weather was good and the days were long. There were nice places to walk and cycle. Catherine and I enjoyed our short cycles to the main shopping street. Although many of the shops were chainstores, there were also some nice local shops, that were different to our local shops in Dublin. People didn't go out as much socially to pubs and restaurants as we do in Dublin. They seemed parsimonious to us but priorities were different. Fundraising for Church and schools seemed to be a perennial issue. Unlike in Dublin, everyone seemed to pay something rather than the few paying more while others pay nothing. Cash was scarce with people; their cash resources were prioritised into their homes and into school fees. Very middle-class, you might say. They say that an Englishman's home is his castle and it is true.

We also saw other parts of Britain for the first time. The countryside seemed so much more mature and manicured than Ireland. Housing seemed much more concentrated in urban centres with large stretches of beautiful countryside free of housing development. It occurred to me that local councils and other authorities were better organised and in control of their local areas, which seemed well cared for. While there was no evidence of major investment programmes, you felt that there was a consistency and maturity about how local authorities operated.

Despite preconceived ideas from my Irish history lessons of the centuries-old enmity between Ireland and England, I rarely experienced anything but goodwill from my English colleagues. Granted, my experience was largely confined to the greater London area, which would tend to be cosmopolitan, however, from my forays wider afield any bad blood would be confined to the odd jibe about Southern Ireland turning a blind eye to the IRA campaign in Northern Ireland. Indeed if anything, I felt that English people in general enjoyed the Irish sense of fun and informality that they themselves found less comfortable.

Our experience with Irish emigrants was interesting; both in mixing as a family and meeting through work and socially. Middle-class professional types tended to be very successful, thriving in the larger pool. In general, they seemed quite anglicised and well adapted to the customs and traditions of their adopted country. Their native land remained important to them if largely symbolically expressed around times of rugby matches and the Cheltenham meeting. Ireland itself seemed to be viewed through a prism of their time growing up. Understandably, they would not be switched on to the trials and tribulations of contemporary Ireland. The chemistry with second-generation Irish immigrants was different. They were inclined to view you in the same light as their Irish parents and particularly viewed your relative success with a tinge of resentment in some cases. I could empathise with this feeling. It may have been born of the fact that their parent(s) had been forced to emigrate to earn a living while those of my own and previous generations avoided the emigrant ship.

Both from this experience of England and my familiarity of Donegal emigration I also became increasingly aware of an issue surrounding the sacrifices made by many Irish emigrants. It was common for them to generously send monies home to help educate younger siblings, just as I had benefited from the generosity of my aunt Annie. Many of these emigrants were now coming to the end of their working lives with inadequate pension and welfare provision only to see these same siblings and offspring much better off than themselves. This is still a sad reality but it is good to see that the Irish government has begun to adopt a more thoughtful and generous approach to these people who have given so much of themselves for those at home.

The experience of living in Ireland gives a feeling of being much closer to the centre of power and the affairs of state generally. For me this makes life far more interesting than living in a place which is part of a much bigger environment.

Additionally, the presence of the monarchy brought an additional and interesting dimension to visiting London. We were fortunate to attend the annual Trooping of the Colour pageant which is held close to Buckingham Palace in the Mall. The sight of the royal family members, the bands, horses and riders in such disciplined formation was a wonder to behold. Mary was a great Princess Diana fan and had the privilege to shake her hand at a local function in the nearby St Alban's Cathedral.

We were also still in London during the 1990 World Cup soccer tournament and I watched the famous penalty shootout, which featured Packie Bonner and David O'Leary, in the offices of solicitors Clifford Chance. We had been attending an important business meeting, but were unable to resist the temptation of catching the final moments of this big match. It was a thrilling match and my English colleagues, too, were all rooting for Ireland. This was in sharp contrast to Ireland, where, in a local pub setting, the majority of patrons might be cheering the opposition if England were playing. This behaviour is all the more surprising when the English Premier League clubs of Liverpool and Manchester United are so popular in the same establishments. I suppose the reasons are to do with our history and the fact that club sides often include Irish football heroes. It may be too early to say, but the recent successful visit of Queen Elizabeth may have softened these anti-English attitudes.

In all our time in England we encountered nothing but goodwill from both colleagues and neighbours. In general, English people are far less obsessed with us than we are with them, which is probably normal for large and small country neighbours. They don't seem to care what we are up to, whereas we take their media and soaps as our staple diet. Unless you read the Irish daily newspapers, you would learn little of Irish affairs barring mention of a terrorist incident in Northern Ireland, in the broadcasting and print media in England. Such was the case then and I imagine it to be little different now. This situation brought home to me the relative unimportance of Ireland in a broader international context, in spite of how we see ourselves. An extreme example of how little thought England's citizens give to Ireland arose when a Barclays colleague Robert Robson paid his first visit to us in Dublin. As I greeted him at the door, he wondered aloud if both our countries were in the same time zone! Witty individual that he is, it was probably a wind-up, but nevertheless it had a ring of reality to it.

There were many things I appreciated about my stay in England, but at the end of my two years, I was glad to be returning home and took some satisfaction in being allowed take up the job I had aimed to do. I had gained valuable professional experience and personally had enjoyed so much of my time there. And, as a family, the experience was rejuvenating.

CHAPTER TWELVE

TOP DOG

Two years in Britain had passed quickly and the time had come for us to return to Dublin. I was duly appointed to succeed David Burke as chief executive of Barclays Bank's Irish operations. Needless to say, I was pleased with this outcome; our decision at the outset to uproot the family for our two-year sojourn in England was vindicated. At 43 years old, the appointment was personally satisfying for me but I was acutely aware of the major challenges and difficulties that lay ahead. One of these emerged very soon after my return to Dublin in August 1990. Big problems began to emerge in the financing of the Irish meat-processing industry and specifically, with the large industry player, the Goodman Group. This group experienced difficulties in recovering monies owed to it by Iraq following the invasion of Kuwait. Among other banks, Barclays was exposed to the tune of several million pounds. As well as our direct lending exposure, the Barclays Group was more deeply exposed by way of an unconventional financial deal with the Goodman Group in conjunction with our finance-house subsidiary, Mercantile Credit Ireland. Following the meat-industry debâcle, against a background of a weak economy, some of the foreign banks involved, including

Barclays, questioned the future viability of their presences in Ireland at that time.

The overwhelming challenges facing me were to manage our way through this crisis in the short term but also to stabilise the longer-term future of the Barclays Irish franchise. Following large bad-debt write-offs, the banks allowed the Goodman meat business to continue under the leadership of Larry Goodman, who surrendered part of his ownership in a business reconstruction. The core meat business proved to be resilient; much of the problems stemmed from poor investment in non meat-processing activities. However, the question remained of how the collapse of the Goodman business had engulfed the banking sector. In my view, in common with other such crises, including the more recent sub-prime debâcle in the United States, the problem arises from ignoring the fundamentals. The progressive Goodman Group managed to create an aura of superior success to the extent that banks became prepared to lend it large sums of money without a rigorous examination of its financial accounts. In the period prior to my London assignment, Goodman's, in the person of the charming Brian Britton, represented the group's clear success so effectively that uniquely, they weren't required to reveal the detail of their finances. This was pretty smart on their behalf, but I could never envisage this situation as a basis for a meaningful business relationship. The result was that we did few transactions together in those days. On my return to Barclays Dublin, I was staggered to learn that several large banks, including ourselves, had competed with each other to virtually throw money at this organisation. I had made my own mistakes in credit judgement, but I was relieved that this was not one of them in view of the scale of funding involved.

The Irish meat-industry crisis had a chastening effect on the banks operating in Ireland. The foreign-owned banks were by far the biggest victims. Barclays was by no means the worst affected of those but we were hurting. Apart from the sheer pain of the inevitable loan write-offs, these kind of problems soak up valuable management time. Thus, the early creditor bank meetings were depressing affairs. The objective of these meetings between all the banks who had lent to the meat industry was to attempt to agree a way forward which balanced the survival chances of the underlying business with the degree of loan write-off pain. What I found interesting and surprising was the discovery that these kind of recovery situations take on a life of their own. Most big banks, especially the London banks, have specialised recovery teams led by individuals, some of whom become legends in their own right. These people have their own jargon and a formulaic approach which they apply. In this case, one of the big lenders, Lloyds Bank, orchestrated the project despite the fact that it was not in their home patch; the advantage was that they were able to bring their tried-and-tested approach to the situation. There was never any question of full recovery of all loans even if the business managed to survive. Survival of the underlying business was crucial to generating cash flow towards at least partial repayment of loans. We were all greatly envious of AIB Bank, whose overdrafts were at a low level when the 'the balloon went up', as they say. It was never clear whether this was fortuitous or if they had read the danger signals early or a combination of both. They weren't the most popular boy in the class, but they were the envy of us all and their deserved smugness was well concealed.

The banks, including Barclays, took the pain and things moved on. Goodman gradually traded out of its problems. Larry Goodman subsequently re-acquired full ownership of the business and once again resumed the role of a highly successful meat processor.

By way of a footnote, it transpired that several years later Goodman's UK banking business was offered to Barclays. The bad taste of our earlier experience lingered, but here was a good business opportunity by objective standards. This now-prosperous company was a big player in the UK meat-processing industry. If Barclays did not take this business opportunity, another competitor surely would. As the Barclays Group senior executive in the home country of Goodman, my support was required to re-enter a business relationship. Although, hard to swallow because of my closeness to the earlier debacle, I decided that based on the merits of the transaction, I would support Barclays reinvolvement.

Barclays was not alone among the foreign banks in reviewing the viability of its presence in Ireland. Was it possible to do viable banking with the corporate sector in Ireland? After all, here was one of the largest Irish corporates possibly going under in pretty unusual circumstances. The Barclays decision-making process about the future of Barclays Bank in Ireland had been in train for some months in autumn and winter 1990. Unknown to me, the powers that be, decided to either completely close Barclays office in Ireland or to downgrade the office to a nominal representative presence employing two or three people.

With the advent of the Dublin International Financial Services Centre (IFSC), at a slower pace and much later in the day than other banks, Barclays had set up a separate company to do IFSC-type transactions. Progress was slow on this front and opportunities were limited to a low volume of large international financing deals. However, despite the unfavourable conditions, we were making progress. Nonetheless, Barclays head office in London seemed to be creating obstacles to these transactions, no matter how good they were, much to the chagrin of our colleague Denis Holland, who was setting up these deals. There had to be an ulterior motive for this odd behaviour and of course, we would later learn that it was about the future of Barclays in Ireland. As a decision to close Barclays Dublin was imminent, head office deemed it pointless to allow these structured deals to proceed as they would shortly have to be unwound. In proceeding with these transactions against this background there was the downside of subsequent damage to the corporate relationships and general reputational damage to the bank.

In January 1991, I received a message from Vice Chairman, Sir Peter Leslie's office in London. This was the same Peter Leslie who had featured in the early period of Barclays in Ireland. The vice chairman position in Barclays was then an ambassadorial role, usually held by a distinguished senior executive who had stepped down from executive duties. Peter was engaged in a visiting programme to a number of Barclays overseas offices, of which Dublin was next on the list. I began the process of putting a programme together for the visit. It was rare enough to have a senior group dignatory visit Barclays Dublin and I was keen to leverage as much mileage as I could for the benefit of the Barclays Ireland business. As is usual in these situations, I arranged meetings for Peter with the two large Irish banks, AIB and Bank of Ireland, at chairman or chief-executive level. I accompanied him to these meetings as well as on a visit to the governor of the Central Bank. For me it was a priority to have Peter meet some customers. I hosted a private dinner in the Shelbourne Hotel for a group of top executives from our large corporate customers, with Peter as guest of honour. The dinner was a great success. Peter was one of the most eloquent and articulate people I have ever encountered. He loved Ireland; I think he may have had Irish connections.

I recall from the discussion that evening that there was little optimism among the guests. The exception was Bill Cullen, who was upbeat. Bill may have had a far-seeing crystal ball giving him an 'exclusive' that the Celtic Tiger was on its way!

The evening was all about Peter's speech, which was to have great subsequent significance for Barclays Dublin. His address was of the highest quality in content and delivery, with warm praise for Ireland and her prospects, despite the prevailing gloom. Peter expressed the strong commitment of the Barclays Group to Ireland and the future of the Barclays presence in Dublin. It was not until a few months later that I learned the impact of Peter's remarks. Apparently, the Barclays Group

Chief Executive was astounded to hear that the Vice Chairman had made such a statement to a key audience. In effect, any plan to close the Irish operation was scuppered by the statement. My then bosses, Terry Jones, the avuncular European director and the sound Chris Duncan regularly travelled to Dublin to attend our quarterly board meetings. On one of their trips, in early 1991, they arranged to see me privately outside the office. We met the morning of their arrival at the private Kildare Street and University Club around the corner from our offices in St Stephen's Green. They fully briefed me on the discussions in London on the future of Barclays in Ireland. Expressing some frustration, Terry explained to me how their plans had been thrown off track by Peter Leslie's intervention. Understandably we agreed that our discussions should remain confidential and particularly that I would not share them with colleagues in the office. There was no point in unsettling staff on what was now a non-issue.

The frustrating dilemma of my London colleagues had my sympathy, but privately I was delighted that such a plan had been thwarted. The plan to close seemed to me like a short-sighted, knee-jerk reaction, which was designed to create the perception of action in the financial media. Now that we had managed to escape closure by our fingernails, I had to lead the business forward in such a way as to support the view that we had a future which was profitable. This was far from a boom time for the Irish economy and consequently not a bouyant time for the revenues of Barclays Bank in Ireland. Much of our good progress was achieved through rigorous cost control and a sustained focus on our lending policies resulting in minimal bad debts. Our success, albeit modest, was a gratifying contrast with the dark clouds that would later gather at a group conference in Bath, of which more later. A lesson here which I had the opportunity to learn repeatedly was that no success is too modest in times of economic turbulence.

1991 was a year of more-than-the-usual quota of high-level visits to Dublin. The next Barclays senior figure to appear was Barclays de Zoete Wedd (BZW) Director, Nigel Lawson, now Lord Lawson, former Chancellor of the Exchequer. He was scheduled to be principal speaker at the annual Irish Financial Services Association dinner, held in April. Again, given the availability of this important guest, I thought that I should take the opportunity to use his Barclays connection to support our profile with a few of our large corporate customers. I called on a few of our customer connections and arranged a private breakfast meeting in the Shelbourne Hotel. Tony O'Reilly, now Sir Anthony O'Reilly was among the guests who accepted my invitation. The invited guests, including Lord Lawson, turned up on time except Sir Anthony. His departure from his Kildare home was, for some unexplained reason, delayed. This absence was a bit embarrassing for me in the presence of my special guest and other senior business leaders. The breakfast got underway but Sir Anthony kept ringing me at intervals to keep us abreast of his present location as he made his way through the morning traffic. What soon dawned on me was that even in his absence, Sir Anthony was taking centre stage at the meeting; he couldn't have planned it better. We all agreed the futility of him trying to make the breakfast at this late stage. As both Lord Lawson and Sir Anthony were flying out of Dublin that morning, they agreed to rendezvous at Dublin Airport. I duly chaufferred Lord Lawson to the airport. We met with Sir Anthony as he alighted from his silver Bentley in the airport VIP car park with a full document case under each arm. He greeted Lord Lawson and apologised for his absence from our meeting. It so happened that Sir Anthony was also flying to London, so he offered Lord Lawson a lift on his private jet, which was idling on the tarmac. Off they went together as I said to myself, 'What a smooth operator.' This was not the first time that I had met the extraordinarily successful and charismatic Sir Anthony. In addition to his business and sporting prowess there is a theatricality to his behaviour which, I believe, sets him apart. The lift offered to the former Chancellor in his private jet seemed like a neat piece of one-upmanship and typical of the O'Reilly magic.

The 1991 Barclays annual European Conference was held in Italy in June. With his wife, Marie, Dick Adams, the Barclays country head in Italy hosted the two-day conference at the Villa d'Este on the shores of Lake Como. Dick had chosen a beautiful hotel in a wonderful location. For Mary and I, the conference was an unforgettable experience in view of the unique location. Futhermore, this was a conference I would not have had the opportunity to attend had earlier events regarding Barclays Ireland taken their intended course. The conference was programmed around senior Barclays speakers from London and an eminent external speaker on a current business topic. Breakout discussion groups were included in the programme. The key in-house speakers were Graham Pimlott, a BZW director and Richard Carden, an influential senior executive in the powerful domestic side of the group. Graham was a seriously able investment banker and clearly on a fast track within the wider organisation. Richard was a career banker, who enjoyed strong connections with one of the founding families of Barclays Bank. A former military man, he was popular with colleagues. Richard was a man who, I guess, might be equally at home on the hunting field as discussing global banking issues. Several years later, Graham was to feature as a key mover when the fate of the Barclays franchise in Ireland was up for determination once again.

Separate leisure activities were laid on for the spouses, some of whom knew each other from previous conferences. The conference dinner was a special treat; we were all ferried across Lake Como to an island restaurant for a most beautiful meal.

The Villa d'Este is one of the most impressive hotels in which I have ever stayed. It was impossible not to run into a Hollywood star there. Among the other guests were Charlton Heston, Zsa Zsa Gabor and Mickey Rooney. Our stay at Villa d'Este was truly unforgettable. However, in sharp contrast to the elegance of the venue, the mood of the conference was downbeat. 1991 transpired to be one of the toughest years ever for the Barclays Group. The conference was overshadowed by cost-cutting programmes and reorganisations taking place in London. Bad-debt provisions arising from the crisis in the property market were looming large and relationships between Barclays UK domestic operations and BZW were unsettled. Morale in the group was at one of its lowest points in my memory. It was hardly surprising, therefore, that European conferences in the immediate aftermath would be held in less salubrious venues nearer bank headquarters. In the following year, the conference was held at the Spa Hotel in Bath. The mood there was even more serious and downbeat. Chief Executive Andrew Buxton pulled no punches in outlining the gravity of the bank's situation. In a private session which included the country heads, he spoke of 'blood on the carpet'. This was one of the toughest messages I had ever witnessed, and worse, I sensed Dublin was among the candidates still in his sights. I found it hard to believe how a company as big and powerful as Barclays could have got itself into so much trouble in the first place.

Later, at the conference dinner, which included spouses, he continued with the same theme in his address. What was unusual about this speech was his demand that the waiting staff withdraw to the kitchens for the duration of the address. I never knew whether it was for confidential reasons or whether the rattling of cutlery was causing interference. You could hear a pin drop. There was one light-hearted incident, when Giles Davison, then head of the strategic German operations, queried the waiter on the pedigree of the wine, tongue in cheek. The well-liked and respected Giles, a wine connoisseur, was one of the group's key executives. However, most people within Giles's earshot thought that he was serious and considered it inappropriate to fuss over wines at such an ominous moment.

Andrew Buxton's much later one-day visit to Dublin, in mid-1996, was, not surprisingly, a more businesslike experience. Far more importantly, it was a visit that was swathed in goodwill, in striking contrast to the Bath experience. However, such a wonderful turn of events was preceded by an extremely difficult hiatus in the early 90s, of which more in the following chapter. It was quite a big deal having a Barclays group chairman visit Ireland for the first time since the Dublin office was initially opened in 1978. The occurrence of the visit was a measure of the high regard in which Barclays Dublin was now held within the corridors of power. A far cry from the situation a few years before when we were in line for the chop. It reflected well on the excellent progress being achieved in the Irish business, so we were all pleased at the prospect of the visit. I was both satisfied and relieved that the our business circumstances had so considerably improved in the meantime.

Andrew Buxton was a serious figure, not alone in Barclays but in the international banking industry. He was a member of one of the founding families of Barclays and it so turned out, the last family member to chair the group. There was quite an amount of liaising with his office to ensure the trip went well. In her usual quiet but efficient way, my then secretary, Eileen Lowe, ensured the arrangements ran smoothly. Both he and Mrs Buxton were dropped by the driver at the Berkley Court Hotel to check in before our schedule of meetings began. The usual candidates, including representatives of key customers, the Governor of the Central Bank, Maurice O'Connell and senior commercial bankers were lined up to meet him, through a programme of meetings and a luncheon. Andrew Buxton greatly impressed those he met in Dublin. His earnestness and general concern about the big economic issues of the day struck a chord. Pat O'Neill, then Chief Executive of the Glanbia group, would later tell me that Andrew had made a very favourable impression. There were, however, few light moments and it was with some relief that on bidding farewell, I personally closed the door of the car bringing the party to the airport in the knowledge that the visit had gone well.

A more relaxed agenda of social functions was provided by the British Embassy in Dublin, which constantly kept in touch with British companies in Ireland and was always supportive of the commercial interests of companies such as Barclays. Our contacts were mainly with the commercial attaché, who would be an experienced diplomat on his or her way to being an ambassador at some stage. I am sure other embassies performed the same role but the British Embassy in Dublin seemed particularly well organised in this respect. This was not surprising in view of the very significant trading relationship between the two countries. During my time as head of Barclays in Ireland, Mary and I had the pleasure of being invited to social functions at the Ambassador's beautiful residence in Glencairn, south County Dublin. This house and extensive grounds was once owned by Boss Croker, a returned Irish emigrant who had made a lot of money in the United States of America. He was a famous character whose horse, Orby, won the 1907 Derby. Orby is buried in the grounds of Glencairn, where his grave is marked by a small tombstone. Boss Croker is buried in a small cemetery in the nearby village of Stepaside.

Another of the social highlights of my job was the privilege of an invitation to Her Majesty the Queen's annual garden party at Buckingham Palace in July 1996. The invitation would have been set up by the local British Embassy in Dublin. Mary and I set out in our best finery and stayed overnight at the Lansdowne Club in London which provided reciprocal facilities to members of a Dublin club to which I belonged. The Lansdowne had the advantage of being convenient to Buckingham Palace and relatively inexpensive. Like many London clubs in those days, its facilities were basic, but comfortable.

We proceeded to the Palace gate at the appointed time, where we were checked through. After being shown through the Palace reception area, we arrived in the extensive gardens at the rear of the Palace to join the throng of people from Britain and from several other countries. The only other guest I recognised was the Ulster Unionist David Trimble, who happened to be standing next to me. I never imagined him to be a gregarious fellow so I was not surprised that he did not engage in small talk. The garden party was a pleasant but somewhat dry affair. We were not among a chosen small handful introduced to Her Majesty, but nonetheless, it was a memorable occasion for Mary and me.

Unlike the Irish banks, Barclays Ireland was not to the forefront in corporate sponsorship. Two sponsorships do, however, remain in my mind. In 1997, we sponsored the Harold Pinter Festival at the Gate Theatre in Dublin, which was arranged by Gate Director, Michael Colgan. The programme of Pinter plays, one in which Harold Pinter himself played a part, was highly successful. Mary and I met the great man and his wife Lady Antonia Fraser. We found them both to be down-to-earth people.

The second event occurred in 1998. It was a horse-racing day at Leopardstown racecourse, in which we sponsored one of the bigger races. The race was won by a horse owned by Moyglare Stud connections. Her Excellency, the British Ambassador Veronica Sutherland, presented the Barclays Prize to the winner.

In June 1997, Martin Taylor, Group Chief Executive, fulfilled a long-standing invitation to visit Barclays Dublin. From my attendance at group conferences in London, I had developed and enjoyed a good relationship with him. I arranged to pick him up early in the morning at Dublin Airport in a specially hired stretch Mercedes. From his body language, I quickly sensed that this car was a mistake, confirming my own reservations about hiring it. Unlike some of the previous visiting senior Barclays executives, he wasn't at all precious and had little appetite for the trappings of corporate power. At the first opportunity, I arranged for this monster of a car to be switched for a standard model so equilibrium was restored. The issue became a standing joke between us for the day. A full day's programme was arranged to include our staff, some key customers, the Press, the Central Bank and AIB Bank, with whom Barclays had a longstanding relationship. I accompanied him to all meetings.

Martin Taylor was a hit with every person we met that day. He enjoyed a glass of wine with the staff and did an informative question and answer session. Discussion with customers, the media and the Central Bank mainly centred around our adoption of the euro as our currency. While he acknowledged the momentum for entry, he clearly articulated the opposing arguments. His principal concern was the loss of our ability to manage the economy through monetary policy. Although the euro has been of great benefit to Ireland, the lack of control over discrete credit growth for Ireland has been a problem in the Celtic-Tiger cycle.

His final call was a business breakfast at AIB Bank Centre with Chief Executive, Tom Mulcahy, where they covered the issues of the day—they got on very well together. As I was due in London that day for a meeting, I joined him on the flight to City Airport, where he was picked up by his regular driver. I took the opportunity of a lift to the head office building with them. The car phone immediately took over and the tensions that went with his job were clearly evident in the phone conversations.

Martin Taylor was one of the nicest and brightest top executives I ever came across in Barclays. He seemed to be most comfortable being treated with the normal respect that you could expect from a fellow human being. I saw no sign of the inflated ego that can often accompany people in high office.

CHAPTER THIRTEEN

Wolf at the Door

While later years would see considerable improvement in Barclays standing, the early 90's was indeed a very tough period for the Barclays Group. As Andrew Buxton had predicted, there was blood on the carpet. While the acute crisis of 1991 had passed, the whole UK banking industry continued to be difficult, but Barclays seemed to be more affected than others. Following a few years respite, the group began to trim its sails and set in train cost-cutting programmes across all business segments. The European corporate banking offices came under the spotlight. Apart from France and Spain, businesses in these other countries were recently established and therefore relatively underdeveloped. The French and Spanish interests were large and autonomous and so were largely spared the scalpel. Dublin, Brussels and Amsterdam were centre stage for this exercise. These businesses operated in relatively small national economies, so the potential upside was regarded as limited. Moreover, the scale and market shares of these operations were small. They were, therefore, less strategic. An immediate hoped for benefit accruing from the termination of these business operations would be an improvement in the Group's high-profile cost/income ratio. Cost/income is an important measure of banks' financial performance used by analysts and professional investors. Therefore banks are sensitive to the issue of keeping them as low as possible. By closing individual businesses with high cost/income ratios, the overall group ratio should be improved.

A significant treasury trading activity was traditionally part of Barclays Dublin's operations. Therefore, as well as having my direct reporting line to the Barclays Europe office in London, I also had a reporting line to the global treasury office there. We were in the closing stages of the annual budgeting process in Autumn 1993, when Dennis Rooke, the senior executive in charge of global treasury services, suggested to me that I cut back Dublin's revenue budget for the following year, but to leave stand the costs projection. Given Dennis's traditional habit of imposing challenging income targets, this turn of events initially threw me somewhat. His reasoning was that he, being in a position to take a macro view of things, anticipated very difficult foreign-exchange and interest-rate markets in 1994 and thus a drop in revenue. I was deeply sceptical of this view and dragged my heels. We both knew that a successful trading operation depended on market risk limits and counterparty limit capacity allocations, which were within Dennis Rooke's gift. (These constraints, which are part and parcel of a money trading unit, in essence mathematically quantify the degree of risk being taken; the extent to which currency and interest rate positions remain unhedged. The less risk-limit capacity available, the less opportunity for growing revenues.) He was, therefore, in a position to force the issue, whether I agreed or not. This was a bitter pill to have to swallow and before doing so, I considered other ways of satisfying Dennis's requirements and dodging this particular bullet. It was not logical to my way of thinking, but I did feel cornered. Our treasury activities were successful and a vital core of our Dublin operations. We had a strong team led by Colm Darling. Indeed, the profitable treasury operations worked as a positive counterweight in the past, when there had been significant bad-debt write-offs in the meat-processing industry and other sectors. Our corporate lending activities were just marking time because the Irish economy continued to be lacklustre, so good quality lending deals were scarce.

It was only much later that, rightly or wrongly, I sensed cynicism in the scenario painted by Dennis. The result of lowering revenue expectations would be to make a decision to shut down the related business unit seem logical and reasonable, and any argument against, seen as pure folly. Furthermore, any cost cuts could be made in Europe, rather than in the central London organisation. In my view, this incomprehensible (to me) interpretation of future events made for a course of action that disadvantaged Dublin. Clearly, therefore, I disagreed with Dennis's version of the crystal ball and dragged my heels on agreeing the following year's budget. Concerns of any potential negative consequences for my career were mitigated by the prospects of being out of a job anyway, if future results were very depressed.

Around this time, Barclays de Zoete Wedd (BZW), the investment-banking arm, had assumed control of the non-retail European businesses of Barclays, of which we were one. In the second half of 1994, they began working on a major rationalisation plan for these businesses. A BZW conference was held in the final quarter of 1994 at the Conrad Hotel in Chelsea Harbour. The conference was chaired by BZW Chief Executive, David Band. At the pre-conference dinner on 29 November 1994, the head of Barclays corporate business in Europe, the widely respected Frenchman, Jacques Rambosson, sidled up to me. Jacques invited me to join him next morning for a private breakfast meeting hosted by himself and the powerful Graham Pimlott. Fellow Irishman Bill Keatinge, who now headed the Amsterdam and Brussels offices, was also invited to attend the breakfast meeting. As I lay sleepless in bed that night a chill ran down my spine. From Jacques's body language, I sensed that a serious message was about to be delivered. I was right. Little food was consumed at the breakfast; the atmosphere in the room was rare and it had nothing to do with the height of the building! Bill and I were informed that later that same day, we would see a conference slide presentation referring to our businesses. The presentation would reveal a decision to close down Barclays corporate banking businesses in Dublin, Amsterdam and Brussels; the closure project would be overseen by Jacques and would commence forthwith. The corporate banking elements in other European offices were also to be terminated. As these particular offices had other elements to their businesses, they would not be closed but rationalised. Therefore, the consequences of these plans were much less serious for them.

I had expected bad news, but not total closure. After all, our business was profitable. We may have escaped the axe in 1991, but was this the final curtain? It was hard for me not to believe that the reason we were earmarked for closure was to do with creating a market perception that the group was taking radical action. Closure in these smaller jurisdictions should be a neat and relatively trouble-free exercise; there was certainly not going to be uproar about it in the House of Commons! I was thinking to myself that given the small scale of the Irish operations, it would make little real impact on the group's prospects whether we remained in business or closed. The sad part was that up to 70 valuable jobs would be lost in Dublin at a time when jobs in Ireland were scarce. At the same time the validity of the reason for destroying the jobs was, to my mind, questionable.

Having digested this unwelcome piece of information, I began to think about how I was going to break the news to staff and about the implementation of this decision. I dreaded the implications, particularly because I just couldn't in my heart believe that the business case for this course of action stood up. For me there were not only the difficult issue of telling staff, but also making arrangements for the termination of hard-won customer relationships, not to mention explaining the decision to the Irish authorities. Barclays was of course entitled to decide the future of its Dublin business, but the decision would be perceived as a big vote of no confidence in Ireland at a time when the government was trying its utmost to promote the idea of Dublin as a financial centre, through the IFSC internationally. Granted, the staff would receive generous redundancy packages, but the prospect of alternative employment was poor. This was pre-Celtic-Tiger Ireland, in which youth emigration was a fact of life. In any event why close a business that was profitable and had potential for further development? I thought this was wrong and said so to Jacques and Graham.

For me personally, there were two choices offered: an equivalent senior position in London, with BZW, or a generous severance package in the form of staged loyalty bonuses so that I would stay around and see out the closure in an orderly way. Graham and Jacques were extremely courteous and personally sympathetic, but there was no doubting the seriousness of their intent. From a purely selfish point of view, I much preferred running my own operation than envisage being a cog, albeit well paid, in a head-office scenario in London. In addition, the more closely I got to observe the BZW environment, the less highly I rated my chances of survival.

It was around this time that Patrick O'Sullivan, Chief Operating Officer at BZW, rang me. Patrick was an Irish-born high flyer, with whom I enjoyed a good relationship. He enquired about my interest in taking a senior position in their new office in Mumbai, India. I would run the Mumbai operation day to day, reporting to a local BZW executive. The job would command a lucrative compensation package. While this was an important position, I felt that there was an element of getting me out of the way in Ireland so that the intended plans to close could proceed. In any event the location held no attraction for me and it was with little regret that I thanked Patrick and passed on the opportunity.

Towards the end of that fateful breakfast meeting, my mind was already beginning to work furiously on a way out. There were two possibilities starting to formulate in my mind. Firstly, would they support me in attempting to find a buyer for the Irish business? Graham did not regard this suggestion as viable. He felt that it would be a messy solution that would take up considerable management time with little probability of a successful outcome. Coming from an experienced corporate financier, I respected his view. My second line of thinking was an internal solution. Would the UK domestic banking division be interested in assuming ownership of the Irish business? After all, there was a very significant trading relationship between Britain and Ireland. This division, the highly profitable powerhouse of the Barclays Group, was led by main board director Bill Gordon, a seriously good banker with a powerful intellect. I knew Bill slightly from having, with others, shared a coach to work from Harpenden during one of the rail strikes. I proposed to my two hosts that I approach Bill with my proposition. Graham and Jacques were clearly taken aback that I would question BZW's edict, which they had just delivered. They held out little hope of any progress with Bill but to be fair to them, they didn't stand in my way.

After our breakfast meeting we joined the conference downstairs. BZW's strategy for 1995 was outlined by the executive team, led by David Band. The fateful slide came up on the screen spelling out the proposed demise of Barclays European corporate banking operations. There would be no immediate general announcement to staff. The closures would be executed under a plan called Project Europe, to be led by Jacques Rambosson and his team in London. Jacques's team would operate in conjunction with the country heads such as myself.

The Bill Gordon angle remained interesting to me, and I saw it as a possible way out of the situation. But I did face a challenge. Bill was a highly astute individual and one of the most senior and respected bankers in Britain. How could I get on to Bill's radar and if I did, I would be lucky to get one shot at a deal? This is where Alex Jablonowski came in to the picture. I had met Alex many years previously at a Barclays senior management course, where he was a speaker. He was one of a select few people who seemed to arrive in the senior echelons of Barclays at an early age. Alex was internationalist in outlook and importantly, was now one of Bill's key executives. Not only that, but his responsibilities included the international operations of the UK banking division. For example the Channel Islands and the Isle of Man were in his domain. I was imagining the inclusion of another island with this lot, namely Ireland!

Having given the problem some more thought, I arranged a meeting with Alex to share my thinking with him. My proposal was that the UK banking division would take over control of Barclays Irish operations from BZW. Within the UK banking division, Ireland would be placed in the international sector alongside the other offshore segments. Alex was initially sceptical. Why would BZW let go of a viable business? Furthermore, in its present relatively small size, the Irish business did not excite him as a prospect. He didn't reject my proposal out of hand, but neither did he seize the opportunity. It was left that we would both reflect on the situation.

My thoughts continued to develop. New strategies began to formulate in my mind. A key plank in my strategy would be that we would leverage Barclays huge UK banking presence to direct their Irish-related business customers to Barclays Dublin. Because Barclays Ireland had always been grouped with the non-UK businesses, we hadn't previously been able meaningfully to tap the trading flows between UK branches and Ireland. If Barclays Ireland was placed within the UK fold, the branches in Britain could be directed to pass their Irish-related customers to Barclays Dublin.

At this time, things were starting to look up on the political front in Northern Ireland. An IRA ceasefire had been declared and political manoeuverings were taking place involving the two governments.

Despite Belfast being a UK city, Barclays did not have a presence there. My proposal to Alex included a plan to open a corporate banking office in Belfast, which would report to me in Dublin.

On the eve of the Ireland/England rugby match at Lansdowne Road on Saturday 21 January 1995, I received what I believe was a useful and timely visit. Mike Pitcher, then Chief Operating Officer and a key executive in Bill Gordon's division, dropped in to St Stephen's Green by way of courtesy visit. Unlike many of my other Barclays callers, Mike had already secured his match ticket courtesy of Allied Irish Banks, where traditionally excellent personal relationships existed at senior level. Indeed, the relationship between Barclays UK and AIB were so good that it was not unheard of that Barclays UK branches introduced their Irish customers to AIB branches rather than Barclays Dublin!

Mike's call was a casual visit but it provided me with another opportunity to promote the case for Barclays UK to adopt Barclays Ireland. We had a good meeting and I'm sure Mike's mood was even better after the match which England won 20-8. I learned subsequently that he had provided favourable feedback on our exchanges to his colleagues on his return to London. In view of Mike's influential position and strong reputation, a good word from him would have done our case no harm at all.

Alex and Bill were beginning to warm to the proposal of assuming Barclays Ireland within their Division, to the extent that they gave me what was effectively an amber light. They agreed that I could develop a business case to form a basis for their decision on whether or not to proceed. We weren't there yet, but I knew that we had reached an important milestone.

With the help and support of my Dublin colleagues and project-management guidance from Alex's London team, I developed a set of business strategies supported by five-year financial projections.

As a critical support, I was fortunate to have Liam Miley, our then Head of Corporate Banking. Liam was a fine corporate banker with a superb work ethic combined with leadership skills. The fundamental underlying assumption we made was that control of our business would immediately transfer to the UK Banking division. With the benefits flowing from the new strategies I was fully confident that we could comfortably grow annual profits by 10%, but this kind of steady if unspectacular growth was not going to be sufficient to achieve buy-in from Bill and Alex. Our cost base was tightly controlled, but I still felt that we had staff who were good enough to add considerably more value to the bottom line. The addition of another corporate manager combined with the existing team would, I believed, help us deliver profit returns close to what I had in mind to be necessary to persuade my London colleagues. With access to substantial additional business flows, a doubling of profits by the end of a three-year period seemed to be achievable. Moreover, it was a convincing statement. So that is what we promised. I distinctly remember one of our senior managers, John Nolan giving me a worried glance when I articulated that profit promise at a meeting. Five years would be a plausible period for a doubling of profits, but three? The way I saw things was that the flow of new accounts from opening up the UK branch network could be very substantial. If we didn't achieve a doubling in three years, we should not be far off that target. If we fell well short, then I would likely be fired. The upsides were that the business would have escaped closure and I would hold my job for a further three years. Furthermore, three years hence, the Barclays internal political and external economic environments would likely have changed for the better and the question of closing would be history.

The big day arrived on 11 April 1995. Bill Gordon and Alex Jablonowski arrived in Dublin to hear our pitch for their support. Our guests came with a positive frame of mind. Our plans were well received. Not only were they convinced by the business case, but they could see no reason why the business should close. They were excited by our proposed strategy and recognised how it dovetailed with the mainstream UK business one. I think Bill and Alex also had a genuine sympathy with our efforts to save the business. They made it a condition of adopting the Dublin business that I would stay and drive the new strategy. Needless to say, I was pleased and flattered by their endorsement of me personally in this role.

With the benefit of hindsight, I realise that a career change at that time to another organisation could have been a good move. I did turn aside an approach from a local headhunter to which I didn't even give a moment's consideration. This was probably the last opportunity that I would have to seriously progress my career; I was just approaching 48 years of age. I was, however, far too blinded by the emotion of the struggle for survival to countenance a move elsewhere. I didn't want to abandon all that I had fought to maintain.

Barclays Dublin had a relatively small but clean loan book. As part of the project to win new ownership, the UK banking division ordered a comprehensive due-diligence report on the quality of our business. By and large, it was clear that apart from the strategic misfit of a small number of loans, they were very satisfied. BZW agreed to retain responsibility for these items. An important issue was how we were going to operate our treasury service under the proposed reporting line. Our highly successful treasury function under the leadership of Colm Darling had, to my regret, just about been disbanded by BZW, leaving us with a skeleton staff. I had thought out a plan as to how we could provide treasury support to our customers. What we proposed was to assemble a small sales team and arrange protocols with BZW, the arm of Barclays where we could source treasury type products on a wholesale basis for our Dublin customers. Our approach would mirror a typical UK regional treasury centre in the way they served Branch customers. Under the new treasury arrangements we would not be permitted to take any risk positions apart from a modest position to cater for daily customer requirements. The profit opportunity from punting foreign currencies and interest rates was for all intents and purposes gone. The upside was that the business risks would be much lower and less volatile.

My treasury team had by now been well and truly depleted, so I needed to bring in corporate dealing expertise. I brought in Sean Blake, an experienced treasury dealer, to lead our new approach to treasury products. Sean's brief was to head a small team in servicing our existing customers and the wave of new customers which I expected our new business strategy to deliver. I worried that BZW's wholesale treasury prices might be higher than if we generated the treasury products ourselves as we had done hitherto. However, aside from the expected initial teething troubles arising from the change of sourcing they worked well. An age-old problem between treasury dealing rooms and corporate sales is the wholesale pricing level of products. Traditionally an antipathy existed in all banks between those dealers purely trading the banks' large-scale positions and the customer-facing people. Due to heavier administration costs associated with smaller ticket items, the large-scale dealers tended to charge more for the smaller corporate transaction thus making life more difficult for the sales people. Thankfully, that particular culture had already changed for the better because of increased transparency in management information.

After the turmoil of recent years, the newly shaped organisation settled down well. Most staff at Barclays Dublin were relieved that their jobs had been saved and were re-energised. Communication lines were opened up with the UK Branch network, our big source of new customers. To lead the drive for this important business segment, I recruited Englishman Simon Howe, an able young manager out of one of the Barclays UK regions. Simon's job was to lead the implementation of our strategy of opening up the UK branch network as a customer source. This he did and the business flowed.

Shortly afterwards, I was rewarded with a personal upgrade in the group staff gradings. On the recommendation of Alex Jablonowski and with the support of Bill Gordon, Group CEO Martin Taylor approved my appointment to senior-executive grade from that of senior management. More valuable in perception than reality, senior executive grade was nevertheless a much-envied one in the Barclays pecking order; as well as being good for me personally it provided further confirmation of the secure position Barclays Ireland now occupied within the Group. My hard work had, it seemed, been vindicated.

By this time, the early shoots of the Celtic Tiger were becoming apparent. Northern Ireland was enjoying the feelgood factor that flowed from the recent IRA ceasefire. The Republic of Ireland benefitted greatly, if indirectly, from this cessation of violence. Dublin was beginning to increasingly emerge as a popular weekend destination for British and continental European tourists. For example, Barclays colleagues from Britain had never been enthusiastic about extending their business visits to Dublin into weekend family leisure breaks. England/Ireland rugby matches were the exception, when we would be overwhelmed with business visits in the preceding week and demands for match tickets. Following the positive developments in Northern Ireland, the behaviour of visiting colleagues completely changed. Now they 'loved' Dublin and couldn't seem to get enough of Ireland.

As the news got better and better for the Irish economy, the number of British companies seeking to be in on the action increased in parallel. Not only did the big-name retailers pour into Ireland, but all kinds of suppliers felt they either needed to be here or at least to sell their products here. When a British company planned to extend their business footprint into Ireland, their first port of call would be their local bank manager. With a significant Barclays share of the England and Wales corporate banking market, it was inevitable that Barclays Dublin would gain many new accounts. With our redesigned business model and strategy we were set fair to capitalise on this surge. What we didn't realise that we were also witnessing the early stages of an economic transformation in Ireland, later to be named the Celtic Tiger.

CHAPTER FOURTEEN

Wheels Deals and Tycoons

In the corporate banking game, you have winners and losers. The relatively small profit margin for the bank on mostly unsecured loans, when measured against potential bad-debt losses, makes corporate lending a pretty tough business. Although the risk factor is increasingly priced into the banks' lending margin, it still takes a lot of margin earnings to recover a large loan write-off. It therefore goes without saying that getting it right in the first place is critical. Consequently, it would not be at all unusual for a banker responsible for large loan losses to experience the demise of a good career or at best, severe damage to it. I found the relationship between risk and reward to be complex but nonetheless stimulating and enjoyed working with some of the key players in Irish business at the time.

Diversification programmes tend to be fashionable in good times and are developed to be a mitigation of the risk associated with just being in a single-business sector. Diversification also allows a company access to sectors with good growth prospects. Circumstances can change quickly, however. Market conditions for either the core business or for the diversification can deteriorate forcing disposal of elements of the total business undertaking. Waterford Glass Group was a prime example of a company caught in such a pincer. The chairman of the company in the mid-1980s was Patrick Hayes, who enjoyed a reputation as a decisive manager. He had been head of the Ford Motor Company's Irish operations, a significant business that had once included motor assembly and distribution. Ford-trained managers enjoyed a strong reputation in Europe and that reputation extended to Hayes.

To help cure Waterford Glass's problems, Hayes set about dismantling their extensive diversification programme. A prime candidate for disposal was the Smith Group. This group had previously been owned and managed by the highly esteemed Con Smith, who had died tragically in the 1972 Staines air crash. The Group had operated the Renault car-distribution franchise in the Republic of Ireland, in addition to other motor-related activities. The Smith Group had been a good business that had been allowed to decline under the Waterford Glass ownership and was now a prime candidate for disposal. The hard part was finding someone who would both be interested in turning around the company and at the same time, have the financial muscle to handle the transaction. Bill Cullen, then a successful Dublin Ford dealer, became the declared choice of Waterford Glass. Patrick Hayes would have known Bill well and witnessed his business generation capabilities from his years at Ford. Gerry Dempsey, a highly respected businessman in his own right, was charged by Hayes to get the Smith's disposal done and it was no easy task. There was so much debt on Smith's balance sheet, that the company had little inherent value. The secret to the successful transfer of Smiths ownership, was the availability of a large-scale financial package and the retention of the Renault car franchise.

David Hogg, then Managing Director of the Barclays-owned Mercantile Credit Company of Ireland, introduced Bill to Barclays Dublin. David knew Bill from doing business with him over many years. Mercantile had provided Bill's Ford dealership with dealer-support finance. David had a high regard for his sales capabilities.

Bill Cullen arrived at the Barclays offices in St Stephen's Green accompanied by Des Peelo, his accountant. Bill was dressed casually and sat on the large leather sofa in the Chief Executive's office. A handsome man, he looked more like a showband star rather than a businessman; a person with presence and panache. Little did I then realise that television stardom ultimately awaited him. I received Bill, along with my colleague, Trevor Jones, then Chief Executive of Barclays Irish operations. Whilst Bill talked incessantly, Des Peelo presented their plans for taking over Smiths and their request for a multi-million financing package. David Hogg's words were ringing true; I could see why this guy could sell cars!

We listened to their story and took a preliminary look at their requirements and particularly, the financial projections presented by Des. In the light of the past performance of the Smith Group, they seemed far too optimistic. Trevor and I both realised that this was a tough proposition, but there were a few positives and we promised to take a closer look. Our credit team did some work on their figures. Frank Perry's input to the numbers was regarded as a positive factor. Frank, the Smith Group's accountant, was well regarded in the financial community and we believed that he understood how motor business finances worked. We concluded that there were a couple of viable businesses in the Smith Group, viz. the Renault distribution franchise and the motor electronic manufacturing plant in Wexford. However, the level of financing required was formidably high.

We needed to get a degree of realism into the figures, so we asked them to revise the sales forecasts downwards to what we considered were more realistic levels. Even these revised forecasts turned out ultimately to be too optimistic. The overall bank-debt requirement was extremely large in relation to the net worth of the business. As there was no significant new equity capital available to inject into the company, this was to be a truly leveraged transaction. This proposition was not bankable on normal bank credit criteria and if it were at all doable, an imaginative financing package would have to be structured. While Bill was bringing his undoubted sales skills and unfettered optimism to the table, he did not have proven management skills for a business of this scale; there was a world of difference between running a car dealership and managing a business the size of Smiths. There was also the challenge of effectively managing the Renault business relationship,

Still, there were redeeming features. There were substantial property and other assets which could be sold to help reduce debt. The Renault distribution side already had a strong management team, comprised of people like Jer Nolan, Donal Clare and John O'Donnell, all of whom I had met and regarded highly. In addition, Brendan Reville, a highly regarded senior motor-industry figure, had joined Smith's board as chairman. Brendan's presence was critical in boosting the credibility of the new setup. Renault was a strong brand even though their model line-up at that time seemed a little tired. Representatives from Renault became involved in the financing negotiations and their support was crucial to a successful outcome. Providing finance to help the company stock the large number of cars being imported was the major challenge, what we refer to as a 'car stocking' loan. In conjunction with Renault and with the engagement of our Barclays Paris colleagues, we structured a Barclays Dublin car stock financing loan supported by the French government export credit agency (COFACE). The essence of this deal was that by far the largest loan element of the total financing risk was underwritten by COFACE. We now were getting closer to a transaction that would work, provided we could rely on Bill and his team to deliver on the sales revenue assumptions.

By virtue of the high leverage and the thin margin for error, this proposition remained a long way from being agreed. However, it was now in a shape to which we in Barclays Dublin, could add our positive recommendation. The next step was to seek the approval of our central advances department in London, the Barclays in-house credit authority for large-scale loan deals. Their initial reaction was negative and the loan-sanctioning executive, Bing Allen, advised us that he planned to turn it down. Paul Nicholson, an experienced corporate banker who worked under Bing, was more positive. We, in Dublin, still believed in the deal and set out to change Bing's mind under the normal appeal system that operated in such cases. I knew we had a battle on our hands, so we decided that a different approach was called for. I would travel to London and make the appeal in person and take David Hogg with me in support. This was deemed a highly unconventional initiative. I judged that because of David's stature within the Group and his record of satisfactory dealings with Bill Cullen over a period of years, his presence could greatly help the case.

We met Bing and put our case to him. He received us courteously and reconsidered the points we made, but we could not persuade him to view the deal in anything but the conventional way. His fundamental problem was the high level of debt in relation to the net value of the business; his stance was of course perfectly logical. There was also the issue of how Bill Cullen could hope to succeed when Waterford Glass had failed to make a real fist of motor distribution. I did feel though that not enough weight was being given to Smith's better prospects under a reinvigorated management This turn of events revealed the typical inbuilt tension, albeit healthy tension between a bank's credit function, which has a vested interest in taking a conservative stance, compared to the front-line people like ourselves trying to develop business activity. And of course this was the bleak 80's. Things were not looking good in the economy.

David and I had a caucus meeting to decide whether we should meekly accept defeat and go home or should we appeal over Bing's head to his boss, John Rutter, who was a Barclays top corporate credit man in London. This was not an easy choice and caused a lot of head-scratching. It seemed most unlikely that John Rutter would go against Bing's decision. Whether or not he would choose to overrule Bing, Barclays Dublin's relationship with the much liked and respected Bing, a key player in our business process, might inevitably suffer. Yes, there were downsides, but as we still believed in the deal, we felt we should have one last throw of the dice. I asked to see John Rutter and I went in to his office to present the deal. Lo and behold, he approved it!

This seemed a great win for Barclays Dublin and David and I both enjoyed the moment. However, any feelings of triumph were quickly tempered by the prospect of having to make the deal work. I realised that I had put my reputation and career on the line for the sake of this transaction, so it badly needed to work. After the initial euphoria there were many difficult days and sleepless nights (for me, whatever about Bill Cullen!) ahead.

The first crisis emerged from nowhere. Shortly after Bill took ownership of Smiths, some of the Renault dealers rebelled against the new regime. Immediately, the important asset of Bill, which was brought to the deal, was being neutralised by the behaviour of these dealers. This was a potentially fatal blow to a company which was so dependent on the sales budgets being realised, with little margin for error. This was not the only crisis but it was the most threatening. This unfortunate development triggered a process in the bank which saw the Smiths banking relationship being 'watch listed'. This resulted in the oversight of the account being moved to a central recoveries team. These central teams tend to be pretty powerful in all banks and are composed of bankers picked for their solid experience rather than for their warm personalities. Barclays was no exception; I had witnessed these guys from several banks at work in the earlier meat industry débâcle. They laid down the law with the customer as to how the business should be run with the prime objective of minimising the banks' credit exposure.

This would have been very difficult for Bill, but even more so for me. Any reserves of goodwill towards me among the recovery team was well and truly undermined by the way I had originally pushed the deal through. The situation was bad, but if anything, these recovery people were inclined to portray the position at its worst. Ironically, in this kind of banking relationship one's career can be at stake with no upside while the loan customer may be better positioned particularly if the business recovers. The battle for survival went on for some time.

Time passed. One by one the bigger problems got solved and the Smiths business began to prosper. I could at last look forward to the rewards to the bank of a long and successful bank relationship with Bill. However, even this was not to be. Soon after Smiths got their head above water and their financial legs became stronger, Bill moved the account to another bank. This was a huge disappointment for me, as I felt I had been through the mill in facilitating his path to success. From Bill's point of view, I suppose he associated Barclays with some tough times, which must have left their mark. While disappointing for me, I could understand why the lure of being loved by your bank from day one could prove an attraction too strong to resist. This was a business decision and indeed, Bill was perfectly within his rights to make a change, but I was sad to see the relationship end.

The clear message for me from the Smith's experience is that you cannot rely on any special payback for going the extra mile. With the benefit of hindsight we should have taken an option on a percentage of the company's shares so that the bank could have had due reward for the additional risk taken at the outset. A deal of this nature nowadays would more routinely have such a proviso in the loan agreement.

Being involved in large corporate finance deals is exciting and can be very fulfilling. They don't all go well. Most frustrating are those deals which have taken up a lot of time to develop but never happen. Others are done but do not completely fulfil their intended rationale.

One such deal was the takeover by the Kilkenny-based food group, Avonmore (now renamed Glanbia) of Waterford Foods in 1997. The two companies were similar in size and business profile, but Avonmore had been the more successful. They both had their roots as farmer dairy co-operatives and were now two of Ireland's largest milk and cheese processors. Waterford Foods had gone on a campaign of company acquisitions, mainly outside of Ireland. As often happens some of these purchases failed to deliver on the expectation which supported the decision in the first place. As a result, Waterford was not generating sufficient surplus cash flow to reduce its debt mountain at the pace expected by the financial community. Both dairy groups would have kept a watching brief on each other as potential merger or acquisition candidates. As Waterford's and Avonmore's dairy and distribution businesses were in adjoining counties, there were obvious economies to be gained from amalgamating elements of each of their activities.

Geoff Meagher, the widely respected Avonmore Finance Director, called me to arrange a briefing on their intention to acquire Waterford. Barclays was one of their lead banks and they wished to test our appetite for underwriting the total financing required to do the transaction. Geoff supplied figures which demonstrated the rationale for the proposed deal. These figures showed the synergy arising from an amalgamation of both business groups. Our credit group examined the financial projections supplied by Geoff and were supportive. Central Advances Department, London, approved the £100 million credit application to enable us to put the financing in place for Avonmore to complete the transaction. The deal turned out to be a mixed blessing for Avonmore, which changed its name to Glanbia after the takeover. On closer examination, several of the acquired businesses turned out to be worth much less in reality than they were worth on paper. This was due to a combination of being overvalued when originally bought and subsequently, not fulfilling growth expectations. Glanbia ultimately emerged a strong and diversified food group, but its position in the immediate aftermath of the Waterford acquisition weakened. The challenges posed by the deal might have defeated a less strong management team than that now led by John Molony.

Another large corporate deal concerned the building of Blanchardstown Shopping Centre. Blanchardstown was then a small town on the western outskirts of Dublin. I knew it well as an awful traffic bottleneck on my way to and from Donegal. Talk of building a new town centre had gone on for years. The concept of new town centres had started in Britain, but it wasn't the kind of town centre you would imagine, but rather, a glorified name for a shopping centre in or closely adjacent to an existing town. Green Property Company owned a large site in Blanchardstown, on which they had earmarked to build the centre. This was the early 90's, when Ireland seemed still to be lodged in the economic doldrums. Large speculative property projects were very difficult to finance. Banks didn't have the confidence that the projects could pay interest on the loans, let alone pay down the bank debt.

Along came Stephen Vernon, a senior figure from a large London commercial estate agent, as new CEO of Green Property. Barclays had been prominent in putting together financing for similar large shopping centres in Britain. We had a specialist team in London, led by Terry Tindall, doing exactly this type of transaction. During my time at Barclays, London, I had been a member of this team, but financing a large shopping centre in a big population centre was one thing. Doing it in a small town outside Dublin in recessionary Ireland, was another.

Stephen Vernon had brought a fresh perspective to the project. Research showed that the project could be viable. After extensive analysis and discussion, Terry's specialist team, in conjunction with ourselves in Barclays Dublin, agreed to underwrite the total project financing for the Blanchardstown centre. Underwriting in this context means that a bank commits to providing the total monies required, with a degree of confidence that you can subsequently persuade other banks to share the risk by putting up a portion of the funds. An underwriting bank might target to be left with as little as a tenth of the total amount of the loan on its own books. In the event, the Irish banks piled into the deal after Barclays had taken the lead and displayed the confidence to do the whole amount. One of the competitive advantages of a large bank such as Barclays is the financial muscle to underwrite very large loan requirements.

Blanchardstown Shopping Centre went on to be successfully developed by Green Property Company. Maurice Greene, an experienced property professional oversaw the successful building project; sadly, Maurice, whom I had known well from his previous job at MEPC Ireland, passed away before the centre was totally complete. As one of the earliest large enclosed centres in Ireland, Blanchardstown created a lot of excitement when it first opened. It soon became a resounding commercial success.

However, not all the stories had happy endings. One of the biggest mistakes with which I was associated was providing a significant amount of finance to the Cambridge Finance Group, an independent Irish leasing company. The Menton brothers were key players in Cambridge. The early years were highly successful. But like many good corporate stories, they overreached themselves by expanding too quickly and diversifying from their core business activity.

My faith in Cambridge was narrowly based, being mainly focused around my knowledge of Kevin Menton, with whom I had been a work colleague in Ulster Investment Bank. Kevin was very successful in those days and was very highly regarded by his superiors. His sports pedigree was a nice add-on: he was a tennis player of international standard, and was also part of the Menton Irish soccer dynasty. Years after I had left the Ulster Bank Group, Kevin gave up his senior executive position in the bank to join his brother Colm in Cambridge. He appeared to be on his way to great things.

Cambridge, by its nature, was heavily reliant on bank finance. When the company entered choppy waters, the lead bank, Ulster Investment Bank, was not any more merciful because one of their own had faltered. Cambridge became a terminal case and the lending banks, including Barclays, shared the eventual bad debt write-offs, which unusually, were not ultimately as bad as earlier feared. My sentiments towards Kevin were of sympathy for him personally but well tinged with annoyance that I had been persuaded to back the ill-fated Cambridge.

During my Barclays career, I was privileged to meet some of the top echelon of Irish business people. Sir Anthony O'Reilly, I have referred to earlier. Another was Sir Michael Smurfit, Chairman and driving force behind the highly successful Smurfit Group. This company had an extensive corporate-banking relationship with Barclays across several countries. In the interests of maintaining and developing these type of relationships, lines of communication between the customer and the bank operated at the highest levels. In that context, I arranged that Jacques Rambosson, our European director, would host a dinner for Sir Michael Smurfit. The dinner was held in a Barclays private room in the restored Royal Mint Court building near Tower Bridge, London.

Jacques was the perfect host for the occasion and as the archetypal Frenchman, his choice of wines could surely be relied upon. This was just as well, as Sir Michael had a reputation for being a wine connoisseur of the highest order. I was relieved that he seemed pleased with Jacques's choice! Our guest arrived with his right-hand man, Paddy Wright. He was immediately into full speaking flow from the moment he walked in the door until he departed the building, mainly about his own business interests. Jacques gave Sir Michael the floor with a display of listening skill that was an example to us all. I couldn't help but wonder how the dinner would have worked had our host been a senior Barclays person with a conversational approach similar to our guest! What stood out for me in Sir Michael was the intensity of his focus around his own businesses, which I have learned to recognise as a hallmark of the truly successful business person. (His major preoccupation in those days was his problems with Irish Telecom, where he had been a highly effective chairman. There was a controversy raging in Dublin at that time over a property which involved Irish Telecom. He was incensed at what he saw as political expediency by the Irish government in requesting him to step aside from the chair during the controversy)

Our relationship with CRH, often referred to as Ireland's most successful industrial company and now a global force in construction materials, stretched across several different countries. In common with other large banks, it was a closely managed relationship and a highly important one. Our main dealings at that time were with the highly respected finance director, Harry Sheridan and also with Myles Lee, now Chief Executive, who then worked with Harry. Don Godson was Chief Executive at the time. Prior to being appointed, Don had overseen an extensive and successful expansion programme in the United States, describing its geography in relation to the 'Mason-Dixon line', the popular term for the division between the northern and southern states of America. I had heard the name in song, but never knew what it meant. I had now learned that it was a geographical reference and it had a ring to it that I enjoyed.

Another highly successful businessman whom I got to know was Donal Geaney, the driving force behind Elan Pharmaceuticals, the company founded by the colourful Don Panoz. Don was an interesting and entertaining individual. Following his involvement with Elan, he set up leisure complexes in Georgia, USA, which included golf courses, a winery and spa. Don promoted the Ireland-America Golf Cup annually at his complex. It was a businesspeople's event that was held in great regard in those days. I never had the opportunity to participate. In my time with Barclays, we began a worthwhile banking relationship with Elan relatively early in the company's lifespan and when few banks would have been queuing at their door. Donal susequently became recognised as a member of Ireland's top business echelon with top-drawer non-executive directorships, including that of inaugural chairman of the National Pension Reserve Fund. Mary and I had the pleasure of attending Elan's party in Dublin Castle celebrating thirty years in business. The occasion was memorable if only because one of the entertainers was Jim Webb, who sang his own composition 'McArthur Park,'a song made famous by Irish actor Richard Harris.

Jack Welch, regarded as one of the world's greatest corporate leaders of his time, visited Ireland after he stepped down as General Electric Chief Executive. Fortune, the US business magazine named him the greatest manager of the twentieth century. In 2001, he gave a private interview before a business audience at the Irish Management Institute in Dublin, which I was privileged to attend. Welch is much admired in management training circles so it was no surprise that he had a full house. The interview and subsequent Question and Answer session was conducted by David McWilliams, the Irish economist and broadcaster. Like most visitors to our shores, Welch was on a publicity tour for his recently launched autobiography, *Jack*. His sales skills were strongly in evidence, aided not a little by parading his Boston-Irish connections. Jack's visit to the Irish Management Institute constituted part of the tour. It was difficult to relate his experience to Irish conditions given the vast difference of scale between Irish companies and General Electric. Nevertheless, the experience of hearing such a 'can do' and upbeat individual was uplifting.

CHAPTER FIFTEEN

Horseback Riding

During the 80/90's, my business life was very full, and there were plenty of challenges. I felt that I needed a hobby which would give me another perspective and a real break from working life. Fortuitously, Liam Kennedy introduced me to Charlie O'Neill at a function in Dublin's Gresham Hotel. This meeting sparked off an exciting new hobby for me and a long and happy association with Charlie.

I had been seeing a lot of Liam Kennedy at this time. Liam was a larger-than-life Irish construction engineer who, at that time, was one of the prime movers in a young civil engineering company, Clonmel Enterprises. The company was a good customer of Barclays. Having enjoyed a successful time in Britain, Liam returned to Ireland in the late 70s with his delightful English-born wife, Nora, and their family. Clonmel Enterprises was the first corporate customer of the newly opened Barclays Dublin office in 1978. George O'Neill, Branch Manager and fellow Tipperary native, had opened the account. They enjoyed a warm personal relationship, which extended to the bank corporate relationship. Liam was a very sociable and entertaining guy. He was well known and liked, not least in the racehorse-owning fraternity of which he was a member.

At the function that night, Liam introduced me to Charlie O'Neill, a great Kildare character. I had always had a lingering interest in riding horses, but had never done anything about it, even though I had ridden as a child. Growing up on the farm, I regularly rode donkeys and ponies. The cost of a saddle was then beyond our reach, so we always rode bareback. I have great memories of riding our chestnut pony and riding at various donkey derbies on Narin Strand and the Ardara Show. John McNelis, our next-door neighbour, always said that I was a useful rider. My cousin Seamus was a good rider and he dominated the local donkey derbies on Conal (William) Shovlin's fine black donkey. Conal was a first cousin of Packie's and my brother Conal's namesake. In addition, Packie was passionate about horses and was a well-regarded horseman in our local area. Sadly, he could never afford to pursue this pleasure once he married and moved out of his childhood home, where a horse was always kept. I regret that my interest in horses didn't blossom until several years after his death. With hindsight, I would loved to have shared this passion with him.

Charlie O'Neill farmed extensively near the village of Clane in County Kildare, where he lived with his wife Mary and family. He was a brilliant and fearless horseman and had been a master of the Kildare hunt. He also had his own cross-country club, the North Kildare Farmers Cross Country Club, which rode out every Sunday afternoon at 2 p.m., from September to March. Members either owned their horses or hired them from livery yards, including Charlie's yard. They would convene each Sunday at a pre-announced location, which was generally in a village or crossroads in the north-Kildare/east-Offaly area. The first meeting of the season took place at Charlie's farm in Clane, from where members rode out en masse across the farm and neighbouring countryside.

An arrangement was made for me to ride out with the North Kildare Farmers Cross Country Club at their Haynestown, Kilcock meeting.

As I arrived at the crossroads where a multitude of horse boxes were parked, horses were being saddled up by both male and female riders of all ages, shapes and sizes. Mary was with me and Liam and Nora were there to support my launch into this new world. Liam exaggerated my social status and general importance to Charlie by way of warning him to 'mind' me. Liam well knew the dangers of this sport and that it is a case of 'every man or woman for himself/herself'. I had only ridden intermittently in the preceding years and most of my riding was of the riding-school variety, mainly taken by bossy women instructors who gave me short shrift should I try anything adventurous such as taking on a jump. Immediately I arrived at the meeting I sensed that this was different. The riders and horses were brimming with attitude. Charlie had his assistant, Tony O'Sullivan, saddle up a monstrous black gelding, which I was assured was an 'armchair'. By this he meant that all I had to do was sit on the saddle and this horse would bring me back safely. Tony demonstrated the value of the neckstrap, which I should hold when an obstacle appeared which had to be jumped. Mary watched in trepidation as I faded into the distance astride this big black gelding.

We soon left the tarmac road behind us and jumped *en masse* into the nearest field. The jumps were coming up thick and fast. The first few were banks, which tend to be jumped from a stationary position. So far I was surviving, but an early fall was inevitable and come it did. Jumping from an elevated bank to a lower level, I was thrown out over my mount's head and landed in a big dirty puddle. My clothes were both filthy and saturated. We were so far out in the country that returning to base was not an option; you can travel miles at this sport in a short period. The only choice was to get back in the saddle and catch up with the rest of the field. That first fall was a baptism of fire. After a struggle, I managed to get back on board. My survival instincts had prevailed. By the end of the run, I had jumped all kinds of obstacles, from banks to uprights to open ditches; a triumph of survival over elegance.

The adrenalin rush was something special. The difference between this experience and equestrian-centre horseback riding was stark. A day's riding with Charlie and the North Kildare Farmers Club was extremely exhilarating. I was going in at the deep end and surviving. In a way, this approach suited my psyche, as I responded better to the immediacy of a big challenge than to a gradual build-up. With Charlie's group, you had to meet head-on whatever obstacles came up in front of you. Should you fall off the horse, the main bunch of riders didn't courteously wait until you remounted. You had to remove the dirt from your eyes, remount quickly, without assistance, and try to catch up with the main bunch.

From that Sunday onwards, I rode with the North Kildare Farmers Cross Country Club as often as I could afford the daily hire charge; it is a pretty expensive sport. Each day out meant a different terrain, which had implications for the kind of jumping in prospect. Jumping, and particularly jumping at speed, was the cream of the experience. Charlie led from the front, closely accompanied by his long-time associate, Pat Murphy, another experienced and fanatical rider. They were a really good combination: like Cervantes' duo of Don Quixote and Sancho Panza. In another literary allusion, Charlie was not unlike the Flurry Knox character in Somerville and Ross's Irish RM. He shouted and roared and, if you were bold or foolish enough to ride ahead of him, you were quickly put in your place. Neither was Pat immune from a lash of Charlie's tongue; a typical shout would be, 'Jaysus Murphy, you couldn't ride Katy Barry'. Pat might demur and seem to take serious exception to Charlie's rant, but they would be as thick as thieves by the end of the day. This repartee was entertainment in itself for the rest of us riders.

In my earlier years with the Club, I hired horses from Charlie's livery yard, by now a thriving business in itself, latterly run by his son Daragh. These horses were as different and as unpredictable as the range of people riding them. They could be fast, slow, easy or hard to control.

What they had in common was an ability to overcome any obstacle that came up in the course of our day out. Plenty of thrills and spills awaited me. Other fellow riders who committed themselves to hire each Sunday from Charlie were in a position to demand the same horse each time. I did not ride out every week, so I didn't have that commitment, but in any event, I was relaxed about varying my mounts due to the resultant improvement in my riding skills. Such varying of hired horses was, however, to contribute to my undoing towards the end of my cross country career.

Rathmore, County Kildare was suitable and popular cross-country territory, which Charlie traditionally covered early in the season. He hired me a lively mare named Cassie for that run. As soon as I mounted this horse, I knew that I was unlikely to survive the day without incident. And come it did. She was a handful. Cassie decided that she would jump up on a dry stone wall and down the other side, rather than jump cleanly over the wall; she treated it like a bank. The wall scattered beneath Cassie and both of us hit the ground and parted company. The mare arose and cantered off in the direction of the bunch. Charlie was thus alerted that one of his horses had got into trouble. His first cry of anguish was, 'Is the horse all right?' There was little concern for me, the unfortunate rider who, after subsequent diagnosis, was found to have suffered a broken collar bone. This was typical Charlie and arguably part of his charm.

Until we moved to London in 1988, I continued to ride intermittently with the club, and as soon as we returned from London in 1991, I resumed my riding with Charlie and his merry band, or Charlie's Angels they were called. The group encompassed a wide occupational range, from medical doctors to airline pilots, coal delivery men, building surveyors, farmers, miscellaneous bankers, hairdressers and others. I soon got back into my stride. In turn, the better financial rewards which came with my new job enabled me to think about having my own horse. At our annual

Prosperous meet, which began in Pat Curry's farm, Charlie hired me a young chestnut mare, which he had recently bought from another Clane man. She was still very young and inexperienced, but after a few outings, I discovered that she was a real pleasure to ride. I also discovered that this mare was for sale, as were all Charlie's horses! Horse-dealing was very much in his blood and every animal had a price. He was famously asked by a prospective purchaser what was the age of a particular horse. Charlie retorted, 'What age would you like him to be'? The horse business is notorious in that respect and Charlie was no exception to this tradition. People are impossible to pin down. In Charlie's case, did it matter what exact age the horse was, whether it was five or six or seven years old, provided that it suited the purpose intended? The values are not high and provided the horse can do the job, there is not much point in quibbling about the age detail, if you can generally trust your supplier. If you are uncomfortable with this kind of uncertainty, then you should avoid anything to do with owning a sports horse.

As well as really enjoying riding this chestnut mare, she looked good, with a delightful action. An aspect that I particularly value is how well a horse responds to the reins; a good mouth or 'steering' as they say. That she was good in this department was no surprise, as she had been schooled by Charlie's then head man, Tony O'Sullivan, a well regarded horseman. Tony named her 'Quality Time'.

I bought the horse in 1994 and paid Charlie 3,500 Irish pounds, which was a full price at the time. He knew how keen I was to have the mare, so he held out for a good price. What I later realised is that the initial outlay is relatively modest compared to the ongoing livery costs. It can safely be said that 'you get what you pay for' when it comes to a horse, so my advice would be, don't hesitate to pay up for an experienced horse. Quality Time turned out to be worth every penny of my investment, giving me enormous pleasure over ten years. Among my many great memories was winning Charlie's annual cross-country race at Clane. This was a horse race over a several-mile-long marked course, which was designed to include natural and artificial jumps. The natural jumps were especially formidable, as they included wide and deep ramparts. You could be going well, but run into traffic particularly at the tough natural jumps where only a single horse could pass at a time. I remember coming up to the second last jump with two horses ahead of me. The second horse, ridden by Colm Gainey, was going well, but Colm mistook the course and went wider than he needed. I now had just one horse to overtake. Because Quality Time went best just behind a lead horse, I was well placed going over the last fence, a hawthorn hedge which was known as 'Big Beechers'. Once we were over this fence, we had the acceleration to pass the lead horse, ridden by Karen Coleman, just before the line. I was sorry that I had denied victory to a member of the Coleman family. Both Diane and John had showed me much kindness on my first ever outing with the North Kildares. However, I enjoyed the moment and Charlie presented me with the magnificent old cup on that unforgettable day. I arrived home to a hero's welcome from Mary and Catherine. As was usual Mary had a wonderful meal prepared which we sat down to enjoy as the perfect end to a perfect day.

There were many other great memories of those days. Completing a clear round over the challenging hunter trials course run by the Kildare Hunt at Punchestown racecourse was thrilling. Days out hunting with the Kildare Hunt were also pretty special. On a day's hunt, it was not unusual to find yourself riding alongside one of the top Irish jockeys, such as Paul Carberry or Michael Kinane, who might hunt during a quiet period in racing. However, the adrenalin rush enjoyed on winter Sunday afternoons riding with the North Kildares was hard to beat. The allure of jumping natural fences often at speed was a real 'blow out', which was great for clearing the head of the week's worries. It was as if doing risky things was good for your mental health.

There was one outstanding challenge which had eluded me for several years, to ride a racehorse in a charity amateur flat race on a real racecourse. These infrequent races are run as the last race of a day's National Hunt racing and are useful fundraisers. With the help of well known horse trainer, Peter McCreery, who provided me with his mare 'Shane's Lady', I rode in the last race at Fairyhouse, in County Meath on Sunday 28 November 1999. It was the most awful day, cold and very wet. Walter Halley, the Turf Club medical officer, was about to disallow my entry, because I was wearing spectacles. Through the intercession of my wife, Mary, I was allowed to participate. Mary and Walter's wife, also called Mary, had both nursed together in the same hospital. For this reason, I believe that the medical officer was a little less officious than he might normally have been. I was grateful.

My weight was borderline on the day, so I had to make do with a very light and small saddle; it seemed like a postage stamp on the horse's back. I found it a real test to get myself settled into this tiny saddle with shorter-than-usual stirrups. There is normally a lot of excitement around these charity races; the thrill of being a real jockey for a day can be almost overwhelming. Peter McCreery and other trainers such as Ted Walsh were busy around the starting line in ensuring that we were all securely mounted.

I came in well down the field but I had finished the race to be photographed by the official race photographer crossing the line. The race was won by Barry Connell, riding his own horse. For me it was participation that mattered and I was thrilled at the opportunity to being a race jockey, just once.

I continued to ride out with the North Kildares for a few more years. My plan was that when Quality Time's hunting career finished, so would mine. Her hunting career's demise came early in 2004, towards the end of the season. The tendon of her left foreleg was damaged, an injury which rarely ever resolves itself fully. After a few month's rest, we tried her once more, but it emerged that she would not be sufficiently strong to hunt again. Quality Time's career had ended, much earlier than I expected.

The following Autumn, I resumed as usual the hunting season with the North Kildares. I was back hiring horses from the O'Neill's and on a fateful day, I was provided with a young grey horse called Kimbal. The meeting was the annual Rathangan outing. As soon as I had mounted, I immediately sensed that this horse was going to prove difficult to control and he was pitting his strength against me; the chemistry between horse and rider was non-existent for some reason. He seemed to have neither steering nor brakes. Unlike most horses, he was only grudgingly doing the small preliminary exercise jumps for me. I was no stranger to challenging mounts and I foolishly thought that, after covering a few miles, he would settle for me. He wasn't settling and I was now considering dismounting and either abandoning the ride, or switching horses with Daragh. I left it too late and disaster struck.

A bunch of riders, including me, was heading towards a narrow artificial fence made from fallen trees. Kimbal was not for waiting his turn. We charged at speed up through the bunch, stopping abruptly at the fence. As they say, I went flying out the front door, over his head, hitting the ground with an almighty thud. Many times in the past I had fallen off horses, but this was different. I could hear my bones crunching, but couldn't detect exactly where. The dreaded prospect of a neck or spine fracture entered my mind. As I lay prostrate but conscious on the ground, I resolved to myself that if I escaped serious injury from this fall, I would not ride with this hunt again.

Dr. Des Day, A GP and regular rider with us was, as always, on hand. He advised me to keep my neck still in case of serious injury until I was checked out in hospital. The St John's Ambulance team, which was on standby, put me in a splint and brought me to the Accident and Emergency unit at Naas Hospital. From preliminary investigation, the

Naas A & E consultant, judging that I had a possible neck fracture, recommended that I immediately be brought by ambulance to a major Dublin hospital. My next challenge was to call Mary with my news! She was neither amused nor surprised but as always, was there when I needed her support.

I was brought to the trauma unit at Tallaght Hospital, where there were orthopaedic specialists on duty. The ambulance journey from Naas to Tallaght seemed to go on forever. The fact that Naas Hospital decided to refer me to a more specialist hospital made me fear the worst. The prevailing thought going through my mind was that a serious neck or spinal injury might turn out to be the price I would now pay for all the pleasure I had had from horse riding. The price could be a high one.

They did the X-rays and to my incredible relief, could find no fracture or other serious damage. There was extensive wear and tear in accordance with my 57 years, mostly resulting from having worked at a desk for most of my life. That seemed ironic after such a bad knock!

Dr. Des was most helpful to me as he has always been to fallers in the hunt. In addition to the X-rays, he also advised me to have a neck scan done privately, which I did. Thankfully, the scan confirmed that no serious damage had been done. However, extensive physiotherapy was needed to help my rehabilitation. Despite my worst fears, the outcome really was not so bad after all. Believe it, or believe it not, my mind began to turn to the idea of resuming my cross-country riding activities! Can you imagine Mary's reaction?

One of the best North Kildares outings was scheduled for Boxing Day 2004. It was to be in Prosperous, County Kildare, setting out from Pat Curry's farm. I failed to resist the lure of getting back to doing something I loved. I asked Charlie and Darragh to fix me up with a decent horse. They provided me with one of their old reliables, Serengeti, a chestnut gelding. My initial reaction was downbeat as I was aware that this animal seemed to have been in Charlie's yard as long as I was going there. Therefore, he was probably going to be slow, but so what, this was my first day back and sure I would be taking it easy, I told myself. Some chance of that happening. The weather was good and we were all in great spirits. There was that post-Christmas feeling of bursting out of the traps after days of over-indulging. The ride was going brilliantly, jumping over the big banks, which were a feature of this meet, and riding at speed in country over which I had ridden many times in the past. The adrenalin was flowing.

An abiding memory of that day was seeing Mary Lambkin, a regular rider with the group, opt to pass through gates rather than take the direct route over large fences. My instant reaction was to feel that she was missing out. On later reflection, I was to revise that opinion completely and to admire her good sense. The end of the hunt was in sight. I was now upfront, in my rightful (!) place, riding alongside Charlie and Pat Murphy. We had just jumped a big open ditch in unison amid shrieks of excitement. This called for 'high-fives' from Charlie and me. He yelled, 'When you're good, you're very good.' This was one of Charlie's stock shouts on the hunt and seemed to refer to the immediate group and primarily himself.

Little did we know, disaster was a mere few hundred yards away. Our day out had been preceded by several days' heavy rain. A water-filled rampart lay between us and a raised bank, leading to our destination. Charlie had just negotiated it successfully and I was right behind him. As my horse jumped, his hind legs began to sink into the waterlogged lower-level bank. His legs continued to sink under our weight. As sure as night follows day, we both toppled over into the freezing cold water, before I was able to dismount. If I was just wet through up to my neck, I would have thought little of it. Sadly, the situation was more serious. As I emerged from the water I immediately sensed that I was once more in trouble. My left leg had got briefly trapped between my stirrup and the side of my horse. I was in some pain and I could feel no support when I put weight on my left leg. Hoping against hope that my leg wasn't broken, I feared the worst. Again, it was the ambulance to Naas Hospital. I was relieved to be spared the embarrassment of meeting the same A & E consultant who had treated me just over two months earlier. I had good reason to feel embarrassed. Here was I taking up a scarce trolley in Naas Hospital A&E with what was, for all intents and purposes, a self-inflicted injury, as Mary had rightly reminded me on my previous visit. This was at a time when a major A&E capacity crisis was raging in Ireland.

I wondered how on earth I could face telephoning her and letting her know about my latest accident on my first day back after the neck episode. I sheepishly made the call; she was livid, and with some justification. The small bone, the fibula, of my left leg was broken just above the ankle. As it was in the Christmas-holiday period, there was no qualified person available in Naas A&E to do a full plaster. They bandaged my leg temporarily until an othopaedic consultant at Tallaght Hospital could give me comprehensive treatment after the holiday period. When orthopaedic consultant, John McElwain, saw me, he immediately hospitalised me. The following morning, he performed an operation which involved splicing the fibula with a metal plate and inserting a metal pin horizontally through the ankle area. I was woken up in the usual way after the operating procedure. The pain was unexpectedly excruciating. They put on a full plaster and detained me in hospital for a further few days. Crutches were supplied which I would need for seven-eight weeks. If I didn't take in the message to quit when my neck was injured, I surely took it on board this time. Almost two months on crutches literally put a stop to my gallop and the immediate future would be spent spectating rather than participating in sport. At last, I gave in to the lure of satellite television and signed up for Premiership football and US PGA golf tournaments. For me, the injury was not life-threatening: I was not paralysed and still alive, but my embarassment at explaining the reason for crutches to friends and relations was acute. Embarassing and all as it was, this accident had worried me much less than the earlier neck injury.

Horseback riding at his level is a hazardous sport. One of the young orthopaedic consultants in Tallaght Hospital jokingly commented to me that if I desired to attend their rooms more often, there was just one other activity I should consider taking up. What was that, I enquired? 'Motor cycling,' said he. However, they did advise me not to be put off by injury, citing the pleasure I derived from the hobby as compensation for the risk involved.

Why, one may ask, do middle-aged persons such as myself undertake such hazardous pastimes? Because it is an incredible buzz, I always tell people. Down the years, I have got so much pleasure from horse riding at this level. This may be difficult for people who have never participated to comprehend. The nearest comparison I imagine, would be other acknowledged exhilarating sports, like skiing and sailing. While these sports may be more fashionable, I would maintain that horse riding is more accessible and natural to Irish people the majority of whom either directly or indirectly have an association with the land. The presence of an element of danger is, I find, very therapeutic. Such is the intense focus arising from the constant risk of a fall, there is no capacity in your mind for residual worries arising from your work or anything else. Now that I no longer have the pressures of full-time work, I have less need for extreme therapies. Golf is now my principal recreational outlet henceforth, but I still ride occasionally. I have taken guest opportunities to ride with the Kildare Hunt, which represents a highly civilised day's riding.

The greatest lesson I learned from my various falls was that having your own horse is critical to safety in this sport. Additionally the more experienced the horse, the safer you are. An experienced horse will refuse to attempt the impossible, no matter how fired up the rider is.

Unsurprisingly, mares are cuter than geldings in refusing to blindly obey their rider. A downside is that as mares age they can become too cute and too careful in taking on obstacles.

Quality Time enjoyed a well-earned retirement in Donegal, where she was inseparable from an aging mare donkey. When the donkey died from old age, we replaced her with a rescue horse, which we obtained from the Irish Horse Welfare Trust. Although she seemed in perfect health, Quality Time died suddenly in late 2010. Most knowledgable people with whom I spoke believed it to be a heart attack.

I feel privileged to have had many enjoyable years of exhilarating riding with Charlie and his North Kildares. Sadly, he passed away in 2011 after a severe illness. He was a uniquely likeable and cheerful character. In addition to his adventurous horsemanship, he was highly entertaining, whether it was me or another rider who might be the butt of his devilment. Charlie worked hard all his life and also raised large amounts of money for charity. He used both his equestrian activities and his Harley Davidson motorbike in this worthy endeavour. He was truly one of the good guys.

Before I hung up my riding boots for good, one of the highlights of my horse-riding exploits was a horseback safari in the Masai Mara game reserve in South Kenya. The Masai Mara Reserve is a continuation of the Serengeti National Park, which stretches from Tanzania northwards across the Mara river. It is regarded as one of the best places in Africa to view a large selection of wild game in their natural habitat. Charlie O'Neill, Corkman Barry Keohane, a stylish Irish banker, and myself decided that we would make this trip in September 2000; this is the dry season, when the great migration of wildebeest across the plains can be witnessed. Therefore, it is an ideal time to go. Barry was also a member of the North Kildares and an experienced rider. We flew to Nairobi via Heathrow and then we boarded a small private plane. We flew south and landed on a grass airstrip in the general Masai region. There we were picked up by a Land Rover driven by a local man, who turned out to be a key member of our safari team leadership. On disembarking the plane, we got our first glimpse of a group of Masai tribespeople. They were all dressed in reddish woollen type shawls. They cut a dignified image with grace and poise notable features of their movements.

After a long and bumpy drive, we arrived at our first camp, to meet horseback safari leader, Mark Laurence, and his team. Ourselves and the eight other riders would be in their care for the two-week safari. The other riders were a diverse group of English and Americans, of both sexes and of varying ages. Most were experienced riders, some of whom had previously been on similar riding holidays. After a light communal meal in the outdoors, we were paired up with our horses and Mark led us on our first rideout, which was a flavour of things to come. The extensive vegetation, particularly the trees, surprised me; I had expected the landscape to be more arid. Our first experience of observing wildlife was that evening, of small monkeys leaping across the treetops. Monkeys are much less visible than you might expect, because they are apparently shy and endeavour to avoid the presence of human activity.

Later that evening, the full group sat down to dinner and began to get to know each other. Some were highly experienced and accomplished horse riders and serious riding was their big objective. Others had limited riding experience, but were really interested in seeing the wildlife from the back of a horse, as distinct from the usual Jeep safari experience. The group ranged from businesspeople to the successful Broadway actor Michael O'Donnell, who had Donegal connections.

We were to live in one- or two-person tents for the duration of the safari. The tents were comfortable and very adequate in the hot climate. Toilet facilities were in separate canvas tents. Going to the toilet during the night in complete darkness could be a hazardous venture, so the dextrous handling of a small torch was essential. There was the threat (albeit unlikely) of being attacked by wildlife seeking food and also the danger of tripping over the myriad stays holding the tents in place.

We would spend no more than two nights in the same base camp before moving on to the next camp location. A team of local men, under Mark's supervision, did all the work of moving and setting up the camps. They operated a convoy of large trucks and Jeeps to move the materials, which included several days' supply of food and water. Despite the absence of refrigeration, the food was excellent, with a plentiful supply of wine and beer. After a hearty early breakfast we would either ride all day if we were moving to a new camp, or, if we were not moving camp Mark would lead us on wild-game-spotting rides, over a few hours, each within a radius of our present camp. The camp team provided us with packed lunches for sustenance on safari. It was customary to tie up the horses in a shaded area around midday. Both horses and riders would rest for an hour or so to avoid the burning midday sun; we were just south of the equator. Temperatures were high but the Mara plains are on a reasonably high altitude, so the heat was never overbearing. You had to be careful to wear a wide-brimmed hat to provide skin cover to avoid dangerous sunburn.

Mark Laurence and his team were highly experienced, so we were afforded the right blend of adventure and safety. The use of horses rather than jeeps allowed us close and privileged access to the wild game. Mark, very much in charge, was the kind of guy who inspired confidence with a quiet but assured demeanour. The sole white person on the team, he was a small, wiry man who seemed to enjoy the outdoor and adventurous life style. The tone of his team was one of cool and efficient professionalism, rather than camaraderie. Delivering a good experience for the riders was the paramount objective.

At home in Ireland, Charlie O'Neill was well used to being the maverick on the hunt. So good was his knowledge of the Irish countryside, that he would regularly lead his own sub-hunt within the main hunt, as it were. If there was a lull in the hunting action, he would go off popping fences. Of course, most riders love jumping fences, so he would quickly have a following. Charlie was used to being top dog and he did challenge Mark's authority on a few occasions by going off jumping across the few obstacles he could find on the plains, such as fallen trees. His adventures were restricted both by the scarcity of jumps but also by the horses' lack of jumping experience; it was not their job. It was clear that Mark was not used to this type of behaviour from the holidaymakers, but at the same time he allowed Charlie leeway. One reason was that he couldn't figure Charlie out, but perhaps another was because of Charlie's popularity within the group. Luckily, no other participant had the confidence, that comes from years of horsemanship, to cut a dash that might have provoked Mark. As usual, Charlie was monopolising the available limelight to the great enjoyment of most of the group.

If Mark perceived it was dangerous to approach wild game on horseback, the open-topped camp Jeeps would be used. Getting close to a pride of lions was a case in point, when the Jeeps would be driven close to the animals so that we could have the best view. A mother and her cubs lying in the shade of the hot sun is a wonderful sight to behold. A male lion with his glorious beard would not be scared in the least by a Jeepful of tourists. These animals are accustomed to seeing the Jeeps and would come so close that, if you knew no better, you could be tempted to pat their manes.

The animal most feared on horseback safari was the water buffalo. This was a surprise to most of us who would have thought that water buffalo were just wild cattle. Apparently their danger threat is connected to their protectiveness of their young. They are very powerful animals and if one of us was unfortunate enough to be head-butted by a water buffalo, he or she would not survive. Their habitat was among the undergrowth along riverbeds so they were difficult to spot. Therefore, they could be perilously close to unsuspecting humans and react violently if they felt threatened. So that we might have a safe glimpse, Mark led our group on foot along a riverbank they were known to inhabit. Unfortunately (or perhaps fortunately), we only caught a brief sight of a herd through dense vegetation. This was the only occasion I saw Mark carry a loaded rifle as protection in case of an attack on our group.

As we rode along the banks of the fast-flowing Mara River, we came upon one of the big crossing points for the wildebeest. As part of their great migrations, they cross the river hundreds at a time. The river crossing is a highly dangerous exercise for the wildebeest. Waiting for them in the waters are crocodiles ready to pounce for their next meal. More wildebeest are slaughtered by the crocodiles than are eaten. The result is that the crossing point is littered with decomposing carcasses. These pollute the river as well as giving off a pungent odour. As the wildebeest are present in such large numbers, there is no danger of them becoming extinct through this type of slaughter. Other predators are the lions which first target the weaker and younger animals in the flock. It is for good reason that the wildebeest are regarded as the larder of the plains.

The families of elephants are a beautiful sight to behold as they make their way across the plains. There is a lovely rhythm to their grazing action as they combine their trunk and foot to good effect. Baby elephants, and particularly the weaker ones, are easy prey for the hyenas. The hyenas can be seen circling their prey menacingly and relentlessly and you know it is only a matter of time before an inevitable strike. There was something in their behaviour that reminded me of the knack school bullies have for picking on the vulnerable child in the playground.

You feel a sense of helplessness and sympathy for the wildebeest and other prey being killed by their fellow creatures. It is of course natural and part of the ecological balance of animal life on the plains. The most eerie sight is the vultures patiently gathering on a nearby tree when a killing is in progress. As soon as the prey is motionless and after the predator, such as a lion, has his fill, they descend in numbers. Again, the vultures serve a purpose, stripping the carcasses to the bone, thus avoiding the unhygienic remnants of decaying flesh. This practical solution to death applies to the Masai people, too.

Apparently they do not bury their dead, but leave the bodies on the plains for natural disposal by the wild game. While this approach initially seemed abhorrent to us it is a logical and ecological solution in the circumstances. Early on one of the last days of the safari, a few of us joined Mark for a routine morning rideout which included a river crossing. We were keen to experience for once the terrain on the other side of the Mara river. Following a short canter from base camp, we had an uneventful river crossing and a most enjoyable ride on the other side. We then made our way back to the river where we eagerly anticipated the thrill of riding the swimming horses back across the flowing waters. All went well until we reached the riverbank. It was pot luck as to whether the water was shallow or deep near the bank and thus whether it would be easy or difficult for the horse to climb out. Unfortunately for me the water was deep, so my horse had no solid jumping-off base from which to leap on to the bank. Rather than try to find a better spot, I wrongly chose to allow him struggle valiantly, but in vain, to establish a footing on the bank. Horse and me tumbled backwards into about seven or eight feet of flowing water. I was submerged under my horse but managed to swim to the surface with my sun hat and spectacles still in place. I didn't cut a pretty sight. Thankfully we emerged from the river before our splashing attracted the attention of either the crocodiles or the hippopotami which were lurking nearby in the Mara. The hippopotami, to my surprise, were regarded as no less a threat to humans than the crocodiles. This was one of those times when I felt that someone was praying for my survival.

I emptied the water from my boots and remounted my horse. During this episode Charlie was bursting his sides laughing at the spectacle of me coming out of the river. He couldn't stop laughing for the rest of the day. Mark and the other riders were astonished at Charlie's reaction. I wasn't at all surprised as I had often witnessed similar bouts of uncontrollable laughter from him when riders took a tumble on the hunt back home. There was something about guys who normally wore business suits taking a tumble that tickled him pink. In sharp contast to Charlie, our fellow riders were chastened by what they had seen, realising that it could just as easily have been one of them. Worse still, one of us could have become victim to the river predators.

The river incident became the story over dinner that evening. There was literally eating and drinking in the story for all. I feigned ignominy but shared in the enormous fun enjoyed by the whole party at my expense. I was fêted with champagne as the hero of the hour and a special poem was penned by one of the more literate among us.

We spent our last few nights at Deloraine House, an old colonial ranch property on 5000 acres with its own grass airstrip. Deloraine is located in the Rift Valley near Nakuru. Deloraine is the home of the Voorspuys, ex-Guardsman Tristan and his wife Lucinda, who had organised our horseback safaris. They had many horses on their ranch also being active on the local polo-playing scene. As we arrived Tristan, was just leaving to lead another safari group among whom was Venetia Williams, a leading National Hunt trainer in England.

Our short stay at Deloraine was not without incident. We ate and drank well, sang songs and generally made merry. On the first morning of our stay Lucinda led a rideout around the ranch. As in the hunts back in Ireland, Charlie and Barry were up at the front with the leader. I was back in the bunch enjoying being out on a horse in the beautiful early morning when suddenly all hell broke loose between Barry and Charlie. I never got to the bottom of it but Barry must have said something that sparked Charlie's temper. He launched an unmerciful tirade against Barry. On subsequent reflection I realised that I should have stepped in to try to pacify them, but laughter took hold of me. It was as if it was the reverse of the Mara river incident. This was an embarrassing event at the time. It is to my eternal shame that I failed to mediate but allowed this altercation to threaten the unique holiday adventure which the three of us had enjoyed. The effects of this blow-up continued until we all arrived in the departure lounge at Nairobi Airport. Barry and Charlie ensured that they travelled to the airport in separate vehicles. I had hoped that we could board the aircraft fairly quickly and avoid embarrassing silences while we sat in wait. Unfortunately, my hopes were thwarted. Our aircraft had a mechanical problem that necessitated a part to be obtained from South Africa. Not only were we delayed, but we were forced to overnight at a local hotel until the plane was repaired and ready to go.

The three of us were forced to spend so much time together at the airport that all the bad feeling had disappeared. Charlie had now bounced back to his irrepressible self. He spotted a very tall black man standing with a wheelchair, which was provided for any disabled passenger needing attention. Charlie hopped into the wheelchair and shouted 'Here Scobie, take me to the aircraft, it's my back again'. 'Scobie' was a form of address I had heard him use often at home; he seemed to reserve it for particular circumstances where he was seeking a favour from a person he had just met. The genial attendant, who was about seven feet in height, duly wheeled a safari-hatted Charlie to the boarding area. Barry and I took the conventional route, but Charlie disappeared down a special corridor. We did catch a glimpse of him whirring past an opening between our corridor and a parallel restricted-access area. It was such a funny scene and a nice prelude to an otherwise uneventful flight to London and eventually back to Dublin after our great African adventure.

CHAPTER SIXTEEN

WEARING THE GREEN JERSEY

In Ireland, 'wearing the green jersey' is associated with doing your bit for the country. The concept relates particularly to Irish managers of multinational companies operating in Ireland. All things being equal, they are expected to help promote the enlargement of the company's footprint in Ireland. Of course, it is understood that the manager's loyalty would be first and foremost to his/her employer.

My principal duty at Barclays was to lead the Barclays Bank Ireland corporate banking operation. I also carried the wider responsibility of being Barclays Group Ireland country head. Thus, for example, if any of the Barclays group divisions, not just corporate banking, had issues in Ireland, they would contact me at an early stage. They would either involve me directly in the issue or keep me informed on a continuous basis. Equally it was my responsibility to initiate discussion with them on any opportunity or threat which I perceived might affect their businesses. Exploiting business opportunities in Ireland fell under this heading and specifically the advent of the Dublin International Financial Services Centre (IFSC). From a purely nationalistic viewpoint, the presence of a local person in multinational corporations can be materially beneficial for the host country. If the local unit is developing and expanding, it is simply good news. On the other hand, the situation can be uncomfortable if the business is declining. Local managers are naturally more alert to local conditions than say, an expatriate country head, whose stay, in the way of things, is likely to be no longer than a couple of years before the next assignment. Moreover, there is the obvious patriotism that a local person will feel in the circumstances where there is a straightforward business case for investment in Ireland.

Our success in the mid-90's in securing the future of the threatened Barclays Ireland banking presence was a modest triumph in helping the Irish unemployment figures. Barclays was, however, a large and diverse business grouping. I had long felt that because of the supply of quality employees, favourable corporate tax rates and respected regulatory regimes, we as a group could do more business in Ireland. The chances of progressing that agenda would be negligible had we terminated the corporate banking franchise with the consequent bad after taste of such an event. Thankfully, with the avoidance of a termination we could now look forward positively and pursue other business possibilities.

One of my proudest achievements during my time at Barclays Ireland was the introduction of a staff profit-sharing scheme in Ireland. Because Ireland was outside the bank's home British jurisdiction, the design of the scheme was particularly challenging and legally complex. Initial legal advice suggested that it wasn't possible, but we stuck with the project. I was very attracted to the idea of the staff having a share in the prosperity of the business unit in which they worked. As a motivational tool it was good for both employer and employees. The scheme, which allowed all staff to buy Barclays shares in a tax-efficient manner, came into being and was a great success. We were the first Barclays office in Europe, outside the UK, of course, to have such a scheme.

The IFSC had already been launched in 1987. Following a difficult struggle initially in carving out a niche in the international financial services industry, it began to gain some traction. Funds-management administration looked like it was going to be the brightest prospect for operations of substance. Large financial transactions were creating momentum and while these were high in value, they tended to be light in employment numbers. We set about presenting the attractions of the IFSC to various Barclays Group constituents. Ian Kenwright, a bright young management trainee, was seconded from head office to Barclays Dublin as part of his training programme. He did a great job in putting together a prospectus on the IFSC. Armed with this comprehensive document, we hawked the benefits of the IFSC around the Barclays Group. Before and during my campaign to keep open our Dublin banking office I had maintained contact with Donald Brydon, Chief Executive of BZW Investment Management (BZWIM). Like many of the best investment professionals, Donald was a Scot. Despite my continued pestering of both Donald and key executive Ron Gould, our good empathy, combined with their lingering curiosity regarding the IFSC, ensured that BZWIM never abandoned Dublin possibilities. It was therefore with some satisfaction for me that BZWIM launched their first IFSC registered funds in May 1995. I supported them on the ground in any way I could, particularly as a founding non-executive director of their first IFSC-registered fund company. I continued to provide that support well beyond my departure date from Barclays Bank. Over this period of time these funds grew steadily to become one of the largest in the IFSC, bringing great economic value to Ireland. Several Dublin back-office fund administrators, professional firms and other suppliers benefitted. Because their business is concentrated outside Ireland these fund companies tend to have a low profile locally but their economic value is considerable. In the light of the subsequent success of the IFSC generally it was always likely that BZWIM would ultimately have established fund management operations in Dublin. Had Barclays however, pulled its corporate banking presence out of the city, the lack of local momentum would at best have resulted in the decision to invest coming much later. The overall success of the IFSC owes a great deal to the relentless efforts of IDA Ireland and Dublin professional firms in promoting the Centre.

In the years that immediately followed, further positive developments occurred. Dialogue commenced between ourselves and Barclaycard International, the credit-card operation of Barclays, run by Barry Fergus. Barclays Group had taken the strategic decision to roll out the Barclaycard brand internationally, recognising that it had global potential. They were considering the best location for a contact centre for their business launches in continental European and African countries. While Barclaycard were not unenthusiastic about Ireland as a service location for these new enterprises, they were reluctant to commit to a major greenfield operation; this would have been their first significant service location let alone outside Britain, but outside their main Northampton office campus. Fortunately, we had some spare office space available in St Stephen's Green which we were able to make available to them for a pilot operation. Our operations director, Donal Moore, and his team provided them with general operational and facilities support. This package of support allowed Barclaycard to incubate their project with a small nucleus of key staff, thus avoiding the risks of a heavy upfront investment in infrastructure. The incubation project was successful and they eventually moved to a large purpose-designed office in Sandyford on the outskirts of Dublin. In their new site Barclaycard International's Irish operations grew to employ over 200 people. It gave me enormous pleasure to attend the official opening of their new Sandyford office. Seamus Brennan, then Minister for Enterprise, performed the opening ceremony in the company of host, Barclaycard Group Chief Executive Bob Potts, and Barry Fergus.

That wasn't all. Things were stirring in the Barclays insurance division, under the leadership of Bob Dench. They had a large project underway with the objective of bringing a heretofore outsourced part of their insurance business back within the Group. The project was part of a large-scale re-organisation of the whole Barclays insurance business, that Bob was undertaking. Adoption of the project plan for the particular insurance element would envisage a separation of the management and underwriting functions from back-office administration. The former would be brought back into the Group while the administration aspect would remain with the external service provider. Ireland seemed a sensible place to consider when setting up these new specialist insurance companies.

I had known Bob Dench from his time as an executive with Barclays Travellers Cheques when I was introduced to him by Liam Delaney, then Barclays Travellers Cheques representative in Ireland. Bob was an impressive-looking guy with a good reputation in Barclays. I originally met him at a corporate golf outing at the Hermitage Golf Club near Dublin. Christy O'Connor Senior, the celebrity for the day, arranged to help entertain guests with exhibition shots at one of the golf holes. A particular memory stands out for me of Christy placing a ball in a divot, taking the driver in hand and hitting the ball down the fairway for over 200 yards; we were all impressed. Bob was a Bill Gordon protégé, so Barclays Ireland's position as part of Bill's empire could neatly pave the way for a good business relationship, if the project proceeded. IDA Ireland led a strong promotional effort to hook the project for Ireland and appreciated our local active encouragement and support. The new companies would not be large employers in themselves, but there were two other very important considerations. Firstly, they were high-value businesses with the consequent Irish corporation-tax take and secondly, they would anchor a large number of back-office jobs with the external service provider based in Shannon.

The vibes coming through from London on the possibility of Dublin as a destination for the project were positive. The decision was taken to set up the companies in Ireland in early 1997

A project outside Britain would be unusual for Barclays Insurance so, if it were possible, Bob was keen to locate it in the environs of an existing

Barclays operation for both operational and governance support. Both Barclays Insurance and the wider group would derive comfort from the close support of an existing Barclays presence. As the Barclaycard nucleus operation had by this stage successfully reached a scale and stability that they required larger premises, we were just about able to facilitate the new insurance business in our St Stephen's Green building. The two specialist insurance companies were incorporated in mid-1997. They prospered from the outset under an effective management which was lead by Eamon Slevin, during my time. Bob Dench asked me to become their non-executive chairman, a position I filled until I retired from Barclays Bank in 2002. I was succeeded by the ubiquitous Billy McCann, former Managing Partner at Price Waterhouse and the doyen of the non-executive director cadre in Ireland.

Both Barclaycard and the insurance businesses settled down to become thriving organisations in their own right. Apart from their obvious benefit to the Irish economy, they directly benefitted the Barclays Bank corporate-banking franchise in Dublin. By sharing infrastructural support, they helped make the totality of Barclays Group operations in Ireland more cost effective through the sharing of central costs. Furthermore, their general banking requirements became valuable account relationships.

By the time I stepped down from Barclays Bank in 2002, Barclays employed 250 people directly and roughly 70 people indirectly at outsourcing suppliers. These figures compared with 70 employees at the time BZW had decided that the Barclays business in Ireland had no future. It was a case of 'from zero to hero' within a few years.

CHAPTER SEVENTEEN

The Beginning of the End

Succession at group chief executive level was a big issue for Barclays in 1999. Martin Taylor had already resigned in 1998. Sir Peter Middleton, then chairman, recruited Mike O'Neill, a former Bank of America executive, but for health reasons, he was unable to take up the appointment. Sir Peter performed the role of acting chief executive, pending a permanent appointment. The unexpected departure of Martin Taylor and the abortive attempt to hire a successor created a great deal of uncertainty around Barclays in the financial markets. Barclays was perceived to have a leadership vacuum and speculation was rife that the group was vulnerable to takeover by a smaller player. The speculation centred around the idea of marrying the potential of the Barclays franchise with incoming management depth from another similar institution. Sir Peter was highly experienced in both public and private sectors. There was a realisation in the group that his steady hand ensured that predators were kept at bay during this period of uncertainty.

Enter 55-year-old Matt Barrett, in October 1999. He had recently stepped down as chairman of the Bank of Montreal. Born in County Kerry, the son of an Irish band leader, Matt Barrett was educated at the local Christian Brothers school in Kells, County Meath. A teenager when he emigrated to London and began a career with the London branch of Bank of Montreal, he soon transferred to Canada with his employer where he enjoyed an outstandingly successful career, reaching the very top. Now, he was to be Barclay's new group chief executive.

My first direct experience of Matt Barrett was in April 2000 at the Barclays Corporate Business Leaders conference in Wembley. He is a fine-looking man and an impressive speaker who uses colourful expressions to get across his message. Sayings such as, 'All hat and no cattle', conveyed the concept of a person given to hype but being of little substance. My colleagues and I were in agreement that he was a motivational leader and looked forward to his growing influence in leading Barclays forward.

This was the first time in Barclays that I saw such an extroverted style used to communicate business messages. Matt Barrett delivered his talk in a pose which reminded me of the comedian Dave Allen: centre stage, spotlit, on a stool. Given his background, there was a lot of Irish interest in Matt Barrett's appointment with Barclays. In a Barclays Ireland context, the favourable publicity was welcome. I was delighted to now see a fellow countryman as top man in my multinational employer. At a meeting at the Department of Finance, the then Minister for Finance, Charlie McCreevy, explained to me the warm regard he held for Matt Barrett. The Minister's acquaintance with Matt preceded Barclays, through his non executive directorship of local state-owned ACC Bank.

I was looking forward to capitalising on the general wave of goodwill in Matt Barrett's favour to promote Barclays interests in Ireland. My earliest conversations, however, considerably dampened my expectations in this regard. These brief exchanges took place at the Chairman's group conference at the Grand Hotel in Brighton in late 1999, a time when he was just about to assume his new role. I had already met him in Dublin when he had spoken at a financial services industry luncheon in his then capacity as Chairman of Bank of Montreal. Although born and raised in Ireland, he had spent most of his working life in Canada so it was not surprising that he seemed essentially Canadian. Moreover, his British audience perhaps attached more gravitas to his later Canadian background than to his earlier Irish years. There tended to be a perception that Irishness was more associated with fun and entertainment back then. Things have changed for the better in the last twenty years but that was then a common perception. I therefore learned pretty fast that neither for sentimental nor for other reasons was Matt Barrett going to take any special interest in Barclays in 'the old sod'. His first and only official trip to Dublin was to brief local equity analysts on Barclays results in early 2000. He planned to drop into St Stephen's Green but Mary and I were on a holiday in Dubai that week, so he never came in. For our staff I was disappointed, because witnessing his charismatic presence would have been motivating. Matt Barrett was a great appointment for Barclays. He re-awakened the group's sense of confidence in itself and provided profile and direction towards greater success.

The year 2000 was an exceptionally good year for Barclays in Ireland. Profits were very substantially increased on the previous year. New corporate-account openings continued year after year under the business strategy adopted in 1995. The bad years had given us practice at keeping the lid on costs with the result that our cost/income ratio was improving rapidly and delivering strongly to the bottom line.

The string of good results copper-fastened my own position and the reputation of the Irish operation was very positive within the group. Our success was the envy of other similar Barclays corporate-banking operations in Europe. We were constantly being visited by representatives from other parts of Barclays and held up as an example for them to emulate.

However, from the time we re-launched the business in 1995, I had not envisaged being in Barclays beyond 2000. I had hoped for circumstances where I could plan my departure in conjunction with my superiors rather than wait around to be ultimately pushed. Being pushed is the inevitable fate that awaits senior executives in roles such as mine. The alternative is to make self preservation a personal mission that takes precedence over all, but which can blind a person to wider personal objectives. I couldn't do that.

Another of the many reorganisations I had seen in my Barclays career was coming over the hill. My London boss, Alex Jablonowski's empire was to be carved up. The European element of Alex's international sector which started with Ireland, was now a substantial business in its own right. By this time Alex had already appointed André Teeuw, a sound, pipe-smoking Dutchman to head up this business group. André was a good colleague with whom I had previously crossed paths. I was to enjoy working with him once more. Oddly enough, Barclays Scotland was now included in our group. This might seem strange as Scotland was in Britain but Barclays had entered the Scottish market at a late stage and so were in a minority market position. There were therefore, similarities with Ireland and other European centres.

More often than not in these re-organisation scenarios, the direct subordinates do not survive a senior divisional executive's demise. Alex, a big-hearted and an unusually uncalculating person, was philosophical about his own position. He supported the concept of constant change and regarded it as a normal state in organisations. Dublin's success alone was a tribute to his vision not to mention his achievements across a broad front. In a way, his work was done. He had been handed several large but fragmented banking businesses, mainly in the offshore segment, which he had re-structured and ultimately passed them to others to lead forward. To use a running analogy, Alex was a sprinter rather than a marathon runner; he was better at creating a short-term momentum for intelligent change rather than the longer time frame of day-to-day management.

Alex came across to Dublin in June 2000 to say goodbye. We presented him with a miniature bronze replica of the wounded Irish hero, Cúchulainn, the original of which stands in the General Post Office in O'Connell Street, Dublin. This gesture was not meant to be analogous to his career situation, but there may have been parallels!

By the end of 2000, I had a new boss, Steve Price. In his thirties, Steve was a young banker who had made his name in the London region as a dynamic corporate-banking executive. He was on the fast track, having already been earmarked as a top-tier executive of the future. Steve gave a hint of the new style of regime by organising a European leadership and coaching conference in Devon. No time was to be lost so the conference was set up for January 2001. I convened with my French, German and other senior colleagues at the Nigel Mansell-owned conference centre in Devon. This was a team-building programme to be comprised of business discussion and 'outward-bound' activities. The programme was led by a specialised consulting firm known to Steve. I saw myself as having the choice of playing along enthusiastically or being true to myself. I decided to be myself, agreeing and disagreeing within our debates as I believed to be right. If my only interest was in maintaining my career, I would have been well advised to go with the flow. Any preliminary thoughts I had about leaving Barclays were now beginning to develop steadily. As a fairly fit 53-year-old, the outdoor challenges were well within my capacity; some were highly enjoyable. What I did find difficult, though, was the motivation to give one hundred per cent when I recognised the futility of what we were doing. Steve wanted to build and mould a team of people in his own image. We were not ever going to function as a team in that way. We were team leaders in our own right in businesses that were not homogenous and in varying degrees of maturity. This is the kind of mistaken thinking I have seen repeated time after time. It typically happens when the person in charge is used to a volume consumer business which can be driven by a simple ramping up of energy being applied. In corporate business across different jurisdictions, cultures and languages, progress needs to be based on a more subtle approach, in my opinion.

My attitude at the team-building conference undoubtedly coloured Steve Prices's assessment of my long-term future with Barclays. Unknown to each other, we were probably thinking along the same lines. I had a sense that this was the beginning of the end.

A new concept of management was now sweeping across Barclays. This was called 'functionalisation', which was meant to have 'the customer experience'at its core. What this meant in practice was that in Dublin and other European capitals, the back-office functions of treasury support, operations and information technology (IT) were henceforth to be managed centrally from Britain, rather by the local country head. Provided the IT support was efficient, functionalisation was a sensible approach. It should have the desired effect as it would enable the Country Head to re-direct management capacity towards the customer and not towards the staff. I could readily see the merit in this approach and I championed its implementation in Dublin. However, for me personally, functionalisation was not good news. If there was any chance of me continuing with Barclays, I would have to revert from general management to the customer-contact role which I had performed years earlier. I do believe that given the appropriate motivation and context, I would again have done this type of job well. The context was not, however, shaping up well.

Every few years we in Barclays Dublin would arrange a business trip to the United States. We had a few American customers and we also a had a couple of Irish companies with substantial businesses in the United States. However, the major objective of these trips was to promote Barclays Ireland with our Barclays colleagues in the major centres as an account destination for their Irish customer connections. In May 2001, I travelled to New York and on to San Francisco, meeting colleagues in both locations. It felt like, and in truth it was, the valedictory tour. This was my first visit to San Francisco, which I thought a beautiful city but with surprisingly little buzz compared to New York. On my return to New York, I detoured to Idaho to see one of our Irish customer's dairy manufacturing facilities there. This is a rural agricultural area, where the roads are straight for miles and miles. I was surprised to see that dairy cow herds were kept in yards rather than grazing freely on pasture, given the vast scope of land available. Most of the people I met there were of the Mormon faith. They made me very welcome and their business acumen impressed me. On my arrival, a board displaying my name and that of Barclays confronted me in the reception area of their offices; a unique and flattering gesture. A distinct impression I picked up from that trip across America was the lax security arrangements at airports at the time. The embarkation procedure seemed little more onerous than taking a bus, which I suppose it was, given the necessity of air travel in that vast country. A mere few months later these weak security procedures had their consequences in the terrible events of September 11th. On that morning I had just plugged into the regular conference call led by Steve Price, when the first airplane crashed into the Twin Towers. Steve and colleague Andrew Kirby had just opened the conference call from the New York hotel where they were staying. I recall Andrew terminating the call because of an explosion at a nearby building. I rushed into our dealing room where the terrible events were unfolding on Sky News. It was hard to believe that what we were seeing was real; it looked like a scene from a disaster movie.

The Barclays re-organisation under Steve Price and his colleagues continued apace. Peter Harvey, Steve's boss, hosted an important corporate banking conference in Derby on 6 June 2001; history was repeating itself here. In one of the key presentations, a telling slide was projected on to the screen. The slide informed all present that the corporate head jobs would disappear in their present form. A new 'head of customer sales' would be appointed. The present Irish corporate banking head, i. e. yours truly, would be free to apply for the new job, as would other applicants. All this was code for creating a situation where existing incumbents could be removed and replaced with a person who would have a different title. To be fair and objective to my senior colleagues, this kind of playing around with the organisational chart represents fairly normal procedure in effecting change at this level. I may not have been informed directly, but we both would understand each other in terms of what was happening. Of course, it is ego-bruising to be on the receiving end but that is life in this kind of corporate environment. Had I not been mentally prepared for the inevitability of having to contemplate leaving Barclays before normal retirement date, this would have been a sobering experience, if not an outright shock. There was a silver lining. If Steve and Peter clearly envisaged my departure it followed that my pension and severance terms would be better than if the desire to part company was confined solely to me. That the severance package could be used to boost my reduced pension due to the retirement date being so far in advance of age 60 was an important consideration for me. I had known Peter for many years and it is fair to say that our good relationship assisted the process of easing me off the pitch.

The prospect of leaving behind the daily grind of my job and the freedom from the serfdom of the bottom line held appeal for me. Despite the stimulation of the job an element of boredom was creeping in. A low boredom threshold has always been one of my weaknesses. There was also an emotional tiredness from the trials and tribulations of fighting to save the business more than once and almost twelve years doing the job was long enough. I had long realised that the apparent high esteem with which I was held in the financial and general business community was more to do with the status of my employer than with me personally. It is not uncommon for people like me in these jobs to mistakenly assume personal magnetism when it is more to do with the mantle one is wearing. Generally, popularity wanes with the shedding of this corporate mantle. Arising from that feeling, I had a desire to reclaim my own personal identity. This modest identity status was likely to be a shadow of the one I had enjoyed as head of Barclays in Ireland. Be that as it may, I preferred not to defer the inevitable if other considerations were favourable. With our mortgage almost repaid, we could now be financially comfortable even on a reduced income. In the back of my mind I had always thought that if I could afford to retire in my mid-fifties, I would do so. The opportunity had arrived and Mary was supportive. As you age, you become increasingly aware that the clock is running down on your time. There were things I wished to do and places we wanted to see. I was keen also to see if I could help out any charitable or philanthropic organisations out of the skills and experience I had accumulated in my career.

Had I opted to apply for the new job, I would surely have failed to get it. If Steve Price or Peter Harvey wanted me to continue, they would have simply re-drafted my job specification. So it would be inappropriate to go through the job application process. In all the circumstances, I was happy to go.

It might have occurred to me to wonder why my superiors wanted me to leave. After all, Barclays Ireland was more successful than it had ever been and with the Celtic Tiger beginning to roar, the prospects for the bank were excellent. I suppose there would be many reasons. A new boss likes to be seen to put his own people in place. I would have been perceived to have gone native; my loyalties would have leant towards the local organisation, away from the centre. My independent-mindedness, stemming from having held the business together in difficult times, could well now be seen as a nuisance factor.

Another more mundane reason could be the availability of a younger colleague who might become available due to a re-organisation elsewhere. Unfortunately, I had no natural successor in Dublin to recommend. The obvious candidate, Liam Miley, had left Barclays a few years earlier; he subsequently went on to become chief executive of a German-owned bank in the Dublin IFSC.

Once the process of my departure began, it inexorably rolled on to its conclusion. Bill Handley, Corporate Director in the Leeds area, was appointed as my successor. This would be Bill's first time to work outside Britain. Bill, a Brixton native, is an enigmatic and streetwise banker who joined Barclays at sixteen years old. When he first arrived, we invited him to our house, where Mary put on a welcoming dinner. The unconventionality of Bill's casual dress code for a senior Barclays manager was novel to us. He appeared in a multi-coloured T-shirt and thick-soled sneakers. Bill regaled us with his life story, barely pausing for breath. Watching Bill and listening to his anecdotes was extremely entertaining.

I set up a programme to introduce Bill to our top customers. Although his style was unconventional, I felt that he could bring an additional dimension to Barclays in Ireland. He seemed highly intelligent and was obviously well regarded by the senior people in London. Bill also had the ability to reveal that rare element of menace which would make him very effective in a credit recovery team.

Peter Harvey and Steve Price attended a customer function in the coach house in Dublin Castle to mark my departure and to introduce Bill. I delivered a speech which provided me with the opportunity to thank the customers for their support as well as the professional firms with which I had worked down the years. Mary and Catherine attended. Mary was presented with a beautiful bouquet of flowers. Peter spoke kind words and presented me with a set of sterling silver cufflinks on behalf of my fellow colleagues on the European business banking executive. I was grateful to Peter and Steve for taking the trouble to attend and for affording me a dignified exit. His Excellency the British Ambassador, Sir Ivor Roberts, also kindly attended.

On an evening before Christmas 2001, we had a small staff party in the nearby Shelbourne Hotel for me to say goodbye to Dublin staff colleagues. Mary and Catherine again joined us. Staff member Mary Garvey's son, Fiachra, and daughter, Niamh, two gifted young musicians, entertained us with piano and violin. It was a great evening for me. After the staff presented us with a gift, I spoke about how much colleagues meant to me. Many of them had been through the good times and tough times with me. Unprecedently, Mary added a few words to reveal that she could speak very effectively in public. Regardless of whether colleagues were pleased to see a change at the top, this evening marked an emotional parting. With Mary and Catherine, I walked out of the Shelbourne that evening feeling liberated and full of anticipation at what lay ahead for the rest of my life.

My 23-year career with Barclays drew to a close. It had been a satisfying one despite the rollercoaster of ups and downs. Barclays had been an excellent employer to me and I hold nothing but goodwill towards the bank. I worked with and made the acquaintance of many fine colleagues in Ireland, Britain and elsewhere in the world. And I wasn't closing the door behind me completely. Barry Fergus, the head of Barclaycard International, kindly allowed me the use of a spare desk at their Dublin contact centre for a period after I left the bank. As a non-executive director with some of Barclays Dublin IFSC Funds, I have continued a rewarding albeit peripheral part-time relationship with Barclays over several further years. Indeed, I was appreciative of Peter Harvey's blessing at the time of my retirement in continuing these relationships.

Barclays Group has continued to progress in recent years under the leadership of John Varley. From the few times I met him as a colleague, I was deeply impressed with his sharp intellect and communication skills; additionally, he comes across as a nice guy. American Bob Diamond has since done an exceptional job in building Barclays Capital into a serious investment-banking force. An impressive, if controversial, figure, Bob has since succeeded John Varley as chief executive. However, his reign was to be cut short as unfortunately, he was overwhelmed by the fallout from historic regulatory issues that emerged in the group. Under their stewardship, Barclays has escaped the fate of government ownership suffered by other UK and large banks elsewhere due to the international financial crisis and property-lending débâcles.

CHAPTER EIGHTEEN

WHERE DID IT ALL GO WRONG?

Where did it all go wrong indeed?

I am referring to the Irish banking industry, of course. Fortuitously, I had departed my role at Barclays before the industry committed it worst lending excesses. I hasten to add that during my time there, and afterwards, as far I can determine, Barclays continued to take a prudent stance in adding property lending exposure in Ireland. The useful lessons that had been learned from the harsh experience of the UK property downturn in the early 90s still applied. Having been attached to the Barclays London property financing team at that time, I also learned some useful lessons. An important one was that commercial property can be very illiquid and can therefore clog up a bank's balance sheet. There are only so many long-term assets such as property that should be financed by customer deposits, which are short term by nature. Additionally the refinance risk is also often underestimated, i.e, that the likelihood is low of the borrower being able to repay the loan by borrowing from another bank without having to sell the property. In that event there is every risk of the market conditions being weak and monies not therefore being readily available to repay the loan from either source. Barclays in Ireland benefitted from the corporate memory of earlier experience. Indeed it is fair to say that the London-based Barclays Group lending policymakers were never convinced as to the endurance of the Celtic Tiger economy.

So much has already been said and written about Ireland's economic problems that there remains little new that can be said. From my perspective, it is, however, worth reflecting on the sea change that took place in banking in the context of the whole economy. The Irish economy got itself on to a steady growth path in the mid to late 90s into the early noughties. As we now know, it was a combination of factors rather than any single factor which contributed to our subsequent economic demise. That combination included government policy, regulatory issues at the macro level and bank lending policies (or lack of) in individual banks. These lending policies turned out to be more grounded in aggressive competitive behaviour than in good economics. I do not pretend to be an economist or indeed to have any other academic competence that qualifies me to provide authoritative answers. My perspective is that of a practitioner in banking. To help me answer to myself the question of how this could have happened—I wrote my thoughts down on the issues in 2006, little knowing that things were to get so much more awful:

'Strong economic growth filling the State's coffers is the holy grail which we have now found. But what could now be called excessive growth is not all it is cracked up to be. There are the obvious downsides: an inadequate health service is one. It seems destined to play catch-up to a burgeoning population further swollen by the immigration needed to sustain this economic growth. Other inadequacies include public transport/road capacity/traffic problems and policing strains. Home prices are stretching beyond the reach of our young people and prices generally are making us less competitive as an economy. There is the consequent poorer quality of life that these frustrations bring. The state services are unable to keep pace with the racing economy. Much of this excessive and unsustainable growth is occurring in the property development and construction industry.

Why, as a sovereign state, can we not harness this wonderful economic progress of the late 90s/early noughties more to our advantage? Surely the true measure of progress is the quality of life for our people? Can we not intervene in moderating this growth so that at least our public services are given a chance to catch up? If we accept as a principle that it might be a good thing to moderate economic growth, we are far from helpless in being able to slow the speed of our economic activity. There is, however, one important intervention mechanism no longer available to us. As a result of joining the euro, the currency/interest rate economic tool once at the Central Bank's disposal is now subsumed into the Frankfurt European Central Bank (ECB) regime. ECB can intervene in a whole-eurozone context, but apparently cannot intervene in individual national economies. Therefore, our central bank, on behalf the government, does not have at its disposal the interest-rate and other market operations, historically available in helping to influence buying power in the economy.

We can, I suggest, do something to moderate growth by acting more forcefully where possible. Government ministers could take a leadership position on the issue and speak out. I do wonder if the financial regulator might, for example, give more robust guidance to mortgage providers in advising sensible levels of personal debt, as well as concentrating on the important prudential stress-testing of the institutions themselves; i.e., detailed and publicised stress testing also for the debt-repayment capacity of the individual borrower. For the institutions themselves, economic sectoral exposure guidance is a tool that could be proactively used to minimise excessive growth levels. For example, the Central Bank might have the banks cap their total loans to some sectors of the economy. The property development sector would be a prime candidate for such capping if the government was so inclined. This should not competitively disadvantage local lending institutions against externally based banks as mortgage products and property-related finance generally tend to be largely provided by local players. Very large externally sourced loans are an exception, but then they are rarely for property-financing purposes. Indeed, had our banks gorged less on this external capital, our country would have been the better off.'

The introduction of the euro has also greatly facilitated the incentive to borrow. Its low-interest-rate regime, welcome in many ways, has resulted in a general switch of benefits, previously enjoyed by savers, to borrowers. This weaker incentive to save in itself fuels growth in spending, including property investment by us at home but also abroad. Why would you invest your money in a savings account with such a low return when you could invest in property transactions (promising hefty returns) at home or abroad? The way things have turned out is that sadly many of these so called attractive property investments have not only not produced a return, but are now worth less than the original investment. To give credit where credit is due, the SSIA scheme and the National Pension Reserve were sensible initiatives in sucking excess cash from the economy. It is a pity not more was done.

On taxation policy, one questions whether zoned-land-related borrowing, should enjoy the same interest allowability that applies to other businesses? Zoned land stock is no ordinary raw material. It is limited in supply, has no obsolescence risk and increases in value (or used to increase in value!) the longer it is held. What that particular point misses of course is that we re-zoned land excessively, thus making zoned land less valuable. However, the tax point remains.

Perhaps the issue boils down to whether we are prepared to take a longer view by modifying growth where possible. As a people we seem pretty intoxicated with our excessive growth in the hope that with all the cash the other bits will fall into place eventually. They should do, but why not try to lessen the pain in the meantime?

Much of the above reasoning may sound naïve with the benefit of hindsight, but it does illustrate what many traditional bankers would have felt at the time, i.e., that it all didn't feel right. I recall a telephone call that I made to a prominent economist in one of the banks at a time when the prevailing wisdom was that a soft landing was assured. I suggested to this person that the property development industry was growing so fast that I feared dangerous oversupply and consequent price collapse ahead. To modify expansion, I suggested that the banks get together with the Central Bank and self impose voluntary annual credit-growth limits. The economist swatted away the idea of credit controls in today's sophisticated economy, suggesting that such thinking was dated and related to an epoch long past. I firmly believe that had the Central Bank and the banking industry met, perhaps under the aegis of the Department of Finance, and implemented voluntary credit-growth control, our country would not today require the support of the IMF led troika.

An irony is that when we had our own currency, the Irish pound, the Central Bank was ever vigilant in helping to manage our economic affairs. After we joined the euro, credit growth and reliance on external funding was left to its own devices, with sorry consequences. With the adoption of the euro we no longer had the worry of managing the fate of our own currency. We would now have the luxury of handing over that awkward responsibility to the European Central Bank. Looking back at the debate (or lack of) I think that we kind of sleepwalked our way into the euro without seriously considering the pros and cons. The political drive to enter the euro may have overshadowed a less convincing economic case.

It does have to be acknowledged that the very damaging international banking crisis which stemmed from the sub-prime situation in the United States was not of our making. It had an enormous impact on our banks, particularly in almost closing down the 'bank-to-bank' lending which is so vital for the liquidity of the banking system. Nevertheless, had we in Ireland been more prudent in our own banking affairs, we would not have been so vulnerable to the sub-prime shock.

Turning to the prevailing bank lending culture of the time, a refrain I had heard many times during my banking career was that 'any fool can lend money'. This was said more in the context of lending for business rather than personal lending, which these days is largely formulaic, being based on levels of wages, job security etc, but it's true to say that in Ireland we seem to have been endowed with a surfeit of such fools! That is not to say that there is no skill or judgement in being a lending banker. There is, of course, much to be learned about bank lending, mainly from hard experience but also academic study. It is, however, the application of this knowledge that is the critical factor.

In the last twenty years or so the business of bank lending has generally become more formula driven. Whether it be gearing ratios or loan-to-value ratios, these tools have gained primacy over the more traditional 'judgement' or 'gut-feeling' factors. In an earlier time, lending activity was minded by the more mature managers within banks, whose view of things would have been conditioned by years of experience, often under highly experienced predecessors. In the Barclays world of my time this element of the credit-risk assessment was symbolised by the key lending criterion 'Character of the Borrower'. While such an approach may appear old fashioned and subjective it is, I believe, still very relevant to the business of lending depositors money carefully. By way of the bank lending process there is another important consideration in decision making and accountability. Decision by credit committee has been in vogue rather than the more traditional sign-off by a single accountable executive in banks. It is obvious that having to personally evidence responsibility for a loan made encourages a deeper concentration by the individual. Committees can well fall foul of all members bowing to the loudest, most articulate or most senior member. If the loan goes wrong it can be nearly impossible to truly track accountability.

The individual banks seemed oblivious to what was going on at the macro level of the economy in the Celtic-Tiger era. The dizzy environment was aided by a chorus of cheerleading economists and journalists who foresaw nothing worse than a soft landing. More sober independent voices were drowned out as potential killjoys. What was not sufficiently realised was that many of these cheerleading economists were employed by banks and had thus gone native. Their real job was to aid the business-building efforts of their lending colleagues in these institutions. It is not that these economists were either asleep or incompetent. In many cases it is rather that they were simply part of the marketing machine for the banks' product sales to their corporate customers.

Furthermore, the banks were dishing out loans to a single economic sector that was inevitably destined to go bust, unless lending policies changed. How can you continue to build offices and houses without being mindful of the future demand for these properties? It has been stated anecdotally that we were employing immigrants to build houses and apartments for immigrants! So, it was like a pyramid scheme in that as soon as the building programme slowed, there would be no jobs for the immigrants and consequently there would be no occupants for the properties. It may not be quite as simple as that, but it is not without an element of truth to it.

In the 90's, Anglo-Irish Bank was developing into a successful niche player mainly providing finance to businesses to enable them to purchase their premises. Indeed Anglo was seen as a positive element in the competitor mix at that time. With the improving economic environment, they moved on to increasingly become a major financier of property development. Such was the scale of Anglo's success that they became a serious competitive challenge to the two leading Irish banks AIB and Bank of Ireland in the narrow but lucrative property-developer sector. Anglo was now setting the pace and metamorphising into a mainstream bank, to the extent that the big banks were tempted to join the party by becoming equally major players in the apparently successful property game.

Ireland's adoption of the euro became an important element in what was happening in the property market. This is true from a number of aspects. Firstly, the substantially lower interest rates brought about by the euro made borrowing so much cheaper and consequently business deals more viable and therefore easier to bank. Combine these lower interest rates with an ample supply of bank credit and you have the rocket fuel to drive a boom. These were times when the international capital markets were flush with cash and pushing it at the Irish banks. This background was providing a feelgood factor that reinforced escalating property prices. Property lending in a rising market offers the banking industry a ready opportunity for the profitable outlay of its plentiful funds. Large commercial-property lending transactions are a quick and easy, if not lazy, way to build up a banking business such is the voracious demand by developers who have little personal financial risk; it is the lenders who are taking the bulk of the risk. Irish developers tended to invest very little equity in a rising market. When they succeeded in their first venture, the rise in their asset value would provide the equity for future deals. In horse-racing parlance it was using the winnings in the first race to back a horse in the next race and so on. In a rising market, it was easy to back winners.

Historically, Ireland's interest rates tended to be too high to enable property-lending deals, with low yields, to meet meet interest payments, let alone to repay large loans. But hey presto! lower European-type interest rates showed property developers and consenting banks that property rentals were now sufficient to meet interest payments, if not to contribute something towards principal repayment. But why worry about principal repayments? After all, wasn't the increasingly valuable property excellent security for the loan? I once heard Sean Fitzpatrick, then Anglo-Irish Bank Chief Executive, expound his lending philosophy in his own folksy way, as: 'Good guys, good cash flow and good security.' By applying such a subjective standard, there was no shortage of the 'good guys!' Unfortunately, the other two criteria were less reliable in changing economic circumstances. Property lending is tempting for banks seeking fast growth; attracting a higher lending margin than regular commercial lending to corporates. Add to that the apparent good security of property. Building a large property loan portfolio can be a quick way to have a highly profitable, albeit unsustainable, bank. The big problem with property from a bank's viewpoint is that it not readily realisable and therefore not liquid. If you need to sell, it is likely that the market environment will have deteriorated and there will be a wait for your money. Moreover, there was a time when pension funds, insurance companies and other long-term asset managers had an investment appetite for completed and let office blocks and shopping centres. With the rapidly increasing supply of these developments and much of them not even fully let, the availability of these investors dwindled. The result was that the banks would be left holding these increasingly illiquid assets whose related rental income was insufficient to pay down the related bank debt. Although this situation was bad enough, it was relatively good compared to pure speculative property development, which would not have ready tenants lined up, and little real prospect of any, given the burgeoning supply.

When the setting-up of NAMA, the National Asset Management Agency, was announced, I thought that it was not the appropriate response. For such an enormous policy decision, it seemed to me to be rushed, on the basis of narrow advice, and to be creating almost a doubling of process and consequently, cost. NAMA seemed to be an additional debt-recovery vehicle to the recovery units of the banks. The banks lent foolishly but they had accumulated skills and experience from decades in the business and they were best equipped to recover debt. Because of the introduction of another party, i. e., NAMA, there is now a necessity for formal valuations and legal intervention with the related high costs. I have not seen anything to change my opinion of NAMA as a concept. The consequent additional cost is hard to justify. Add to the equation the immediate front-loading of the bad debt provisions in the books of the banks, creating instant insolvency. By all means establish a unit to supervise the banks' recovery-management process, but don't take over their recovery function. Rather than funding the banks through takeover of their property portfolios, why not inject the capital straight into the banks as required? Perhaps setting NAMA up was necessary way to enable European funds to be sourced. Otherwise, it is difficult to see its logic.

Despite the recent disasters in Irish banking, the business and practice of banking remains a vital activity for the country and a worthy occupation. Not so very long ago, parents would be delighted to see their children take up banking. When I joined the Ulster Bank shortly after school, I wondered at how conservative the then prevailing Presbyterian banking values were. These sound values and good ethics thawed away over time. How I longed for them in the wake of the destruction of great Irish banks. The 90's were probably the zenith of Irish banking, when our larger ones became international players and were a significant source of good employment for our young people. Sadly, the institutions that have survived are now but shadows of what they were.

In the future, perhaps our banks should become local utilities with the sole aim of serving the banking needs of our people and economy. They should be sensibly regulated and allowed to make profits that would enable them to pay a reasonable annual dividend to their shareholders. Any ambitions of becoming internationally expanding companies with the hope of speedily rising share prices are probably not for the foreseeable future. Even though the likelihood of having this choice open to them is not on the horizon a solid national banking policy ought to be in place in ready protection for a time when the recent disasters are a distant memory. Already good progress is being made by the authorities in stabilising the banking sector with declining dependence for funding from the European Central Bank. The failed institutions are now in a liquidation process, an approach combined with depositor guarantees that perhaps should have been adopted at the time of the blanket Government guarantee in September 2008. Of course, in saying this I enjoy the benefit of hindsight which those decisiontakers did not.

EPILOGUE

When people ask me what I do, I am faced with a minor dilemma. My short answer is that I am retired, but that is not the full story. Although I am retired from full-time employment, I have not retired from doing work. Even in advancing years, I find that the words of Noel Coward hold true: 'Work is more fun than fun'. What I do now is wholly different and varied from banking, although I still retain a minor role in financial services. I have become fairly active in the voluntary sector. Oxfam Ireland, an all-island developing world charity were seeking to appoint a member to its council who had financial experience and so I was asked to join them as honorary treasurer in 2005. It has been both a great privilege and indeed a learning experience being an Oxfam Ireland volunteer, albeit not in the field. I have met the most dedicated and competent people working on overseas development. What has pleasantly surprised me is the thoughtfulness with which they approach the challenges in the developing world. I believe that what Oxfam Ireland do really well is to provide leadership locally in those locations. They are good at identifying small, locally controlled NGOs and then partnering with them in humanitarian and other efforts. For these NGOs, the involvement of Oxfam Ireland not only brings some funding, but perhaps more importantly, provides a badge of credibility which assists them in sourcing local government and other international-funder support.

In late 2009, I undertook the challenging inaugural Oxfam Ireland Trailtrekker 100-kilometre walk. This annual fundraiser involves around a hundred teams of four people walking continuously, on through the night, in hill and road terrain in the spectacular Mourne and Cooley mountains. It is not a 'relay', as each team member has to walk the total 100k. I was greatly helped in this endeavour by Tom Milligan, who is perhaps Ireland's greatest living hillwalker, by my good friend Frank Coyne and by Belfast university lecturer Gerry McAleavy. Against the advice of my wise GP, Dr Tiernan Murray, I participated and finished the walk in a respectable 27 hours. Foot blisters and shin splints were suffered but the feeling of achievement was worth it. Thanks to my many kind supporters, we were the fundraising team that raised the most money.

Another significant volunteering involvement for me is with the RDS, or Royal Dublin Society, a Dublin-based organisation that was founded over 280 years ago. The RDS is known mainly as an exhibition and event centre but less known are its important foundation programmes in the areas of agriculture/rural affairs/equestrianism, arts, industry and science. Indeed, the RDS is somewhat of an unsung hero, particularly in its work with the younger generations. There are currently active plans increasingly to promote these altruistic endeavours. The far-seeing founders of the RDS initially caused to establish such great Irish institutions as the National Library, the National Museum, the National Gallery and the National Botanic Gardens. It continues to have connections with these important national institutions through the nomination of RDS members on their various boards. It is through this connection that I enjoy current membership of the National Library board. The National Library of Ireland is not just a book reading library. It is the primary repository of Ireland's documentary heritage; such treasures as the James Joyce and Seamus Heaney collections are but two of these important archives.

Being able to enjoy music has been one of the great pleasures of my retirement, due in no small part to the contribution of well-regarded music teacher, musician and no mean wordsmith, Dubliner Ken Shellard. He has uniquely introduced a new word to the English language—'cantaparolation'. This word embraces everything to do with the 'singing' of words. 'The speaking of words is referred to as 'diction', but it is also commonly used to define words when sung. Cantaparolation seeks to discretely differentiate the singing of words from the speaking of words. To describe the wonder of music I find almost impossible. To that end, I quote from the great composer Felix Mendelssohn, who I think had a vivid way of putting it: 'People usually complain that music is so ambiguous; that it is so doubtful what they ought to think when they hear it; whereas everyone understands words. With me it is entirely the converse. And not only with regard to an entire speech, but also with individual words; these, too, seem to me to be so ambiguous, so vague, and so easily misunderstood in comparison with genuine music, which fills the soul with a thousand things better than words.'

My first experience of music was in Mrs McGill's classroom in Beagh school, when I must have been around six years of age. The McGill family were extremely gifted musically. She was the only primary teacher who tried to give me the opportunity to learn music. She used a tuning fork and did the scales with us. The tuning fork has fascinated me ever since: a simple piece of metal with such a fundamental application. As a young boy, my musical experience was confined to céilí music, which was used for dancing classes. Dancing classes were popular and given by a young John Molloy in the old AOH Hall in Kilclooney. John subsequently became a highly successful businessman. Ardara and the surrounding area was well supplied with traditional Irish musicians. Many houses had a traditional fiddle on the kitchen mantelpiece, which a member of the older generation could play by ear. These musicians came into their own at house and school dances which were the predecessors to dances in local halls. Ardara had a strong musical heritage and could readily field a dance band; the names of John 'the tae' Gallagher, Josie McHugh,

John Whoriskey and Thomas Campbell were prominent. Of course, the acclaimed Johnny Doherty from the neighbouring Glenties parish was well known in Ardara, where he had strong family connections.

The radio programme 'Take the Floor' was very popular all over Ireland in my boyhood. Apart from the news bulletin, it was one of the few programmes which country people especially valued and enjoyed.

As I grew up, being deprived of music tuition was in a strange way a relief, as music was seen as an activity for cissies. On the plus side, St Eunan's College was a rare beacon of music culture in Donegal. It staged a Gilbert and Sullivan opera each year in December. Director Michael Mason, a Derryman, did auditions before rehearsals commenced. I almost got picked for the chorus until Mr Mason realised that I didn't know what singing in tune was supposed to mean. Anyone with musical knowledge who ever heard me try to sing a song concluded that I was without an ear for music even though the sound quality was all right.

It was not until after I met my wife Mary that my musical tastes developed beyond rock and country music. Mary had a good musical education and has more sophisticated music tastes than I have. This consequently helped lift my level of music appreciation. As a result we now both enjoy attending concerts at Dublin's National Concert Hall. Our interest is in the lighter end of the classical music spectrum. I enjoy hearing singing, especially the traditional ballad; I particularly enjoy the American baritone Thomas Hampson singing Steven Foster material. Gradually, and much to Mary's relief, I have been weaned from a diet of country music and rock 'n' roll. The country artistes who continue to appeal to me are American singers Johnny Cash, Waylon Jennings, Maria Muldaur and the Irish country singer Ray Lynam.

One of the objectives I had for my retirement was to further develop my musical education so as to enhance my enjoyment of it. Shortly after I gave up full-time work I was fortunate enough to be introduced to the aforementioned eminent music teacher, Ken Shellard by my good friends, the musically talented Conaghan family. Ken is a highly respected piano accompanist and singing teacher who taught at the Dublin Institute of Technology. He stepped down from his college job some time ago and now teaches privately. His pupils regularly take honours at Feis Ceoil, Ireland's premier annual music competition. In his spare time, Ken acts as musical director and organist to the choir in St Patrick's Church of Ireland, Dalkey, County Dublin. He is regarded as having achieved a remarkably high standard with this amateur group. In Ken, I found a gifted professional whose whole life was musical excellence. And what's more, he was prepared to attempt to teach me, whose musical tastes were pretty primal, and moreover who was long judged to have no ear for music.

By means of diagram and physical demonstration, Ken showed me how human breathing functions (such function is so natural that people rarely give it a thought). References were made to the similarity in the relationship of bow-to-violin and breath-to-vocal chords. The partial or full-length application of the violin bow relates, too, to the application of breath to vocal chords, an enormous amount of discretion being applied to the degree of application in the case of both instruments. Continuing the analogy, Ken showed me just how much the resonant properties of both instruments are so enhanced by the skill with which air or bow is deployed.

My main vocal difficulty when first auditioned by Ken was what is commonly called tone-deafness. Ken explained to me that the normal reaction to such an impediment would be to advise the candidate to explore alternative avenues of endeavour! But Ken hastened to assure me that he was eager to take me on for a serious investigation into the nature of tone-deafness, and the possibilities of either by-passing it or even overcoming it. So that was the nature of the contract to which we both signed up.

It would take time and multiple paragraphs to describe the approach which we adopted. Suffice it to say that after much trial and error, and even more of the same, we evolved a *modus operandi* that led, in time, to a moment of triumph when Ken rang my wife Mary, put her 'on speaker' and I sang to her 'The Mountains of Mourne' with perfect intonation. My recollection is that she was quite overcome. Coming from our different perspectives, I think that stamina and a phenomenal degree of persistence saw us through to this moment of justifiable euphoria. Those methods, once evolved, have continued to serve, and a small repertoire is building up.

Learning to sing, albeit to a modest standard has been a wonderful experience for me. There is far more to the craft than you could imagine at the outset. It is a journey of learning and therapy. The little bit of knowledge I have gained has helped me to appreciate the endless hours that professional musicians dedicate to their craft. I can only stand in awe at the art of reading music and playing the piano. My musical journey has opened up another exciting dimension to my life by stimulating my curiosity about the world of music. I am so much better equipped to enjoy the music of the great composers such as Mozart and others. To illustrate their value as a therapy, I can say that singing and listening to nice music is as therapeutic in its own way as riding a good horse over a challenging fence.

When I first took singing lessons, I tended to be quite secretive about it. I feared that it would be interpreted in the same vein as dressing up in women's clothes! This, I know, is a ridiculous notion but it is a measure of how some of us consider that a wonderful activity such as singing is not for grown men. For anyone who has the slightest compulsion to sing, if only to themselves privately, I would strongly recommend it as a hobby. The challenge is to find a competent singing teacher who is sufficiently broadminded to work with you in developing the skill. This is not as easy as it sounds as the top teachers are naturally inclined to work with pupils who have high potential. In finding Ken Shellard, I was extremely fortunate in unearthing a top professional as well as a fine human being.

My lifetime has witnessed great changes and advances in society. Apart from the enormous advances in technology the most unanticipated change in Ireland is the accelerating decline in respect for monolithic institutions that dominated the country of my youth viz. The Roman Catholic Church, the Fianna Fáil Party, the banks, the gardaí. In my childhood, weekly worship was almost 100%, compared to the present 63%, according to some studies. Fianna Fáil dominated politics for much of the 20th century, and is now in a minority parliamentary position. The current absence of a kind of general fear that pervaded many aspects of life in the mid-20th century is another great contrast; for example, fear of hell, fear of the teacher's cane and fear of the police. While there was a kind of comfort in the old certainties their demise was inevitable. Nevertheless the consequent empowerment has not always been well used, as was evident in the disastrous excesses of the Celtic Tiger economy.

With the advent of cheap international flights, travel abroad has become an increasing feature of all our lives and particularly the twilight years. We live longer now and are better off than our parents ever were, and this has allowed us great freedom. Mary and I are no exception. We have visited quite a few places; most out of curiosity rather than aiming for leisurely holidays. Some of the more interesting destinations have been Russia, western Canada and South Africa. In Russia, we visited both Moscow and St Petersburg, two very contrasting cities. Moscow with its incredibly wide streets, bustling with activity, seemed a young people's city. St. Petersburg seemed much more sedate and less self-confident, despite its great history and heritage of churches, art galleries and palaces. Our well-informed tour guide arranged a most interesting trip to a seminary complex outside Moscow where Russian Orthodox priests are trained. There you see young clerics swooshing around in ancient-looking black garb, while at the same time talking animatedly on their mobile phones! On our way to this seminary the tour guide also arranged for us to visit a typical rural homestead. There we met an elderly lady who lived with her son in very modest circumstances. A large picture of Stalin had pride of place on her kitchen wall. It was hard for us to believe how this cruel dictator was being still revered almost 50 years after his death.

But the most riveting experience of all was our visit to Auschwitz and the neighbouring Birkenau, the Nazi death camps in Poland. You could see the remnants of the gas chambers where so many innocent ordinary folk were murdered. The horrible accommodation with communal toilets for example, that afforded no dignity, can still be seen. Like many people, I find it almost impossible to believe that humans treated each other in such a systematically despicable way.

Of course, no matter how far I travel, there is nowhere I have been that beats the beauty of Ireland. Whether it is Wicklow, at Dublin's back door or Donegal, the scenery alone, not to mention the nature of the people, is hard to beat. For me all roads eventually lead to Sandfield. My good friend Kevin Haughey likes to reference The Eagles when he says that we may have checked out of the place, but we never left. This would seem to be true, not just of Donegal folk, but of many Irish people, who remain emotionally attached to their birthplace for all of their lives.

ACKNOWLEDGEMENTS

There are inevitably a few people to whom I owe a debt of gratitude in helping me to reach publication. To my wife, Mary, a very special thanks for the love and unconditional support she has given me not just in the writing of this book but in making all the many wonderful things in my life possible throughout our time together. To my daughter Catherine and her husband Ken for both themselves and the gift of our lovely grandchildren, Alex and Zara. To my only sibling, my brother Conal, I acknowledge the positive part he has played in my life, from a shared childhood to the present day. I would also like to pay tribute and express my gratitude to colleagues in Barclays Dublin, without whose hard work and commitment I would have been able to accomplish so much less in my career. I should also acknowledge the wonderful friendships I have made across the Barclays organisation, with colleagues in Ulster Bank Group and indeed in the Irish Customs service during my short stay there. Sean Donnelly, I wish to acknowledge for reinforcing the idea that publishing online was a viable option and to Brian Hegarty, for his general advice on publishing a book.

I should also be quick to acknowledge the generous slices of luck I have enjoyed all throughout my life.

I would particularly like to thank my editor Alison Walsh for her good-humoured help and patience in bringing this book to a state where it could be published.

Finally, I wish to acknowledge the generous assistance from my good friend John Kelly in reviewing the text and providing invaluable feedback to me.

Every effort has been made to ensure that the book contains no factual error. If any mistake has made it into print, such error is solely my responsibility.

Printed in Great Britain
by Amazon.co.uk, Ltd.,
Marston Gate.